Also by Daniel Sekulich

Ocean Titans: Journeys in Search of the Soul of a Ship

TERROR ON THE SEAS

TRUE TALES OF MODERN-DAY PIRATES

DANIEL SEKULICH

THOMAS DUNNE BOOKS
ST. MARTIN'S PRESS ⚇ NEW YORK

The names and identifying characteristics of some individuals
depicted in this book have been changed.

THOMAS DUNNE BOOKS.
An imprint of St. Martin's Press.

TERROR ON THE SEAS. Copyright © 2009 by Daniel Sekulich. All rights reserved.
Printed in the United States of America. For information, address St. Martin's Press,
175 Fifth Avenue, New York, N.Y. 10010.

www.thomasdunnebooks.com
www.stmartins.com

Library of Congress Cataloging-in-Publication Data

Sekulich, Daniel.
    Terror on the seas : true tales of modern-day pirates / Daniel Sekulich. — 1st ed.
        p. cm.
    Includes bibliographical references and index.
    ISBN-13: 978-0-312-37582-9
    ISBN-10: 0-312-37582-4
    1. Pirates—Anecdotes. 2. Piracy—Anecdotes. 3. Sekulich, Daniel—Anecdotes.
    I. Title.
    G535.S434 2009
    910.4'5—dc22

                                2009007590

First Edition: June 2009

10   9   8   7   6   5   4   3   2   1

For Arla Jean

CONTENTS

ACKNOWLEDGMENTS IX

PROLOGUE: HASSAN'S STORY 1

1 THE BRETHREN OF THE COAST 15

2 SEA GHOSTS 43

3 PIRACY, INC. 79

4 THE DRAGON'S TEETH 113

5 NEW LIBERTALIA 139

6 FEASTS AND FAMINES 169

7 SIX DEGREES OF SEPARATION 197

8 PIRATE TALES 229

9 REVELATIONS 249

AFTERWORD 275

NOTES 279

BIBLIOGRAPHY 295

INDEX 299

ACKNOWLEDGMENTS

I have been immeasurably grateful for the confidence and advice given to me by numerous individuals on almost every continent of the globe, without which I would never have been able to complete this book. Unfortunately, a number of them cannot be named for a variety of reasons—including their own personal safety—but I hope that these people know I remain in their debt. And to anyone I have overlooked here, please accept my humblest apologies.

My list of thanks begins in Canada, with Jerry Johnson of *The Globe & Mail* newspaper, who commissioned me to write a couple of features on piracy in East Africa. William Andrews again proved his mettle as one of the finest travel agents around by getting me in and out of four continents as efficiently, and safely, as possible. I am indebted to the Canadian navy's Lieutenant Commander Marie-Claude Gagné and Commander Mike Considine, John Morris at the Department of National Defence in Ottawa, Dona Fitzpatrick at MSOC Ottawa, Gord Helm at the Port of Halifax, Rick Gates, Paul and Mitch Rudden, Jack Gallagher, Chris Cooper, and Ron Bayer. Closer to home, I received great support from Alice Hopton, Susan Meisner, Kristen Colle, Richard O'Regan, Phil Desjardins, Nick DePencier, Shelley Saywell, and the brave Somali-born journalist Sahal Abdulle. Special gratitude must be extended to Deborah Palloway, my family, and my son, Gavin.

In the United States, I acknowledge the advice and insights from Kimberley Thachuk, Tamara Shie, Geoffrey Gil, Akiva Lorenz, Lieutenant Denise Garcia with the U.S. Navy's Fifth Fleet, Doina Cornell at Noonsite, Herb McCormick at *Cruising World*, Jim Puckett, and David Rigsby. In Great Britain, I thank Jonathan Olley, Julie Lithgow, Girish Lele, Ieuan Dolby, Sam Dawson and John Bainbridge at the ITF, with a special mention of Andrew Linington at Nautilus UK and the work that organization has carried out on behalf of mariners. Barry Wain, Andrew Symon, Joshua Ho, Satnam Kumar, and Reverend Mervyn Moore generously provided support in Singapore.

Elsewhere, I would like to thank Angele Luh at the UN's Environmental Programme in Nairobi, Johanna Straub in Berlin, Michael Storgaard and Senior Captain Henrik Solmer at A. P. Moller-Maersk in Copenhagen, to say nothing of Captain Jørgen Sonnichsen and the entire crew of the MV *Emma Maersk*, plus the companionship of Damir Chytil and Ed Lundy on that particular voyage from Asia to Europe.

There are many mariners who have contacted me about their own experiences with pirates, including a large number of recreational sailors. Forgive me if I do not list everyone by name as doing so would make these acknowledgments too lengthy, but please accept my thanks for your candor and recollections.

This book could never have gotten off the ground without the prodding of my incredible agents at TLA, Don Sedgwick and Shaun

Bradley. Their creative eyes saw something that I did not, and I thank them from the bottom of my heart for pushing me to develop it and for supporting my work through thick and thin. The encouragement of Naomi Wittes Reichstein was equally invaluable as I struggled to find my way, and I only wish we'd been able to work together longer. Finally, I must thank St. Martin's Press for its support of this project and for pairing me up with an incomparable, insightful, and patient editor, Peter Joseph.

PROLOGUE

HASSAN'S STORY

MOST PEOPLE BARELY notice Kisauni as they drive north from Mombasa toward the resorts that line the Kenyan coast along the Indian Ocean. It's an overcrowded slum with garbage-strewn laneways and clusters of unemployed men who pass the time together at roadside stalls that sell cheap beer and soft drinks, not the type of place a tourist would venture into. On a cloudless, late-September morning, though, Kisauni's sprawl doesn't appear quite as depressing as some other places, for instance the shantytowns of Mumbai or the favellas of São Paulo, but life is clearly hard here.[1] While Kenya is better off than many other parts of the continent, the opportunities to find work and support a family are still not great in this part of Africa, so people will take almost any job offered, even if it means risking their life.

Down a muddy alley, past a small, white mosque, the beat-up Toyota taxi I'm riding in pulls up outside a simple one-story concrete and brick structure. The driver seems uncertain of the location, but my interpreter speaks to the man quickly and then gestures for me to get out, saying this is the place. A trio of young boys pause in their barefoot game of soccer to smile and wave at me, while a toddler plays in the dirt with a cardboard box. I'm uncertain where to go until I see my interpreter chatting with someone standing in a nearby doorway, a man who watches me impassively. He is tall, with large hands, a broad nose, and gaunt features; I guess he must be about forty. This is Hassan Abdalla.

As we're introduced, Hassan quietly welcomes me with the traditional Swahili greeting, "Jambo." I'm beckoned to come inside, and following my translator's lead, I remove my shoes and enter a darkened passageway lined with a half-dozen doors that ends at a small cooking area, where two women are preparing lunch over an open fire. Hassan heads into the tiny room he shares with his wife and infant daughter, a space barely ten by fifteen feet square filled with a couple of chairs, a sofa, bed, dresser, and bassinet. With its peeling blue paint, lack of decorations, single lightbulb, and barred window, the room feels less like a home than a prison cell. We sit in silence for a few minutes, knee-to-knee, as he sizes me up.

"You want to know about the pirates, hmmm?" Hassan says in English. I nod. He nods back. More silence. He looks at me with eyes both hesitant and sad, making me wonder what is wrong. Before coming here, I'd been told there was a sailor who would talk about a pirate incident, nothing more. How bad could it be? I wondered.

Hassan interrupts my thoughts, speaking so quietly that I have to lean forward. "I remember it like yesterday. Maybe too much." He pauses to smile, but I notice it's forced and quickly fades. Then, apologizing for his English and switching to Swahili, Hassan begins his story.

"For ten years I have been a sailor, working all along the coast—

Zanzibar, Dar es Salaam, Mozambique, Somalia, and here, Mombasa. I was bosun, in charge of the crew, important job. It was a good job—I make about one hundred American dollars a month—and there was never any trouble, even when we went to Somalia before. It was a good life."

Hassan reaches over to grab a small duffel bag lying in the corner, pulling out a stack of dog-eared photographs that are his memories of working at sea. He flips through them, smiling more warmly now as he passes them over to me. There are pictures of Hassan with crewmates, snapshots as he poses beside various ships, and other glimpses of better times. But then the smile again fades, and his face becomes stony as he takes back the photos, shoving them away inside the bag. Hassan takes a moment to collect his thoughts, then starts speaking in a slow and deliberate manner, revisiting events that few of us can comprehend and some might think untrue.

"My story . . . It was June of 2005 when it all began." Hassan is no longer looking at me; he is somewhere else. "I was on a freighter sailing from Mombasa with a load of rice, and we were four days out when the pirates attacked. It was just before 2000 hours (8:00 P.M.), and I was in my cabin. We were about thirty-five nautical miles offshore, in international waters. The seas were very calm that night, I remember, and it was hot. I heard some noises from outside, like *pop-pop-pop*. Then I heard voices, shouting, outside my cabin, and then there was banging on my door. I opened it and saw a man holding an AK-47 pointed at me, and he was telling me to go to the bridge with the rest of the crew.

"I knew right away they were pirates. They had surrounded the ship in some small boats and swarmed aboard so quickly, this all took maybe fifteen or twenty minutes. There were fifteen men, with AKs and RPGs [rocket-propelled grenade launchers], and they had us all sit on the floor with our hands on our heads while their leader questioned us. He spoke some English, and wanted to know our religion. I told him I am Muslim. Most of us were, except our captain, who was Hindu. I thought maybe that was good for me, because they were Muslims, too.

"I was scared because the pirates had weapons and were singing and laughing, happy to have conquered us. It was strange. Then their leader became very angry with us, shouting and threatening with his gun. They called themselves Somali Marines and said we were carrying illegal weapons, that was why they had boarded us. Our captain told them, 'No, we are carrying rice on a humanitarian mission for the United Nations, not weapons.' But the leader did not believe him. That was when I first became worried, because we were supposed to be helping the people [of Somalia]. When the pirates went to check the cargo holds, they saw we had only rice, but were still angry. Maybe from chewing the khat.[2]

"Meanwhile the looting had begun. Pirates were going through our cabins, stealing whatever they wanted: watches, mobile phones, anything. We had to sit there while they robbed us. The leader put his gun to the head of our captain and made him open the ship's safe and took all the money there—$8,500 American. So much money. Then they ordered the captain to take the ship toward the coast and our torture really began.

"You must know that I had never been in such a place. These men were bad people. I hoped—we all hoped—it would be over quickly. Wouldn't you? And the pirates kept telling us this; they used our emotions. On the first day, they took the radio and the satellite telephone to begin negotiating with the owners for our release, but the discussions kept breaking down. So one week, two weeks, then a month went by, and nothing happened. We had to stay inside the ship and could not be in groups of more than three.

The pirates watched us all the time with their guns. The food and water began to get low, so we began to ration. We even took some of the rice from the cargo to cook.

"Then, one day, the pirates' frustration with negotiations became too much. They took their weapons and began to shoot up the ship, smashing the windows, and we were very afraid. They said we had to tell the owner to pay the ransom or something bad would happen, and we worried they might begin to execute someone. By now we had been held hostage for over two months, and all of us were getting desperate. We had hunger and boredom and no news from the outside. Nothing. I tried not to think of my family, because I knew if I did, I would become depressed. It was like this for all of us: silence, no thoughts, no emotions. This was a psychological torture from the pirates.

"Just when we didn't think it could get any worse, the pirates ordered us to raise the anchor and get the engines working. They wanted to head to sea because they had seen another ship out there and decided to hijack it, using our vessel as a mother ship. It was very tense since no one knew if a naval ship might be in the area and come after us. You know, maybe they might try to sink us with guns. Luckily for us, nothing like that happened. But not lucky for the other crew, who also became prisoners of the pirates.

"All this time they kept moving our ship from place to place along the coast. The pirates were cautious; they made sure we never sailed in international waters, where someone might have rescued us. One night, some of us came up with a plan to throw a beacon overboard, to show our position. But there was no chance. It was too dangerous.

"Then, as quickly as it began, it was over. On October 3 they said we were free; they had received the ransom money. I do not know how much exactly, but they told us earlier they were demanding 38 million Kenyan shillings [over $500,000 U.S.]. I knew they would hijack again, because ransom money is sweet—once you've tasted it, you want more.

"So we headed home to Mombasa, and I remember thanking God for keeping me safe. Our original trip was supposed to be twenty days; instead, we were held prisoner by the pirates for a hundred days. But it was over."

Hassan pauses, then looks me in the eyes, his features hard. "Why did this happen to me? I do not know. What did I ever do to those people? What? Nothing is the same; everything has changed for me. All because of pirates. After this all ended, what did I get in compensation? One hundred American dollars. A dollar for every day I was in captivity."

We're suddenly interrupted by the appearance of Hassan's wife and infant daughter. The little girl is an obvious source of pride for him, and he puts on a brave face in front of his wife as he shows me some newspaper clippings from his arrival home in Mombasa. In the photos, Hassan sports a bushy beard and lean physique from three months spent with little food or water. But he also appears healthier than the man sitting in front of me in this tiny room in a Mombasa slum. Except for a short spell working in a local shipyard shortly after his release, Hassan has not been able to hold down a job for over a year and a half. His hundred-day stint as a pirate prisoner has left Hassan Abdalla a broken man.

And as I look at this broken mariner cradling his infant daughter, I keep thinking of what he just told me: a dollar a day.

The most shocking thing about Hassan's story is that it is not unique. Far from it, for piracy is alive and well today, thriving on the waters of our planet as never before. Incidents like the kidnapping of

Hassan Abdalla occur on a frighteningly regular basis, with attacks being recorded on an almost daily basis worldwide. Every year, thousands of people are assaulted, are injured, go missing, or are murdered by pirates. These attacks occur off Africa, Asia, the Middle East, the Indian subcontinent, South America, and throughout the Caribbean. They cost the global economies billions annually and the targets of pirates include coastal freighters, oil tankers, containerships, fishing boats, passenger ferries, private yachts, and even luxury cruise liners.

To be talking of piracy in the twenty-first century may seem slightly preposterous, what one might consider a small aberration overblown by the media. The common perception is that piracy was long ago relegated to the history books, the source of countless novels, movies, plays, and Halloween costumes that hark back to bygone eras when ships of sail roamed the seas, armed with cannons and crewed by outlaws bearing cutlasses, intent on enriching themselves through pillaging. Of course, one can always find criminals in any day and age, but the concept that piracy is widespread in today's age strikes most people as a tad far-fetched.

However, ask any professional mariner about the subject and you will quickly discover a chilling reality: After centuries of decline, piracy has reemerged as one of the most serious threats facing those who go down to the sea in ships. This type of criminal activity runs rampant around the world, to the concern of nation-states, navies, international organizations, businesses, and individuals like Hassan. It is a deadly enterprise enveloped in the most base of human actions: preying upon the weak. Of all the man-made threats that lurk upon the seas, without a doubt the most frightening is coming face-to-face with armed men intent on boarding your vessel. In simple terms, someone—somewhere—was attacked by pirates today, and it's almost certain that violence was involved.

Seafaring has fascinated us for thousands of years, ever since someone rode a tree trunk down the shore and then returned to tell the other villagers about the experience. It's a world full of mystery, drama, and the unknown, something that few ever really see, even today. Some of the greatest works of literature and art have dealt with the lives of mariners, from Homer's *Odyssey* to Joseph Conrad's *Heart of Darkness*. And the dark side of seafaring—the pirates, buccaneers, and privateers—is no less attractive, for the stories of outlaws entertain those of us who live ordered lives, allowing us the vicarious pleasure of indulging our fantasies without ever leaving home.

Three hundred years ago the exploits of Scottish pirates, English corsairs, American privateers, French buccaneers, Dutch freebooters, and Spanish raiders entertained many, selling books and newspapers and fueling conversations in back-alley bars. The late seventeenth and early eighteenth centuries were known as the golden age of piracy, when the likes of Blackbeard and Captain Kidd preyed on merchant shipping. But compared with today, that era was a mere bronze age: modern pirates surpass their predecessors in numbers, riches, and violence. Since the end of the cold war, piracy has become far more prevalent than at any other time in history, developing into a business with multinational impact, multibillion-dollar cost, and a deadly human toll.

All of which now begs the question: if piracy is such a serious problem, why do we hear so little about it?

The simple answer is that piracy usually takes place far from major centers—especially in the West—and the victims are most often professional mariners, people with whom landlubbers have little, if any, contact. Compounding this is the fact that in a world in which image is everything, there are very few opportunities for a news crew to capture footage of pirates in action, or even the aftermath of an attack. Besides, the world seems more concerned with Iraq and Afghanistan, hot spots that involve thousands of foreign soldiers engaged in battle with shadowy opponents.

Pirates are also members of a criminal subculture who prefer to remain well out of the limelight. One must dig and dig to find the truth about piracy and this can take years to do, as I found out the hard way. You cannot just arrive in some far-off village and ask to meet the nearest pirate—nor should you. But the threat that piracy poses means we should be more aware of the situation.

It's difficult to glamorize the exploits of those who kidnap, assault, and murder, and that is not my purpose here. I feel little remorse for anyone who holds another person hostage for a hundred days merely to make money, though I've come to understand the reasons one would do such a despicable act. The story of modern-day piracy is steeped in its own seven deadly sins: poverty, desperation, hunger, opportunity, violence, envy, and greed. Some of today's pirates are little better than petty thieves, others are brutal thugs, and a large number are members of well-organized gangs using the Internet, fax machines, satellite phones, and GPS units to coordinate their assaults. The sophistication of today's pirate gangs is such that some operate like multinational corporations, with hundreds of "employees" and business contacts working in several countries at any given time. Other gangs have grown so powerful that they have taken on the trappings of ministates, influencing recognized governments, dispensing fishing licenses, regulating shipping, and effectively controlling vast expanses of oceans.

Today's pirates have intuitively refined the lessons learned from their forebears, realizing opportunities that could only have been dreamed of in times gone by. They utilize high-tech forms of communication that allow the coordination of attacks over immense areas. They have the ability to muster weaponry far more effective than their predecessors, from assault rifles like the famous Kalashnikov AK-47 (and its variants) to rocket-propelled grenade launchers. They have the ability to hijack a vessel worth millions of dollars and make her essentially disappear, along with her crew and cargo.

The dark side of seafaring has attracted countless opportunists, corrupt officials, and organized crime syndicates, all seeking to cash in on the global boom in shipping and the inability of anyone to effectively safeguard the seas. Among those drawn to the world of maritime crime are some of the most-feared individuals in the modern era: terrorists. The extent of terrorist involvement in modern piracy is an extremely touchy subject for many in the maritime and security communities. In some quarters it is dismissed as inconsequential, while in others it is considered the next threat to national security. The arguments have far-ranging impacts, as the types of terrorist attacks are numerous and their potential targets great. They might commandeer a supertanker and sink her in a major shipping lane or place a weapon of mass destruction in a shipping container bound for some Western port. No one can be certain these events might happen, but no one expected the horrific destruction of the World Trade Center towers, either.

What is undeniable, though, is that terrorist groups have been engaging in maritime operations in the last few years. Al Qaeda has claimed responsibility for two deadly attacks by suicide bombers in the Red Sea, Filipino terrorists killed over a hundred passengers on a ferry that had just left Manila, and Tamil separatists have turned the waters off northern Sri Lanka into a very real war zone.

Piracy is technically just one aspect of maritime crime, along with such other acts as armed robbery. The most common definition in use today is that found in article 101 of the 1982 United Nations Convention on the Law of the Sea (UNCLOS), which states, in part, that piracy consists of "any illegal acts of violence or detention, or any act of depredation, committed for private ends . . . on the high seas." The same article defines armed robbery against ships to mean "any unlawful act of violence or detention or any act of depredation, or threat thereof, other than an act of 'piracy' . . . within a State's jurisdiction over such offences."[3]

It's important to note the difference between the UNCLOS definition of piracy and that of maritime armed robbery: the former occurs on the "high seas," while the latter is within a nation's sovereign waters. High seas—which represent 50 percent of the Earth's surface—are separated from sovereign waters by an invisible line that lies twelve nautical miles off the coast of a country, so by this application someone who boards a ship thirteen miles out is engaging in piracy, but if he attacks a vessel in port he is merely robbing it. I say "merely" because the word "robbery" carries far less emotional weight than "piracy."

In reality, both acts are exactly the same. They always mean the invasion of private property, often involve violence, and sometimes lead to murder. So, to the disapproval of purists, I make little distinction here based on the hairsplitting in legal codes. However no apologies are offered, for I feel that a broader description makes it easier for people to approach the subject of this global problem. I think a better definition comes from the well-respected nongovernmental International Maritime Bureau (IMB), which considers piracy, and armed robbery, to be "any act of boarding or attempting to board any ship with the apparent intent to commit theft or any other crime and with the apparent intent or capability to use force in the furtherance of that act." (It should be noted that "terrorism" has no firm legal definition in international law, though it has been addressed in the codes of many individual countries.)

By using the IMB's definition, it does not matter whether a vessel is in port or on the high seas: any attack on her should be considered an act of piracy. The real issue isn't determining the sovereignty of the seas but recognizing that criminal elements are committing violent deeds upon those waters so regularly. Setting aside the arguments about what constitutes an act of piracy or sea robbery, let us consider the perpetrators. We call them pirates, buccaneers, sea robbers, thieves, murderers, gangsters, and a plethora of other colorful descriptions. Here we are freed from any legal constraints, for those who engage in maritime crime have never been firmly defined in our modern era. The most fitting definition for these criminals comes from the Roman statesman and philosopher Cicero. Over two thousand years ago, he decided that pirates and their ilk should be considered *hostis humani generis*, enemies of the human race, enemies to all mankind.

I often wonder what Cicero would make of our world if he knew that the scourge of piracy continues. Perhaps he would agree with a perspective on the situation that I have developed: Piracy is the world's longest-running armed conflict, a de facto low-level war that has simmered on the seas for thousands of years, since well before the Roman statesman was born. The victims of this conflict are members of a community with its own history, traditions, and language, a nomadic people related not by birth or nationality but by the sea. We don't usually think of mariners in those terms, but they truly constitute a distinct group in our planet's history, a group that has been preyed upon, robbed, and murdered for millennia, merely because they chose to set out upon the water. For this community to have endured violent attacks in the past is terrible. That they are still being targeted today is unconscionable.

For seafarers, the impact of these violent assaults is not unlike the combat stress experienced by soldiers, something that very few of us not personally involved can really comprehend. As I took my leave of Hassan Abdalla in Kisauni, he told me that what happened in Somalia had created a special bond between the men held hostage by their pirate captors. "Only if you have lived through that can you understand this," he said. "People must know the truth."

1

THE BRETHREN OF THE COAST

My Lord, it is a very hard Sentence. For my Part, I am the innocentest Person of them all, only I have been sworn against by perjured Persons.

—CAPTAIN WILLIAM KIDD, MAY 1701

THREE HUNDRED YEARS ago one of the most famous outlaws of his era stood before an Admiralty Sessions convened at London's Old Bailey Courthouse to utter these meek words of defense.[1] Captain Kidd had been found guilty of "Pyracy and Robbery on the High Seas," as well as murder, capping a brief three-year career as a buccaneer that had come to fascinate the general public. He'd been neither the most successful pirate of the time nor the most feared; indeed, he was actually somewhat amateurish in his attempts at plundering ships off the Malabar coast of India and his crew had actually mutinied against what they saw as an incompetent leader. Captured in Boston and sent back to England to face justice, Kidd was in his mid-fifties when his roving days came to a close.

Yet Kidd was undeniably legendary back then, and part of the reason for his notoriety was that he had turned his back on a life of genteel opportunity to become a roving pirate. The Scots-born son of a Presbyterian minister, William Kidd set off for the New World, where he made a name for himself as a member of the colonial elite in New York City, with a house on Wall Street and a wealthy bride. But for reasons that have never been made clear, he soon grew bored with his refined life in America and decided to embark on a series of privateering expeditions, possibly yearning for adventure—and the chance to make some easy money.

Privateers are not pirates, at least not legally. The difference between the two is important, as a privateer operates within the laws of a nation, while a pirate does not. Traditionally, privateers received a document from their government known as a "letter of marque" that allowed them to legally attack the merchant shipping of an enemy state. Armed with such a letter and suitable weaponry, privateers were expected to return a portion of any profits plundered to the authorities. Kidd got his own letter of marque from the British and sallied forth to attack French shipping but then got greedy and turned from privateering to outright piracy against any vessels he encountered, English or foreign. To the authorities in London this was unacceptable for a variety of reasons, not the least because it sullied the reputations of recognized privateers. Perhaps more important, though, Kidd's feats set a dangerous precedent, showing that piracy could appeal not only to the poor and dispossessed but also to the gentry. When someone of his upbringing decided to go "on the account" and take to pirating, the Admiralty had to deal with it quickly. He could not be allowed to become a hero or role model for anyone thinking about piracy.

So it was that Captain William Kidd was tried for his crimes during a brief two-day session in the Old Bailey, found guilty of all charges, and sentenced to death. Barely two weeks later, on May

23, 1701, he was bundled aboard a horse-drawn cart and traveled from Newgate Prison in the City of London toward the then suburb of Wapping and a place known as Execution Dock. Located at a bend on the north side of the Thames River not far from the Tower of London, this was where convicted pirates were traditionally hanged. With a crowd watching onshore and from sightseeing boats on the river, the most infamous pirate of the day was led to the gallows at Execution Dock, continuing to protest his innocence. By most accounts he was blind drunk as the hangmen put the noose around his neck. This was probably just as well, for it took two tries to kill him: the rope broke on the first fall and he lay wallowing in the river mud before he was led back to the gallows and the sentence was finally carried out. Admiralty law then proscribed that his body be tarred, bound in irons, and hung from a gibbet farther downriver at Tilbury Point for all to see, rotting there for years afterward as warning to other would-be pirates.

Modern Wapping is today, like much of the Docklands area, awash with redevelopments turning a historic part of London into upscale condos and offices. Execution Dock is long gone—its last use as a killing ground was in 1830—and it's difficult to find the site today. Walking along the narrow confines of Wapping High Road, I find no historical markers or other indications of this macabre part of London's history. The street is separated from the Thames by buildings old and new, with a couple of parkettes offering riverside views of Tower Bridge, but little else.

Stopping at a pub to ask the bartender if he knows where Execution Dock is, I'm told it's right next door, and I head down a small laneway to the river's edge, the closest one can get to the actual location. There is really nothing much to see beyond tour boats plying the Thames on this late-summer morning and bits of rubbish floating toward the sea, not that I'd expected relics to be lingering after several hundred years. But the effort to see where Captain Kidd and so many others like him met their demise makes me realize that the reality of pirate life has often been kept hidden from us.

For instance, one of the forgotten aspects of London's history is the wealth that it received from pirates and privateers and the degree to which piracy was considered a legitimate, or quasi-legitimate, form of maritime life. For hundreds of years, the bounty plundered by Sir Francis Drake, Sir Henry Morgan, and countless regular sailors helped make London's waterfront teem with brothels, bars, and gaming parlors where one's newfound, illicit wealth could be spent. The same held true for New York City, Boston, Nassau, Havana, and numerous ports around the world. Even with the threat of Execution Dock's gallows looming nearby, the allure of a supposedly easy life of maritime crime would have been strong for the impoverished men sitting in Wapping's pubs centuries ago.

I've come to London not just to see the historical site where pirates like Captain Kidd were executed but also to begin understanding how piracy could remain such a problem in today's day and age while being virtually unknown to most people. One of the best places to start is at the IMB. It is not a governmental organization but a division of the Paris-based International Chamber of Commerce, an organization founded in 1919 to promote business interests and global trade. The IMB itself was established in 1981 to help combat commercial crime in the maritime world and is funded by a variety of shipping firms, insurance companies, and others concerned about the issue. It is one of the groups at the forefront of dealing with global piracy today and, ironically, is headquartered within sight of the old Execution Dock here in Wapping.

The IMB's director is Pottengal Mukundan, a professional mariner who rose to become a captain before coming ashore to take a desk job with the IMB when it was set up. A trim, bespectacled man, he speaks in the calm, deliberate manner of a master mariner. Mukundan works tirelessly to publicize the threats posed by pirates and maritime criminals, crisscrossing the globe to speak at conferences, meet with government officials and military officers, and persuade the shipping industry to address the problem.

"Why does someone become a pirate? Well, purely for financial gain," Mukundan tells me when we meet. "Everything that we see is economic piracy and most of the incidents take place in countries with economic problems. As long as there has been maritime commerce, there has been piracy. Pirates in the old days were . . . criminals of the lowest kind who preyed on the weak and showed no mercy at all. Pirates today are exactly the same, though violence has increased and the types of attacks have become more dangerous. The problem now is that pirates are using guns, knives, and even grenade launchers, and the types of attacks have become more dangerous—today very often you have four or five boats, converging on the target vessel from different directions, making it very difficult for the people on the bridge of the merchant ship to avoid the pirate boats, and in that confusion [pirates] will fire on the bridge and then get on board, from the stern typically, and take control of the ship."

Mukundan explains that the IMB began to look more closely at piracy, as opposed to general maritime crime, back in 1991. The following year, they opened the IMB Piracy Reporting Centre in Kuala Lumpur, Malaysia, which collects information about incidents from the shipping industry, government organizations, the media, and even individual mariners. Before that time, no one had bothered to assess the global threat of piracy in such a comprehensive manner, and they continually update their information on a regular basis. The IMB's records are considered the most complete source of information on piracy in the world, used by the United

Nations and various governments and businesses. The results of the IMB's analyses make it clear that piracy is not just alive and well but getting worse.

"Since we began looking at piracy, we have seen the attacks steadily go up. For instance, in 1994 there were only 90 actual or attempted attacks reported to us, but by 2000 that figure had risen to 469. The attacks went down a bit in 2005–2006, but then began to increase again: we had 198 reported attacks in the first nine months of 2007, up 14% from the same period a year earlier. But, and this is something I must emphasize, there are a very large number of attacks which go unreported, particularly in West Africa, South Africa, and South America. The real figures are much higher. We know that in some cases, there have been forty to fifty attacks in a country that are not reported."

As laid out in detailed reports the IMB has been publishing on a regular basis, there have been pirate incidents in the waters off 82 countries around the world in the last decade and a half, involving vessels from 112 different nationalities.[2] If you consider that the United Nations lists 192 Member States as belonging to that global body, the IMB's statistics reveal that pirates have attacked vessels flying the flags of over half the nations on Earth.

The reports are meticulous, providing accounts of each individual pirate attack reported to the IMB, a list of the regions where piracy is occurring, the types of vessels involved, the weapons used, and a breakdown of the types of violence crews faced. It is the latter set of statistics, known as Table 8 in the IMB reports, that is most chilling to read, for they outline just what mariners endure on the seas. The headings read: "Taken Hostage," "Kidnap/Ransom," "Threatened," "Assaulted," "Injured," "Killed," "Missing." Beside each is a row of figures that adds up to over five thousand incidents of violence committed by pirates in the last decade. These include over 2,800 hostage takings, 303 murders, and 167 unsolved disappearances of mariners, an annual average of 321 pirate incidents, 280 people taken prisoner and 30 individuals killed. Since the real figures are assumed to be much higher—Mukundan tells me that doubling them would be entirely plausible—this begins to reveal the scope of the threat that looms out there.

I pick up the IMB report for the first half of 2007 and flip through its catalogue of pirate attacks:

Nigeria, 8 January: Danish product tanker was attacked by armed pirates while anchored at position Latitude 06:19 North and Longitude 003:23 East. Five pirates armed with guns and knives boarded at approximately 2335 Local Time. They attacked the duty crew Bosun who sustained injuries to his left hand. They then tied him up and stole his personal effects. The pirates then threatened to cut off his ears if he did not reveal the code for the locks to the Cargo Control Room and how much money was aboard.

Bangladesh, 29 March: Dutch container vessel was anchored in Chittagong Roads when two robbers using grappling hooks with ropes boarded from a small boat near the stern. The alarm was raised by the deck watchmen who were attacked by the robbers armed with knives. The crew sustained serious cuts to their hands. The robbers jumped into the water and the small boat moved away.

India, 13 April: Singapore tug was towing a barge off Trivandrum at position 08:20 N 076:32 E when about 100 pirates including fishermen armed with long knives boarded the barge. They stole cargo and escaped.

Spratly Islands, South China Sea, 26 April: Armed pirates boarded Chinese fishing vessel at time unknown and robbed it of its catch while it was taking shelter due to engine trouble. The Master informed his family about the robbery and that another vessel was approaching it. All contact with the fishing vessel was lost since the Master's last call. The fate of the vessel and crew members is unknown.

Somalia, 14 May: United Arab Emirates–owned general cargo ship attacked while 180 nautical miles off coast at 1530 Local [Time]. Pirates armed with machine guns and rocket launchers approached and ordered the ship to stop and started firing towards the bridge. Master took evasive action when he saw pirates preparing to fire rocket-propelled grenades. The ship was hit and accommodation caught fire and was extensively damaged. Attack lasted for one hour before pirates aborted.

These incidents—involving a containership, a tanker, a tugboat, a cargo ship, and a fishing boat—are just 5 out of 126 that had been reported to the IMB between January and July of 2007, but they are a good cross section of the types of pirate attacks that occur on the seas today. Mukundan assures me that these are by no means the worst reports they've received. Descriptions of gangs large and small, violence to crews, abductions, petty thefts, disappeared ships, rocket-propelled grenades—these are the sorts of things he finds waiting in his morning e-mails each day he comes to work. Though he's not inured to the continual barrage of incident reports that filter in from all corners of the world, Mukundan takes pains to maintain a professional demeanor when looking at piracy: "Of course I get angry when I hear about these attacks. Who wouldn't? The lives of people are at stake here, but just getting angry will not solve this problem."

The IMB director stresses the importance of collecting information, sifting through it for developing trends, and sharing what they have learned with others so that mariners and governments can be aware of the situation. After establishing the Piracy Reporting Centre in Malaysia, the organization set out to pinpoint the root causes of regional maritime crime, and by looking at the data compiled since then they were able to establish three key factors that lead to piracy: a desire to make money, a lack of strong law enforcement, and unarmed vessels plying nearby waters. Or, to put it another way, greed, lawlessness, and opportunity.

"If you look at any of the hot spots of piracy today, you will find these conditions present. For example, in Somalia there is no national government or law enforcement infrastructure, no one for the victims to turn to for assistance, there is poverty from the fighting and chaos in the country, and there is [shipping] traffic along the coastline. So it's a combination of social conditions, economic conditions, and the way law enforcement is done that allows piracy to flourish."

The hot spots that Mukundan is referring to are those places around the globe that are the most dangerous for mariners, as shown by reports of pirate attacks received by the IMB. He highlights the waters off Somalia and Nigeria as being the worst places seafarers can find themselves today, though his list also includes Indonesia, Tanzania, West Africa, the Red Sea, the port of Santos in Brazil, and Bangladesh. In all of these locations, vessels have been attacked while anchored and also while steaming.

For most of the past decade, the most notorious area infested by pirates has been the Strait of Malacca, between Indonesia and Malaysia. Because it is a crucial sea-lane connecting East Asia with the West and transited by thousands of vessels each year, the numerous pirate attacks on shipping in this region have attracted a lot of attention. When I ask him about the situation there today, Mukundan relaxes a bit after having provided me with such a bleak assessment of the worldwide piracy situation. He explains that though the Strait is still prone to pirate attacks, the situation there is much better than it was a few years ago. Years of prodding by the IMB and other groups finally forced the three nations that control the waters, Malaysia, Indonesia, and Singapore, to become more forceful in dealing with the threat.

"We have the odd attack in Southeast Asia, either in the Malacca Straits or east of Singapore, which indicates that the gangs doing the serious attacks—the hijacking of ships—are still present. There was an attack, for example, against a product tanker in March. The ship was actually hijacked and the hijackers took control of the ship and tried to sail it towards an Indonesian island. The engines failed and they became so frustrated that they left the vessel after seven hours. The crew then freed themselves, restarted the engines, and went back to Singapore. Overall things are much safer there, though we still recommend vigilance by crews."

Having looked at the root causes of modern-day piracy, the IMB next began to analyze what sorts of groups were engaging in attacks. In truth, there are many incidents that essentially involve a couple of guys climbing aboard a ship while she's anchored in port and trying to steal whatever they can get their hands on: paint, ropes, tools, and anything else that the crew might have left out in the open. These are like smash-and-grab thefts in cities, albeit without so much smashing. Because of this, a number of observers have derided pirates as nothing more than mere thugs, not worthy of a great degree of notice.

But ask any criminologist about petty crime and you'll see that there's a slippery slope involved here. If it's that easy to make some money stealing paint cans off a vessel, there's a definite risk that the individuals involved will decide to try something more brazen, like robbing a mariner of his wallet, stealing the contents of a ship's safe, or holding the crew for ransom. Pottengal Mukundan says that what the IMB has discovered is that there are distinct types of pirate attacks that can be separated by their intent.

"At the bottom end of the scale you have mugging at sea, where low-level criminals try to get on board a ship and try to steal whatever they can within a period of about forty minutes to an hour and then take off. At the other end of the scale you have the organized-crime attack, which is really aimed at hijacking the multimillion-dollar ship and its multimillion-dollar cargo. That's a very well-resourced attack. They use automatic weapons like rocket-propelled grenade launchers, they will change the name of the ship, kill the crew or set them adrift, and then they take the vessel to a new port, under a false name, and discharge the cargo. And then, once the cargo is discharged, they have control of the empty vessel, which they use as a criminal vessel, a pirate vessel, what we call a phantom ship."

In between these extremes is the most serious type of piracy, where ships are attacked not to steal the cargo but to abduct the crew and hold them until a ransom is paid. In some places, pirates only target the senior officers, such as the captains and chief engineers, while in other spots they keep the entire crew hostage, as happened to Hassan Abdalla off Somalia. According to Mukundan, these attacks are carried out by well-organized gangs who have a knowledge of how the shipping industry works. Their ability to pinpoint a vessel at sea, board her and abduct crew members, and then carry out negotiations with shipowners for ransom requires much more sophistication than these gangs are often given credit for.

"The taking of hostages is not opportunistic; it is a very well-planned attack: they are well resourced, well armed. They take over the ship and hold the crew for ransom. Organized-crime syndicates are actively involved and they've always been, because it's a hugely profitable exercise for them. You might get $50,000 (U.S.) for a crew; you might get a half-million dollars for the entire ship. So, there is a lot of money involved."

The IMB director goes on to say that the networks used to organize hijackings involve more than a few guys with a small boat and some weapons. Pirates today monitor radio frequencies and the Internet, receive information from spies in ports and confederates within the shipping industry, and get assistance from mariners willing to betray their shipmates. An incident in late May of 2007 is an example of how sophisticated the IMB has seen pirate gangs become.

In the wee hours of Tuesday, May 22, the tanker MT *Thanadol 4* was steaming about thirty miles off the east coast of Thailand in the Gulf of Siam (also known as the Gulf of Thailand). The ship was laden with hundreds of thousands of liters of fuel oil for fishing vessels working the surrounding seas when she was approached by a small boat piloted by a former crew member from the tanker. He boarded the *Thanadol 4* and said he was hijacking her. The idea seems to have been to sail the tanker to an undisclosed location and off-load the cargo of fuel oil so it could likely be sold on the black market.

Apparently, the pirate hoped to convince the crew to help him and his land-based accomplices with the plan—maybe the pirate gang thought the seafarers aboard the tanker were so poorly paid that some extra cash would be enough of an inducement to join in the plot. Unfortunately for the would-be hijacker, the crew of the *Thanadol 4* balked at becoming pirates themselves and, in retaliation, their former comrade shot and killed the captain, throwing his body into the sea.

Three members of the tanker's crew managed to escape and jump overboard. Picked up by a passing fishing boat, the escapees notified the Thai authorities that their ship had been hijacked, and naval aircraft and patrol boats were dispatched to find the phantom ship. Within a short time, they'd located the ship and, as the noose tightened, the pirate aboard the *Thanadol 4* fled from the ship, only to be captured by marine police.

Someone obviously doesn't set out to hijack an oil tanker on his own. The ability to locate a commercial vessel while it's sailing thirty miles offshore means there was intelligence gathered about when the tanker was departing port and where she was planning to sail. Believing the crew could be co-opted to participate in the plot points to an insider's take on their mind-set. And disposing of thousands of liters of fuel oil requires coordination with other vessels, such as barges, to off-load the cargo from the tanker, as well as the business connections to sell the booty. So, though only one person was arrested in this particular incident, there must have been many others involved in its planning and execution who are still at large.

According to Mukundan, these types of events receive little notice in the media because they so often happen in some far-off locale and involve small numbers of mariners from non-Western nations. As he puts it, when a passenger plane is hijacked it often has hundreds of passengers aboard, with a good chance there are at least a few from some major nation, while on a typical ship "you might have just twenty crew members, from places like India, the Philippines, China, or Indonesia, and they don't get the attention they should."

For someone who began his career as a professional mariner, modern-day piracy is more than just a collection of statistics in annual reports; it is an ever-present threat to the lives of those who are fellow members of the global fraternity of seafarers. Mukundan expresses some disappointment that the issue is still downplayed by various governments and elements in the shipping industry, as though piracy were just another of the costs of doing business today.

"It is very serious for the unfortunate victims," Mukundan says, quickly adding, "You must remember that a ship is a person's home; it is more than a place where you go to work. When people invade at night and take over a vessel, the crew members know that no one is going to come to their assistance while the pirates are on board. At sea, on a ship, nobody is going to help them. So they know for that time they are completely at the mercy of the pirates. And many seafarers who survive these attacks, the serious attacks, probably will not go back to sea again; they've given up the life at sea because the experience is very traumatic. I don't think it should be the cost of doing business."

If records like the IMB's are to be believed, there are only a few hundred pirate attacks occurring every year, which, in the harsh reality of life today, does not seem to constitute a problem serious enough to warrant greater attention. But even Pottengal Mukundan believes the real figures are much higher, as he had told me earlier.

Wondering why so many incidents would go unreported, I head off to Southwark, on London's south bank of the Thames, to meet with a shipping insider. Like a number of individuals I would speak to while looking into modern-day piracy, he preferred to remain anonymous. In some cases this was because of the sensitive nature of what they had to say, and I have protected their true identities to safeguard them. In other cases, like this, the individual I was talking to worked in the shipping industry, which is highly competitive and notoriously secretive about its activities, as I'd found when working on a previous book about commercial seafaring.[3] Until last year, this man—"Ian"—had been working as an officer on commercial vessels in the Far East and off Africa. Family commitments led him to return home to Britain, where he now works in the London office of an international shipping firm. Preferring I not swing by his workplace to talk, he'd suggested we meet beside the replica of Sir Francis Drake's galleon, the *Golden Hinde*, which is berthed near London Bridge, telling me in an e-mail: "Well, if you want to talk about pirates, let's begin at Drake's ship. I'm a bit of a history buff about those days."

Early for our meeting, I take a few moments to wander around the wooden galleon, which lies in a special dock adjacent to the Thames. Perhaps because it's almost noon on a Thursday, there are few people paying much attention to the ship, and she's not nearly as famous a tourist attraction as the cruiser HMS *Belfast* (moored within sight of the *Golden Hinde*) or even the *Cutty Sark* (found downriver in Greenwich and currently undergoing repairs after a disastrous fire in May 2007). The *Golden Hinde* is not even the only replica of Drake's original ship to be found in England: there's another one, called the *Golden Hind*, maintained in southwestern Devon's Brixham Harbour.

Looking at this vessel, moored beneath the shadows of an office tower, one could be forgiven for thinking she was a Disneyfied creation of some designer seeking to add maritime color to an otherwise bland urban courtyard. Her dark hull is accented with spirals of red and yellow trim, while a large blue and white depiction of a deer emblazons the rear of her aftcastle (this being a tribute to one of Drake's sponsors, whose family crest included a deer—or "hinde"). Above the deer can be seen the royal moniker "ER," for Elizabeth Regina, Elizabeth I.

Compared to modern seagoing vessels, which are predominantly utilitarian in design and virtually devoid of decorative finishes, the *Golden Hinde* seems comically cartoonish. But looks can be deceiving, for the *Golden Hinde* under Sir Francis Drake was the most successful pirate ship that ever sailed, in terms of both the booty acquired and the global impact of her voyages.

"Tiny-looking ship, eh?" a voice says to me as I'm staring at the

Golden Hinde. It's Ian, extending his hand in friendship while forcing me to listen carefully to his particularly thick Northern accent. Ian looks nothing like a professional mariner—he's slight of build, wearing the nondescript office uniform of dress shirt and tie, and can only be described as a generally gregarious, outgoing guy. Many mariners I've encountered tend to be quite reserved and quiet when first we meet, so Ian's demeanor is refreshing. As we stand beside the galleon, he launches into an exuberant spiel about the original *Golden Hinde*, an Elizabethan-era wooden ship that had taken Francis Drake and his crew on a circumnavigation of the globe between 1577 and 1580. That event was a remarkable seafaring achievement in itself, yet the voyage was not just about exploring new worlds.

"This was one of the most fearsome vessels on the waters when she sailed, or, at least, the original one was," Ian says while staring raptly at the *Golden Hinde*. "That voyage of Drake's created great concern, in Spain, Africa, South America, Mexico, and Southeast Asia. Four continents feared her, and just look at the ship—she's puny. Less than twenty feet across, something like a hundred and twenty feet long, she's the size of a couple of double-decker buses. Yet with her, Drake had as big an impact on late-sixteenth-century European politics as Osama bin Laden has had today."

Ian's enthusiastic comparison to modern terrorists is not just hyperbole. The myth of Sir Francis Drake's three-year global odyssey has become one in which he helped England to establish its seafaring credentials at a time when it was the Spanish and Portuguese who were the masters of the waters (albeit often with help from foreign mariners such as the Italian Columbus), and much has been made of Drake's ability to circumnavigate the planet, explore the west coast of present-day America, and cross the Pacific. But there was more— much more—than just a voyage of discovery and national pride taking place here.

In reality, Drake's expedition was a state-sanctioned part of a complex political struggle going on between England and Spain. In the 1500s, Spain was the most powerful political entity on the planet, ruled by Philip II and with a realm that spread from Europe to the New World and beyond. It was wealthy and confident and had the upper hand in terms of military, scientific, and economic supremacy at the time. And Spain had formed powerful alliances with other European rulers that allowed Philip to control a vast empire spread across several continents.

Meanwhile England, under Elizabeth, was still struggling to come to grips with its break from the Catholic Church (carried out by Elizabeth's father, Henry VIII), as dramatic an event in Europe as when Lenin and the Bolsheviks would turn Russia away from imperial rule in 1917. When she ascended the throne in 1558, England had just endured a politico-religious conflict that had created much internal strife; it had few allies, many formidable adversaries, and a huge budgetary shortfall; Elizabeth's military and naval capabilities were stretched to the limits and vastly inferior to those of Spain; and a myriad of intrigues made everyday life in her court a decidedly dangerous endeavor.

The most apt comparison of the relationship of these two countries is to that of the USSR and the United States during the cold war, neither willing to confront the other in outright war but each actively seeking to contain its opponent's power. One might compare Philip's Spain to the United States in the 1950s: a strong nation feeling a sense of purpose in its actions. By comparison, Elizabethan England could be considered akin to the Soviet Union in the years immediately after World War Two: a nation growing in power and seeking to establish its place in the world while dealing with the lingering memories of conflict, suspicions about its citizens, and the constraints of a smaller economy.

In the midst of Elizabethan rule, England could but look on in envy as Spain grew ever wealthier from its far-flung imperial outposts, especially the ones in Central and South America. The amount of silver and gold being extracted by slave labor and shipped across the Atlantic was staggering: each convoy that arrived in Spain increased Philip's coffers with the equivalent of millions, perhaps billions, of dollars' worth of precious metals. So it was only inevitable that some individuals in England would seek to acquire some of that wealth, for their own good and also for that of Good Queen Bess.

Throughout the 1560s and 1570s, a number of expeditions were mounted by English privateers in the Caribbean, with the intention of harrying the Spanish Main and plundering vessels. These little proxy conflicts brought England some much-needed revenue. They also filled the hearts of the Protestant elite with glee as their hated Catholic adversaries saw that Spain now had a serious political opponent. Still, there was a growing sense that England needed to make a bigger statement about its intentions, something on a grander scale than these quasi-legal pinpricks against imperial Spain in the Americas.

And so it was that a syndicate of men came up with the idea of a grand voyage into waters known and unknown, through all the regions claimed by Philip, which would irrevocably show that Elizabethan England was ready to assume a new mantle. The time had come for British mariners to take their place on the global scene, and this syndicate convinced Elizabeth to allow Francis Drake to set out from Plymouth on December 13, 1577, aboard the one-hundred-ton *Pelican* (which he would soon rename the *Golden Hinde*). In the course of the *Golden Hinde*'s three-year global odyssey, Drake captured Spanish vessels in the Atlantic and Pacific oceans and attacked towns and villages along the coast of South America, returning home with a rich horde of plundered wealth. For those who had invested in Drake's voyage (like the queen), this amounted to a return of £47 for every £1 they had put up. As he had established English nautical prowess and made a lot of money, Elizabeth promptly knighted Drake when he arrived home.

As Ian puts it, the Spanish considered Drake nothing more than a pirate: "They called him 'el Draque'—the Dragon—which was also a play on his name," says my companion, while to the English "he was a heroic privateer." Well, actually, not quite, as Ian reluctantly concedes. Drake, in fact, did not have a privateer's letter of marque when he embarked from Portsmouth, though he did have the tacit approval of the queen. Somehow, in the midst of Tudor-era politics this did not seem to matter, as he had succeeded in returning a profit to his backers.

I had assumed Ian chose the *Golden Hinde* as our rendezvous because of Drake's reputation as one of the most successful English privateers ever but am told that's just one of the reasons. "Drake's voyage with the *Golden Hinde* was shrouded in secrecy," the amateur historian says as we wander to a nearby coffee shop. "This was because of the political situation at the time and the relations with the Spanish. There've been books and whatnot written about his journey. Some think he sailed as far up the Pacific coast of America as your Vancouver Island, even up to Alaska. But we don't really know exactly, because Good Queen Bess had all sorts of the ship's documents made what we'd call 'top secret,' and they were stashed away, never to be seen again. Y'see? Seafaring, piracy, politics, business—they're all shrouded in secrecy. Always have been."

The secrecy he speaks of continues to this day in a business that Ian describes as "cutthroat, libertarian, and profit minded to a degree unlike many others." There are close to fifty thousand merchant vessels plying the seas and carrying over 90 percent of the world's commerce on a regular basis, with thousands of shipping-related companies all vying for a piece of the action.[4] It's an expensive business, what with the costs of building ships, maintaining them, chartering them, insuring them, hiring crews, and providing fuel and supplies. Still, there's a lot of money to be made if you manage your operations properly.

"The most crucial aspect of the [shipping] industry is your ability to attract customers," says Ian as we settle on a bench on the promenade overlooking the Thames. "You've got to be able to deliver on their demands in an efficient manner, pure and simple. If they're happy, they'll stay with you. So companies want to show [that] their operations are run smoothly, with no problems. Shippers, and their customers, don't like chaos or problems. There are enough problems with seafaring to begin with: the weather, regulations, delivery schedules, delays in port, competent crews, those sorts of things. Now what does this have to do with piracy? Well, a lot, because it's all about the fear of losing money."

What Ian has observed in his professional career as a mariner is that some shipping firms prefer not to report pirate attacks on their vessels for fear of the impact on their financial bottom lines. "If the news gets out that a ship of yours has been pirated, customers might decide to not use your company anymore. You know, they don't want to see their cargoes stolen or delayed getting to a port, do they? Say you're contracted to deliver some consumer goods from Japan to Europe by such-and-such a date, but your ship is attacked in the South China Sea. If the captain heads to the nearest port to file a report afterwards, that could see the ship stuck there for days while the crew is interviewed by police and an investigation is done, meaning the TV sets or whatever you're carrying are late reaching the market. That can be a black mark against your business reputation. And God forbid you should have more than one of your vessels attacked—that could turn you into a pariah firm that no one wants to work with."

A second reason attacks go unreported is the increased costs of insuring vessels that can result. All commercial ships must be insured, against loss or damage, as must their crews and their cargoes. If a shipper makes a claim to an insurance company for losses incurred by a pirate attack, they may find their premiums going up. As well, insurance rates can be higher if your vessel is sailing in waters known to be prone to pirate attacks.

"A couple of years ago," Ian recalls, "I was working out of Singapore on a contract. This was when things in the Strait of Malacca were still considered dangerous because of piracy. As a result, the insurance companies here in London, like Lloyd's, decided that the Strait would be considered like a war zone, like Iraq, and they hiked the rates they charged shippers. Nobody was happy about that, let me tell you. That lasted about a year, until the summer of 2006, I think."

I pull out the IMB's recent piracy reports and show Ian the statistics. Peering at the figures, he nods glumly at the tallies, then flips to the 2006 records for West Africa—the last place he sailed before coming home—and counts up the listed incidents. According to this report, there were twenty-seven actual attacks and five more attempted ones for the entire year. With a look of disdain on his face, Ian glances at me and says, "Bullshit." Based on his experience, the real figures are at least double what's printed out here and could be three or four times higher. As for the global total of 239 reported pirate incidents for all of 2006, he just shakes his head in disgust.

"I know IMB, IMO,[5] and other groups are doing their best to get the word out about piracy," he says with a sigh, "but these figures aren't real. No way. I can't say as they've been 'sanitized,' but

I'd be willing to bet they're more in line with what the shipping industry wants them to look like. These [figures] look like what a colleague of mine would call 'acceptable levels of risk.' One pirate attack every two or three days somewhere out there—that's okay. Three attacks every day—not good."

Ian puts it this way: You can't hide that there are pirate attacks occurring, because everyone's heard the stories of hijackings and assaults and murders. So there have to be incident reports; there has to be a paper trail; otherwise it would look like a huge cover-up. But at some point, as the statistics begin to pile up and the real picture emerges of how serious the situation is, people in places of influence will become nervous that the threat will tarnish their business.

To me, it seems highly improbable that organizations like the IMB or the IMO are doctoring the statistics on piracy attacks. Since they can only collect information based on what is actually reported to them, it seems more likely that groups like these are simply not being told about every incident that occurs. Ian agrees, dismissing any theories about a grand cover-up going on in the seafaring world.

"Is there a conspiracy going on within the shipping industry? I doubt it. The idea of a group of owners sitting in some boardroom and ordering the suppression of information is a little far-fetched. Most of these guys hate one another; they're competitors who would love nothing more than to steal each other's business. I do think they all know the unwritten rules of merchant shipping, though, and one of those is to keep a low profile. You know, right now the commercial shipping industry is in the midst of a huge boom; it has really never been better in any time in history. There is a *lot* of money at stake here. No one wants to jeopardize that by scaring people about pirates."

It is, he feels, not so much a conspiracy as a tacit understanding between interested parties that "the less said the better." I wonder if this leads shipping firms to put as little resources as possible into preventative measures. Ian disagrees: "Most shipping companies or ship management firms are on top of this, as best they can. All of the big firms have security plans in place and train their crews in anti-piracy measures. I don't mean to paint a picture of an entire industry that is shoddy. I'll admit there are . . . parts of the merchant shipping world that don't take [piracy] seriously enough, okay? I'd never work for one of those companies, but I know a lot of mariners don't have a choice. A job's a job, especially if you live in a place like Indonesia or Sri Lanka or the Philippines. Those are the blokes that have a rough time of things."

A text message on Ian's cell phone reminds him he has to get back to the office soon, but I can tell he's not quite done talking. We silently watch some barges pass on the river, heading upstream slowly against the current. "You know, it pains me to say this as a professional mariner, but seafaring can be a pretty ugly business. There are so many 'dodgy' elements within it that I sometimes wonder if I'd do it all over again if I had to. You meet some exceedingly . . . unscrupulous people. Watch yourself out there," Ian says solemnly. "It's a funny old world, piracy is."

That evening, I end up in a Chinese restaurant in Soho, poring over my notes and making preparations to leave the next day. My understanding of the scope of modern-day piracy is already enlarging from speaking with the likes of Pottengal Mukundan at the IMB and Ian the seafarer, especially the influences of greed, lawlessness, and targets of opportunity. The most recent IMB piracy report before me shows that in the last seven days there have been attacks reported off Indonesia, Jamaica, Guyana, and Somalia and in the Strait of Malacca. Relatively speaking, it was a quiet week, with no one kidnapped or injured in these attacks in Asia, Africa, and the Americas. Maybe that's why an earlier Google search came up with only a few listings of these incidents, primarily on shipping-related sites.

This brings to mind a conversation I had in Canada with a friend who asked me, "Why should piracy be important to me? How does it affect *me*?" She was right in quizzing me, for it does appear that this is a problem with little real resonance in Toronto, New York, or London. Then, while mulling the effects of piracy on those of us living comfortably in the West, I find an example of its impact hovering nearby from a most unlikely source: my waiter.

As the man brings me a fresh pot of tea, he notices the piracy-related documents laid out on the table and gives me an odd look. When I'm done eating and go to pay, he's standing at the register and, after I've settled the bill, asks me if I'm working on a paper for a university. "My son is studying economics at Sheffield [University]," he reveals. I explain what I'm doing and he tells me, in short, clipped sentences, that it's unfortunate I cannot be in London longer, since I should speak with his son's girlfriend. "She is from Vietnam but is [ethnic] Chinese. She came with her family in the 1980s. It was very bad. Do you know? They came in small boats. Many people die. They remember pirates. I remember. Many people do."

What he is referring to is the darkest period in modern-day maritime crime, a time of vivid cruelty inflicted by pirates on those most in need. It began in 1975 when decades of war in Indochina finally ended with the communist victories in Vietnam, Cambodia, and Laos. In the immediate aftermath, thousands of refugees sought to escape to parts of noncommunist Southeast Asia, primarily Thailand, Hong Kong, Singapore, the Philippines, and Malaysia. The majority were Vietnamese, and by land and by sea in the first three years after the fighting ended they fled abroad any way they could. As the routes through the jungles became increasingly difficult to traverse, the asylum seekers took to the seas in vessels of every size, and the crisis of the Boat People was born.

The trickle of destitute refugees soon turned into an exodus—almost two hundred thousand fled Vietnam in 1979 alone—but their journeys through the South China Sea forced them through a gauntlet of thugs eager to rob, kidnap, murder, and rape them. These pirates were fishermen from neighboring countries, ordinary criminals, and organized gangs; all you needed was a boat, some weapons, and the willingness to attack unarmed men, women, and children.

It's difficult to fathom what the Boat People went through: Having survived a ten-thousand-day war, they then chose to flee their homelands with what few possessions they could carry on leaky vessels that were often barely seaworthy. Without knowing exactly where they were going, they set out through all sorts of weather conditions, enduring storms, high seas, and intense heat that sapped young and old alike. But all of these conditions may have paled in comparison to the appearance of a pirate boat on the horizon, for this would have been the most vulnerable time for the refugees. With no one in sight to protect them, they knew their very lives depended on the mood of the attackers.

The stories of what the pirates did to the Boat People are horrific. Anything of value was, of course, immediately stolen from the refugees. Those who tried to escape by jumping in the water might find the pirates using them for target practice. Some pirates would club the men on the boats unconscious and then ax them to death, dumping the bodies in the sea. Women and girls were separated and then raped, at times by gangs of men who cared not whether the victim was alive or dead. Other girls were taken aboard the pirate ships, never to be seen again. And once the orgy of violence had ended, it was not uncommon for the pirates to sink the victims' boats.

Back in 1981, the Office of the United Nations High Commissioner for Refugees (UNHCR) compiled some grim statistics on these pirate attacks: They looked at 15,479 Vietnamese refugees who had arrived in Thailand and found that of the 452 boats that made the journey, 349 had each been attacked an average of three times during the crossing.[6] There were 881 dead or missing and 228 women abducted by pirates and 578 who had been raped. This was in one year and only covered those who fled to Thailand.

The initial response to the crisis can only be called apathetic. Like Darfur, the plight of the Boat People was known for several years, but an effective reaction was mired in politics. Some commercial vessels that plied the waters of the South China Sea did come to the assistance of boats that they happened upon, taking the refugees aboard, feeding them, giving them shelter, and delivering them to authorities in ports like Hong Kong. It wasn't until 1982, though, that the United Nations finally set up an anti-piracy program in the region to combat the attacks. Meanwhile, governments in Southeast Asia were becoming less welcoming to the new arrivals. At times, naval forces were ordered to push back the boats, in the vain hope the refugees would turn around and return home. (This brings to mind the manner in which the United States has dealt with Cuban and Haitian refugees off the Florida coast and the way Italy and Spain have reacted to Africans trying to land.)

By the mid-1980s, the outcry to do something to stop the attacks forced a response. The Royal Thai Navy was given the resources to begin mounting anti-piracy patrols, and in concert with other forces this led to a decline in attacks on the refugees. There was also a crackdown on the criminals onshore, with a series of arrests and convictions. Then, despite the crackdown, piracy in the South China Sea began increasing in the late 1980s. It was soon determined that these attacks were being carried out by hardened gangs of professionals, not the fishermen who had been part-time pirates. Within a few years, though, these gangs turned their attention to other ventures, mainly because the flood of refugees had been reduced to a trickle by 1996,[7] so it just wasn't profitable anymore. Besides, with the skills they had honed murdering, raping, and pillaging the Boat People, the pirates could embark on far more profitable operations, such as attacking commercial vessels.

Shunned by governments, defended by few, and preyed upon by many, the Boat People of Indochina endured an odyssey of terror that has largely been forgotten three decades after it occurred. To some, their plight has been surpassed—if that's the right word—by Pol Pot's holocaust in Cambodia (Kampuchea), ethnic cleansing in the Balkans, genocide in Rwanda, and various other recent examples of man's inhumanity to his fellow man.

To some, the saga of the Boat People is a quarter century old, it's history now, and there's only so much bad news we can retain in our collective consciousness. But death, displacement, or rape should not be viewed as a competition in which numerical superiority is the final arbiter of what constitutes something of historical note. The life of each of those refugees has value and merit, as do the lives of everyone else who has been attacked by modern-day pirates. The issue is not about numbers; it is about individuals and their personal stories. Clearly, as a Chinese waiter in London has revealed to me, the stories of what the Boat People endured are not distant history. They may remain hidden from view but nonetheless linger just beneath the surface, seared into the memories of these victims of piracy.

2

SEA GHOSTS

Compared with [Malay pirates], the buccaneers of the Spanish Main were gentle and amiable creatures.

—OWEN RUTTER, *THE PIRATE WIND: TALES OF THE SEA ROBBERS OF MALAYA*, 1930

I KNOW IT must have seemed like a good idea when I thought of it, but sitting in a small, open fishing boat as it flits across the choppy waves of the Strait of Malacca is beginning to worry me. It's not the storm clouds brooding over the western horizon, the increasing swells on the sea, or the immense oil tankers that we have to dodge around as we race to shore that are of concern; nor is it the fact that we have no radio or lifejackets out here and my back is killing me from the pounding the boat's been taking all day. No, it's the speed with which we are approaching the coast that's nagging at me. That and the seeming indifference of the skipper to our imminent demise. A glance over my shoulder shows him sitting nonchalantly with one hand on the tiller and the other holding a cigarette as he stares off to the north, not toward our beachhead. His assistant squats up by the bow and appears to be sending a text message to someone on his mobile phone, equally uninterested.

Ahead of us, the shoreline is getting nearer and I can see that it's crowded with fishing boats that have already come in. I've no idea where the skipper intends to land us, or how, but he hasn't throttled back on the 30 HP outboard engine one bit. At the last moment he makes a slight course adjustment, aiming for a small opening among the other boats, and I grip the gunwale with one hand and jam my feet against the hull in anticipation of the impact, while thinking, This is crazy. Then, as the bow hits the sand, the skipper cuts the engine, lifts the prop out of the water, and the boat slides onto the gently sloping beach until it's completely clear of the water.

While I'm still recovering from this novel technique of landing, the skipper has already unfastened the outboard engine from the boat's transom and is lugging it into a storage locker built from scraps of wood. The younger man grabs the net full of fish that sits by my feet and hefts it ashore as I sit there uselessly. A couple of fish plop onto my feet as he does this, causing the skipper— Abdul Salleh—to start laughing. As do a half-dozen other fishermen sitting nearby. "Fish like you!" he tells me. "Okay, you can get out now. You home. All okay."

Abdul's assistant, a young Malaysian named Kamarudeen, offers me his hand to get up. "You worried, mmm? Boat go too fast?" He gestures at the skipper: "Normal, is normal. He do all the time like this."

"Yes, normal," Abdul assures me. "This way of fisherman. Come; we still have work."

After four hours at sea in the small fiberglass boat—what they call a *perahu* in the local Malay language—my body aches and my legs are rubbery as they touch dry land again. Abdul and another man approach carrying long wooden poles, which are passed through rope loops attached to the *perahu's* gunwales. I join Abdul, Kamarudeen, and the other man as we heft the poles on our shoulders, lifting the boat up, turning it so the bow faces the sea, and backing it farther onto the beach, above the high-water mark.

Abdul and Kamarudeen take their net and join a group of other fishermen as everyone begins sorting through their day's catches, tossing the valuable fish into plastic bins full of ice, throwing the rest aside (some of which will be used as bait). There are nine sitting on the beach, all working their hands through the nets to expertly pluck fish out while yammering away among themselves, making jokes, poking fun at one another, and generally passing the time at the end of a long day. Fishermen have done this for thousands of years all over the globe, and it's refreshing to see the tradition continues still.

The bins begin to fill up with the bounty from the sea: There are some *ikan duri,* also known as goat catfish, *malong* (yellow pike congers), a few *ikan pari* (stingrays), and a nice collection of red snapper, or what the fishermen call *jenahak.* Everyone is happiest about the snapper, since it will fetch the most at market.

I notice that the wind has picked up considerably since we got in, snapping at the flags used by the fishermen to gauge its direction and rustling the palms that line the beach. There is a dark bank of menacing clouds coming at us from the Indonesian side of the Strait, and all the other fishing boats have made it home safely, except for one straggler that is idled in the seas about a mile offshore, either hauling in the last net or fiddling with a cranky outboard engine. From the comments of some of the other villagers, it doesn't look like anyone will be heading out tomorrow, which is fortunate for me, as I need some downtime to recover from several days spent seeing how these men make their livelihoods. Abdul pauses from his work to scan the horizon. "Storm come. No fish tomorrow. No money," he says, holding a conger eel in his hands. "I think no pirates come. That good, yes?"

Meeting with these fishermen had been a mistake, but not because of the way they treated me or any real fears for my well-being. Rather, it was a bit of an accident.

I arrived in Southeast Asia a week earlier, intent on finding out more about a rash of recent pirate attacks endured by fishermen along the Malaysian coast of the Strait of Malacca, especially in one village near the historic city of Melaka.[1] According to reports, things had gotten so bad there that in July of 2006 the fishermen stopped going to sea for a while, worried about their safety. They'd been robbed, beaten, and wounded by pirates brandishing automatic weapons and had had enough. One report said that of three hundred locals who made their livelihoods off the sea, at least half were refusing to head out into the Strait until the Malaysian government did something to protect them from pirate attacks.

Landing in Singapore in the middle of the night, I was greeted in a most unique manner: a lunar eclipse was visible out my window as the 747 jumbo jet was making its final approaches to Changi International Airport. The sight of the Earth's shadow on the face of the Moon was extraordinary to watch, but I also knew that in some cultures it is considered a bad omen: When I was traveling in India, a villager once told me that when there was a lunar eclipse he would throw away any uneaten food, because it would be poisoned by the angry Moon, while I remembered an old wives' tale from my youth warning pregnant women not to touch their bellies during such an event lest their child be born with a noticeable birthmark. Though my rational mind discounted these as mere superstitions, they nagged at me as I waited for my luggage to appear on the arrivals area carousel. Watching all the other passengers grab their bags and aided by jet lag, I began to wonder, Had the lunar eclipse caused my baggage to be lost? Well, no, it was just the last piece to be unloaded.

Later that same morning I stumble into the Singapore rail station, a crumbling relic of the British colonial period, to board an express train bound for central Malaysia. The route winds its way through lush green forests and endless plantations of palm trees; from time to time we pass small clearings scattered alongside the rail line that reveal simple farms with goats, chickens, and water buffalo wandering near orchards laden with durian.[2] Alighting in the midst of a tropical downpour at a desolate rail stop in the middle of nowhere, I eventually convinced the lone taxi driver parked beside the tracks to take me to the coast. He spoke no English and I speak no Malay, but I showed him the name of where I intended to go and an hour later I was staring at the Strait of Malacca cursing myself.

After making supposedly meticulous plans and trekking halfway around the globe with planes, trains, and automobiles, I'd ended up in the wrong Malaysian coastal village, probably because the taxi driver could not read the handwriting on my note. I'd intended to make for a place called Tanjung Ketapang, which lies east of Melaka, but was now standing with my bags in Tanjung *Kling*. The taxi was long gone and it was already late afternoon, so after berating myself for the mistake, I decided to adapt to the changing circumstances, a necessary part of doing this type of work. I figured I would spend a couple of days here—in the village of Tanjung Kling—getting familiar with life beside the Strait and then head off to where the fishermen had really been battling pirates, in Tanjung Ketapang. Little did I know how widespread the problem was along the entire Malaysian coast.

Tanjung Kling is located on the west coast of the Malaysian

peninsula facing the Strait of Malacca, one of the most important shipping lanes in the world and one of the most pirate infested. For much of the last fifteen years, the Strait has been well known as the site of thousands of attacks on commercial ships and local fishermen up and down its five-hundred-mile (eight-hundred-kilometer) length.[3] It bisects lower Thailand and peninsular Malaysia from the Indonesian island of Sumatra, with the tiny island nation of Singapore at the southern end of the peninsula. Its notoriety is such that the Strait of Malacca has become virtually synonymous with modern-day piracy, making it a magnet for those looking at the problem and attracting the attention of governments, naval forces, the shipping industry, and, yes, journalists. If you're looking into piracy, this has been the one place you have to visit.

Keeping in mind the three factors required for piracy to flourish—greed, lawlessness, and opportunity—the region around the Strait of Malacca has had each in spades for decades. Indonesia, Thailand, and Malaysia have all struggled to cope with large populations subsisting on meager incomes, more so in the first country. While the situation has improved recently, especially in Malaysia, there are still millions of poor people living along the coastlines of the Strait.

As to maritime law enforcement, well, let's just say that until the last few years it was virtually nonexistent. Years of bickering, corruption, internal strife, and poorly equipped sailors, soldiers, and police left the waterway barely patrolled against piracy. Indeed, reports have circulated in the past of the complicity of local naval units with pirate gangs, though the reality may have been that criminals were using uniforms as a means of getting close to vessels and then boarding them.

Singapore, it should be noted, has never been considered a part of the modern piracy problem in the Strait, being a stable, prosperous city-state with strong security forces. The problem with the

Strait has always centered on Indonesia first, Malaysia second, and Thailand third.

But the biggest reason for piracy here is the sheer number of vessels one finds transiting through the waterway. The Strait of Malacca is known as one of the world's major shipping lanes of communication, seeing some fifty thousand vessels passing through it every year, carrying about a third of global commerce and half the planet's oil trade. The Strait is a choke point for all this shipping, about 155 miles (250 kilometers) across at the northern tip and 40 miles (65 kilometers) at the southern end, though the shipping lanes are, in places, barely a mile wide, so vessels have to slow down on this maritime superhighway.

On my first day here, all that traffic is on vivid display as I stand on a rocky beach at the south end of the village. I'd found a small two-room cabin to rent—two rooms if you count the bathroom—complete with thatched roof, shuttered, glassless windows, and a veranda that looks out toward the Strait. The elderly ethnic Indian couple who owned the small collection of "vacation cottages" seemed quite happy by my unannounced arrival, perhaps because all the huts were currently vacant.

From the shore, I can see a trio of barges being pulled by tugs and heading southbound, toward Singapore, and a small product tanker. A couple of immense containerships are heading in the opposite direction, far out to sea, followed by some other vessels lost in the haze. Closer in, a large oil tanker appears inbound for the nearby PETRONAS[4] terminal, while a half-dozen fishing boats skitter about on the murky waters. The only other waterway I've seen that's as busy as this is the Dover Strait between Britain and France.

The Strait in front of me is strewn with bits of wood, plastic bottles, and coconuts, the water cloudy and brown from all the sediment churned up by the strong current that flows through this shallow waterway. It's far from a tropical paradise, though I'd been told there is a nice sandy beach a bit farther up the shore where you can go swimming. Off to my left, however, I notice a man walking through the waist-deep water toward me. As he gets closer, I can see that he's got to be in his fifties, at least, and is pushing two long bamboo poles through the water. He wears a checkered shirt and tan baseball cap and keeps glancing behind him as he plods along. I've no idea what the guy's up to, but he seems intent on his task and is clearly not out for a dip in the sea.

As I take all this in, the sun begins to set and a warm, dry breeze washes over me from the southwest, helping to erase the effects of international jet lag. High above, two white-bellied sea eagles soar on the thermals with their wings outstretched, effortlessly gliding in concentric circles over the coastal shallows before heading off to the north. Darkness comes quickly this close to the equator, revealing stars and a lone bat flitting about, while the cry of a muezzin can be heard over the rustling of the palm trees. It all seems very peaceful—there is nothing in the least dangerous or threatening about this place, no indication that danger looms nearby. At least not on the surface.

To visit the Strait today in search of pirates can be a bit futile, for it is no longer the cesspool of violence it was a few years ago. If you go by official reports, the Strait was the scene of at least seventy-five serious incidents in the year 2000 and pirates roamed these waters at will, attacking all manner of vessels and robbing, kidnapping, and murdering. As late as 2004 there were over three dozen officially reported attacks on commercial vessels in the waterway and, as Ian had told me in London, the violence led maritime insurers to consider the Strait like a war zone and raise the premiums on vessels sailing through the region. By 2006, though, the number of pirate attacks had supposedly fallen to eleven, thanks in part to the increased presence of naval patrols.

Captains worth their salt will still make sure that they take suitable precautions when sailing through the waterway. This usually involves having the crew monitor the radar and keep an eye posted for suspicious craft, keeping the vessel lit up at night like a Christmas tree (pirates don't like to be seen), locking all the doors into the main accommodation housing, and placing fire hoses at the ready near any place a pirate might try to board. The most common place to climb aboard a ship is at the stern, which is often the closest to the waterline and a sort of "blind spot" at the rear (the sides of some vessels also offer possibilities). The hoses are meant to be turned on and used to spray any attackers who might appear with high-pressure water, a crude, but effective, means of repelling boarders.

Despite the reported decrease in attacks, the Strait continues to be considered dangerous waters, and two weeks before I arrived here a couple of mariners were kidnapped and a third was killed by pirates in an attack northwest of Tanjung Kling. I'd heard various recent stories that the pirates of the Strait were switching their attacks from commercial ships to more vulnerable local fishermen, attacks that were getting little attention because they did not involve international shipping and foreign crews. It appeared that if these tales were true, it was those at the bottom of the maritime world who were bearing the brunt of the problem here—hardworking fishermen[5] in small boats out there trying to make a living off the sea's bounty.

That evening, I sit on the small veranda of my cabin under the watchful eye of a couple of curious geckos clinging to the shutters while bats flitter around in the night sky. The open-air restaurant next door to where I'm staying is full of Malaysian families enjoying the end of a three-day weekend to celebrate Independence Day, so I periodically look up from my work to find a couple of children smiling and waving my way, shouting, "Hallo!" exuberantly at the only Westerner around.

I'm immersed in leafing through piles of reports from official sources and media outlets. One of the most horrific incidents happened in February of 2004, when a small oil tanker was attacked northwest of here. A month earlier, the *Cherry 201* had been making a routine run to Belawan in northern Sumatra, the gateway to Indonesia's war-torn Aceh Province.[6] She carried a crew of thirteen and a thousand tonnes of palm oil as she motored toward Indonesia's second-busiest harbor, and although the crew was aware of the pirate risk, as well as the fighting between the army and the Aceh rebels, they had made the run before without incident. But on Monday, January 5, their luck ran out when a speedboat darted from the shoreline and took up position alongside the tanker. Grappling hooks were thrown and men with automatic weapons climbed aboard, making for the wheelhouse.

The *Cherry* was defenseless—merchant vessels rarely carry weapons—and the pirates quickly overwhelmed the crew and ordered the captain to go ashore, contact the vessel's owners, and demand a ransom of 400 million Indonesian rupiah (about $50,000 U.S.). The tanker and her crew, plus the remaining pirate captors, simply disappeared, perhaps to one of the many inlets that riddle the area.

For weeks the negotiating went on, possibly as the *Cherry*'s owners tried to buy time so Indonesian forces could find their vessel and her crew. The owners first talked the pirates down to 100 million rupiah and then finally settled on 70 million (less than $9,000). But after five weeks without being paid, the pirates' frustrations boiled over: they grabbed four of the crew, executed them, and dumped the bodies in the sea before abandoning the rest and fleeing. The pirates have yet to be caught.

The *Cherry 201* garnered notice because of the gruesome murders, but at the same time attention was being focused on this incident there were at least three other fishing boats with nine fishermen also being held hostage. Indeed, in looking at the most recent incident reports for the Malacca Strait, I can see a large number involve fishing boats: "Seven pirates armed with long knives boarded boat underway. They took hostage two crew and stole cash." "Pirates stole equipment from a fishing boat." "Five armed pirates attacked fishing boat and kidnapped crewmembers, demanding a ransom for their release." "Pirates attacked fishing boat and kidnapped one crewmember." These local working people were enduring their own version of the low-level conflict that is modern-day piracy.

The next morning, I walk down to where the fishing boats are based in Tanjung Kling, only to discover that all but one are currently out in the Strait. The port, such as it is, is really nothing more than a small strip of sandy beach maybe twenty yards wide, hemmed in by towering palm trees. Plugs of volcanic rock protrude here and there in the shallows near a ramshackle row of shelters where the fishermen keep their boats and gear, empty but for some nets and other gear. Behind all this, close to the road through the village, is an open low-walled concrete structure that looks like a meeting place or maybe a market of some sort. A couple of older men sit on plastic lawn chairs beneath its corrugated tin roof intently watching television. When I walk over, it turns out they're watching professional wrestling, the ostentatious American kind, and laughing as someone is body slammed onto the mat.

At the far end of the beach I can see two men huddled over the only boat onshore, tinkering with something. It's a long, white fiberglass craft, about twenty feet long, with a sharply pointed, rather graceful-looking prow. They look up from their work and nod at me as I approach. One of them is sharpening a knife with a whetstone while the other holds lengths of rope that they are splicing together.

The younger man—he might be in his late twenties—stares at me somewhat suspiciously, as does his slightly older knife-wielding partner. As I quickly discover, it's not because they are doing anything untoward, just that few tourists wander this way. Fishing villages like Tanjung Kling are not prime attractions for vacationers.

The guy with the knife is the boat's owner, Abdul Salleh. He wears a short-sleeved blue shirt with "Toyota Leasing #1 Team Leader" emblazoned on it and, most incongruously, a Los Angeles Kings ball cap. I'm quite certain this man has never seen a hockey game in his life, but the Canadian in me takes this as a good omen.

Abdul's English is poor, so it's his friend who does most of the talking as they work. Kamarudeen—or Deen, as he likes to be called—lives across the road with his family, as does Salleh. Deen has a shaved head and intense, questioning eyes framed by a gentle face. Both men come from families with long traditions of fishing in the sea—Abdul can trace back at least four generations on both his parents' sides, a century of seafaring, and he's been putting out into the Strait for over ten years; Deen's family has been tied to the sea for almost as long.

As Abdul continues to sharpen the knife blade, Deen tells me there are about thirty-five villagers here who make their living on the Strait, using sixteen boats that head out with mostly two-man crews. Deen himself is only a part-time fisherman; he normally works at a nearby hotel doing maintenance, but whenever he gets a chance he also goes out onto the sea, helping anyone who needs an extra hand.

He loves fishing—the independence, the fresh air, and the money you can make doing it. Though he'll never grow rich doing it, fishing still pays better than his hotel job and, more important, it's a tradition in his family that he wants to carry on if he can. His dream, he tells me, is to one day have his own boat, so he's been saving as much money as he can for the last few years. He figures he needs to have 11,000 Malaysian ringgit (about $3,100 U.S.) for a second-hand *perahu* as well as a used outboard motor and all the fishing gear required. It will take him a decade to save the money.

The men begin discussing the relative merits of fiberglass versus wood boats. Abdul is adamant that wooden sampans are far more seaworthy and durable, though much more expensive. Deen thinks the newer types of *perahu* are more efficient and, being cheaper, make it easier for more villagers to continue fishing.

While they finish splicing the lines together, I ask Deen what they know about the pirate attacks on the fishermen east of Melaka. He speaks to Abdul in Malay for a moment before telling me that they call the attackers *perompak* or *pencuri*—thieves or robbers.

"Ah . . . yes . . . yes, was big problem. No one want to fish. No boats go from here for maybe few days."

No boats from here? Abdul puts down his knife and glares from beneath his baseball cap. "Pirates . . . everywhere," he says while reaching into the *perahu*. He lifts a floorboard and retrieves a slightly rusty machete from its hiding place. There's also a wooden club lying down there.

"*Perompak* come, use parang," the skipper says, his voice rising as he slashes the machete—or parang—through the air. "*Perompak* come when fish. *Perompak* come here. Yes, here." He gestures at the sharpened blade of the machete, and it's clear he would use the weapon to defend himself if the need arose. For a fleeting moment

I remember every pirate story I'd read where the crew brandish cutlasses to ward off buccaneers; then Abdul's anger abates and he returns the machete to its hiding place.

Though I'd been asking about another village, both men inform me that the problem of pirate attacks is a troubling issue for fishermen up and down the coast and say this wasn't something confined to 2006 down east of Melaka: there have been incidents every few weeks up and down the coast since then, including a nighttime raid by Indonesian pirates on this very beach just last month.

Deen points to where the fishing boats are stored and says that in the middle of the night someone heard a large boat with a loud engine by the beach. Because some men will go out night fishing, no one thought too much about it until morning came.

"Last month, village have seven boats and five outboard motors stolen," Deen says, holding up his fingers so I get the numbers correct. "Right here. We think they come from Indonesia, because this is [what] happen in other villages. Everyone is sleeping. A large *perahu*, double-engine motor, with fourteen Indonesians come here. Maybe half hour they are here. They take *perahus*—boats—and motors and leave. Bad for everyone."

Abdul says that everyone believes the Indonesians were aided by a spy, someone who had reconnoitered the area beforehand and then called his accomplices on a cell phone. Because there's little to physically differentiate Malaysians from Indonesians and since they speak essentially the same language, it would be easy for someone from Sumatra to go unnoticed here.

The impact of this late-night theft cannot be underestimated in a small fishing community like Tanjung Kling. In North America we would shrug this sort of thing off easily. After all, how many cars are stolen every night in cities across the continent? But here it's different: Almost half the village's fleet of boats were stolen that night, and none of these fishermen have insurance to cover the losses. Most would have saved a decade to get their first boat and then worked hard to make fishing worthwhile, so this one attack has wiped out the dreams and financial investments of many in Tanjung Kling.

We're joined by another, older fisherman, one of the guys I'd seen watching wrestling on the television. His name is Ali and he's been a fisherman here in Tanjung Kling for twenty years. Short and stocky, Ali is clad in the manner that all the fishermen here are: athletic shorts, sports shirt, baseball cap, and a carryall slung over his shoulder. I haven't seen a sarong or other form of traditional clothing anywhere around here; it's all been replaced by Western influences.

As Ali lights a cigarette, I notice he bears the occupational wounds inflicted from decades of working these waters, with numerous scars across his forearms and on the backs of his hands. Normally he'd be out fishing on the Strait, but he lost his outboard motor in last month's attack so must now share an engine with another villager. With little in the way of savings, Ali has no idea how he will replace the expensive motor and is frustrated that, at fifty-one, he's got to start over again. At least, he says, the pirates didn't take his boat.

Deen, Abdul, and Ali list the nearby villages that have been hit by pirates—five boats stolen here, a dozen there, six engines in another—and assure me that these events have all occurred in the last few months. In most cases, the incidents were reported to local police, but as Abdul says with a shrug, "*Perahu* gone. Motor gone. Police can no [help]. Many time pass and police come. *Perompak* go home."

In the aftermath of the thefts, the fishermen of Tanjung Kling pooled their meager resources to help one another and decided to set up a watch-keeping system: each man spends one night keeping guard over the village's fleet of boats. It's a tiring task after a day spent out on the waters but a necessary precaution against further attacks. Ali's turn was two nights ago; Abdul will be on guard duty tomorrow.

Throughout history, pirates have preyed upon not only vessels at sea but also on coastal communities. Henry Morgan struck fear into Spanish settlers living in present-day Cuba and Panama back in the seventeenth century, while Blackbeard and his pirates blockaded Charleston, South Carolina, a few decades later, terrorizing its in-habitants as they marauded openly through the streets.

Criminals, for the most part, prefer an easy mark to something more complicated, and pirates are no exception. It matters little whether the target of opportunity is a vessel at sea or a community onshore; it's all about power, with the key factor being the defense-less nature of the target. Ironically for the fishermen of Tanjung Kling, this is something their forebears knew well, for they were some of the fiercest pirates ever to sail the Strait. Indeed, it is en-tirely conceivable that among Abdul Salleh's distant ancestors were at least one or two who took to their *perahus* not to fish but to rob and pillage.

One shouldn't assume that piracy is a recent phenomenon in this part of Southeast Asia; it goes back hundreds of years, if not longer, and was long considered a normal part of the lives of those who inhabited the coastal villages. The famous Chinese explorer Admiral Zheng He[7] encountered pirates in the Strait when he sailed through here with his immense flotilla between 1405 and 1407. As recounted in the museum devoted to the admiral in the old part of downtown Melaka, Zheng He was forced to engage the sea bandits in battle, apparently with great success. This was likely the first instance of intervention by foreign naval forces against local pirates, but it would be far from the last.

Zheng He's voyages were intended to expand the Ming Dynasty's influence politically, militarily, and, most important, economically. Like the current doctrine of modern China, the Ming rulers decided on an ambitious plan to create regional trading partners who would become political allies. By accident, Zheng He's arrival in Melaka coincided with the growth of the community from a sleepy fishing village into a powerful trading state, which would be aided, in part, by the economic relationship that soon developed with the Chinese. Melaka's ruler at the time was Parameswara, a Hindu prince born across the Strait in Sumatra who had opted to settle on the island of Temasek, as Singapore was then known. Parameswara used Temasek as a base to begin pirating passing vessels, eventually incurring the wrath of nearby leaders and being forced to flee north to Melaka, where he reestablished his piracy operations.

Clearly an opportunist, the Hindu prince saw the arrival of Zheng He's fleet as the perfect chance to "go legit" and establish himself as well as make Melaka the premier commercial trading center in the region. It had one of the finest harbors along the coast, the perfect place to provision vessels and establish markets, making it well suited to become a vital stopping place for foreigners sailing through the Strait. In order to do that, though, Parameswara needed to pacify the various pirate villages along the nearby coastline, the ones he had so recently abetted. This would allow trading vessels to safely come and go, something that Admiral Zheng He was keenly interested in fostering, having his own vested interests in the maritime stability of the Strait.

With the might of the Chinese fleet helping to secure the sea, Melaka grew into a prosperous town, becoming arguably the most important commercial center in Southeast Asia at the time. Its wealth attracted traders from India and China, created places of learning and art, and allowed Melaka to flourish as a multicultural, multireligious center. Though Melaka officially adopted Islam as its state religion, it tolerated Buddhism and Hinduism. And then the Europeans showed up.

On the one hand, the arrival of Portuguese vessels in 1509 may have surprised the Melakans, but on the other hand, they had been used to foreign ships coming and going for years, so the initial thinking may have been somewhat pragmatic: here were potential new trading partners. Whatever the Melakans' thoughts, the relationship soured within two years, and under the leadership of *fidalgo* (nobleman) Alfonso de Albuquerque the Portuguese besieged the city, forced its sultan to flee, and established European control over Melaka, control that would remain for four and a half centuries. Once the town was conquered, they built a grand fortress—called A Famosa—and then an entire walled city that rivaled those in medieval Europe. Settlers soon followed, as did businessmen and Catholic missionaries, including the future saint Francis Xavier.[8] However, the Portuguese found themselves in almost constant conflict with the locals, and this period of instability saw a return of piracy in the Strait as the locals fought back against the intruders.

A century after the Portuguese had captured Melaka, the Dutch arrived and promptly laid their own siege to the town. This was one of those situations where European rivalries were being played out between ascending and descending powers. The Dutch took control of Melaka for the next century and a half. Like their Portuguese predecessors, the new rulers set about imprinting their own style on the city. You can still wander the old part of Melaka and see the distinctly Dutch architecture, complete with the dark red Stadthuys (town hall).

The problems with piracy continued to simmer during this period as the Dutch attempted to consolidate control over the Strait from their base in Melaka. They mounted patrols with gunboats in the Strait, sent cruisers to do battle by distant islands, and disembarked soldiers to burn villages, but the pirate threat refused to abate. To some observers it grew stronger: reports came in of hundreds of pirates fighting the Europeans and their might, refusing to back down in the face of cannons and muskets. Maybe the native people felt they had nothing to lose or maybe they were angered beyond reason, but the incidents began to take their toll on an expatriate community far, far from their homeland of Holland. Luckily—for the Dutch—the political situation in Europe changed again and by 1824 the regional problems were left to the last foreign power to hold sway over the Strait of Malacca: Great Britain.

At the time the British replaced the Dutch as colonial rulers of Melaka, they had already established one outpost at the south end of the Strait, Singapore, and a second at its northern mouth, Penang. With the addition of Melaka, these three outposts came to be known as the Straits Settlements and allowed the Royal Navy to become the dominant naval power in the waterway for over a century. Britain was maturing into the most powerful empire the world had ever seen, one that would not countenance rebellious natives anywhere.

The period of British rule over Malaya saw some of the fiercest battles fought between government forces and pirates, though at the time piracy here never received as much publicity as the Caribbean buccaneers did (perhaps owing to the longer time it took for news to reach Britain from Southeast Asia or, more likely, because the pirates of the Americas were mainly European rogues). As the British writer Owen Rutter put it back in 1930 in his book *The Pirate Wind*, "A century ago, and for more than half a century before that, piracy was rife in the Malayan seas." This was a typically British understatement.

The immediate necessity of securing the Strait of Malacca for commercial shipping was clear to the new British authorities—it was a vital link between their colonial outposts in the Far East and the Jewel of the Empire, India.[9] Their initial attempts at combating pirates by using large armed vessels proved fruitless. The deep drafts of the Royal Navy's brigs and cruisers could never allow the warships to venture into the coves and close to the villages where pirates lurked. Besides, the Malayan buccaneers were smart enough to avoid direct confrontation with these vessels, preferring to retreat into mangrove swamps in their small *perahus*.

Eventually, the British adapted to the situation and began using their own small boats similar to the locals in order to take the fight to the pirates. An early version of guerrilla warfare was occurring here, the beginning of something that would plague Southeast Asia for the next 150 years. From the Straits Settlements, teams of British sailors, marines, and soldiers set out to attack suspected pirate lairs, engaging the Malays in vicious fighting. In just one example of the battles, in 1836, over a hundred pirates were killed in an engagement not far from present-day Tanjung Kling. This was not an isolated incident, and the war being fought here far outclassed any engagements that had occurred in the Caribbean.

Like so many other conflicts in so many other places, the attempts by a foreign power to enforce its rule over a local population met with only limited success here and was never complete. Throughout the nineteenth century, the British would deploy sailors and soldiers equipped with the most technologically advanced weaponry available to suppress piracy in Southeast Asia. And while their efforts would manage to contain it in one area, piracy would often crop up in another place soon afterward. The fact that Owen Rutter was writing about pirates in 1930 and they continue to stalk the Strait today suggests that British efforts were, in the end, a failure.

Looking back on things from a modern perspective, one can see how villagers in coastal Malayan communities would have considered piracy to be just another means of making ends meet. This doesn't excuse what they did, merely observes that for them the sea was a source of bounty, whether that meant fish or passing vessels. And they certainly lived in harsh times, when the whim of a sultan or prince or governor or admiral might mean destruction and death. The foreigners definitely felt threatened by those who practiced piracy in the region, and reacted harshly to the problem. One must wonder, though, what the locals thought when those vessels arrived, full of strange men with weapons intent on attacking their villages and boats. Domination of the Strait—be it by the Chinese, Portuguese, Dutch, or British—was attempted at the point of a gun and a cutlass; in this context you might say that one person's pirate fleet is another's navy.

When Deen meets up with me a few days after our first encounter, I ask him about the legacy of colonial rule, native resistance, and piracy on the Strait. He looks at me dumbfounded.

"The history of my country is long, very long. Yes, but these things you say, I can no speak. I am no teacher, yes? Maybe I show you someone else, to talk of this."

We head back toward the village, across the road from the fishing beach, to a small hut cobbled together from plywood, bricks, and corrugated tin. At the back of the hut, there's a small table under an awning, beneath which an older woman sits surrounded by what appear to be hamburger patties. Deen introduces me to Makcik— "Auntie"—a woman well into her seventies with sullen eyes who wears a blue bandana on her head and a brilliant red apron. She sits on a wooden crate, working a mushy pulp of prawns into cakes

known as *belacan* that are sold locally. She does this by hand, methodically grabbing some of the shrimp mush from a plastic tub,
spreading it into a circular form, and flattening it out. Laid out on
old newspapers, the *belacan* will dry under the tropical sun on platforms behind her, near where a clutch of chickens cluck.

It turns out that the prawns are local, very local: they come
from the shallows of the Strait not a hundred yards away. For a
week or two every few months, fishermen are allowed to harvest
the small crustaceans by walking through the water and dragging a
net behind them—no motorization is allowed for this traditional
work. The man I'd seen on my first day in Tanjung Kling walking
back and forth in the murky water had been a prawn harvester. It's
something these people have been doing for hundreds of years.

Makcik barely pauses from her work when I get Deen to ask
her what she knows about the history of British attempts to suppress piracy here. She slaps at the prawn cakes with her hands and
spits out answers in a rapid-fire manner: "That history is wrong.
We live from the sea. We always live from the sea. The others [for-
eigners] not understand us. Pirates? Yes, men go to sea to rob boats
in past. This normal. Now it is different. Now pirates come here."

The woman stops pounding the prawn mix as a tiny girl who
might be about five stumbles out of the nearby hut, wearing a
faded print dress and tottering around the yard in a pair of high-
heeled shoes much too large for her feet, nattering away in the
manner that little girls do while playacting. Wiping a hand across
her brow, Makcik sternly tells the girl to go back inside.

"All in the past," Makcik sighs. "I am old. Do not ask me about
pirates. You want to know the ancient history? I remember when the
Japanese arrived.[10] They walked down this road. And the British
were over there. That is ancient history, hah! Pirates . . . no . . ."

Auntie returns to her task as Deen gently takes my arm and leads me away after we say good-bye. Once out of earshot, he explains that the woman lost her husband years ago, killed by pirates while fishing on the Strait. Now she must help support her extended family by churning out *belacan* cakes whenever she can and selling them for the equivalent of twenty-five cents apiece in local markets.

Kamarudeen and I walk to a little snack bar stall up by the main highway. He points out the *belacan* patties for sale there, maybe from Makcik's little operation, but we ignore those in favor of a handful of *duku* fruit and a couple of lukewarm plastic bottles of Coca-Cola, which we take to a picnic table to consume. Sort of like lychees, *duku* are golf ball–sized fruit with a glorious, tangy flavor not unlike that of grapefruit. The colas are nothing more than bland sugar and water in comparison.

Any romanticized image I may have had of a traditional fishing village in Southeast Asia is nothing like what I found in places like Tanjung Kling. There are no wooden houses with thatched roofs built on stilts over the water here; instead you find concrete and brick bungalows with satellite dishes and all modern conveniences. The inhabitants are not Luddites clinging to the past but entrepreneurs struggling with the present.

Around us, traffic whizzes by on the highway and I can see construction cranes at work on what is to become a new time-share vacation complex. There is already an immense hotel-condominium tower just south of the village, which is hemmed in on the other side by an oil terminal. According to Deen, villages like Tanjung Kling are under increasing pressure from commercial developers and business operations, as Malaysia seeks to expand its economy. The capital, Kuala Lumpur, is but two hours away by car, so there are some who want to turn this part of the coast into a retreat for wealthy vacationers. It gives Deen pause to ponder whether his village will be able to survive into the future.

"Fishing, it is a good life," he says, peeling a *duku* open. "But there are many changes now. Some in village think it the old way, maybe we should do other work, for better money. You sell house, property, maybe make enough for children. Others think no; these are the most of us, I think. We want to keep tradition—the life of the sea—here. Many pressure: the developer, the government, and, yes, the pirate. To live in my village and be fishermen is . . . some think is sadness."

I think he means "madness," but he corrects me: "No, is hard to do this, to keep old ways. It is task on . . ." Deen searches for the English words, fails, and taps at his heart. What he really means is that the price of being a traditional community tied to the sea in the modern era can be a costly burden to bear. It's no wonder that, hemmed in by hotels, highways, and tourists, inundated by mass-produced "culture," and preyed upon by armed men, someone might think twice in coastal Malaysia about wanting to make his or her life from fishing in the Strait of Malacca. There's a fragile balance going on here, with a small village struggling to maintain its historical balance with the ecosystem that surrounds it.

The people of Tanjung Kling don't decimate the seas with large ships or factory vessels and they don't take more than they need from the Strait, but they are still punished for their work. Their fishermen are robbed, beaten, kidnapped, and sometimes murdered by pirates. Yet they still go on. When I ask Deen why, he answers, "Only way you know is to come fish."

Just past eight the next morning, I'm back on the beach watching as Abdul and Deen load up the *perahu*. The skies are overcast and there's a warm offshore breeze blowing in that has covered the beach in a smoky blue haze. Someone is burning brush up near the little point of land that juts into the sea, just past where the boats are stored, but this is nothing compared to when large-scale fires are set across the Strait. Deen says that the Indonesians do this from time to time to clear the land on Sumatra and that the smog created can be very bad once it blows over to the Malaysian side.

The fishermen call for me to help push the *perahu* into the muddy green surf; then I leap in atop the bundle of fishing net as the outboard is fired up. Before I've even gotten myself settled in, the boat surges forward, washing me with the spray from the sea. Deen is nestled down forward grinning at me, while Abdul steers the craft quickly westward. A couple of other boats have also set out at the same time, all of us racing to the fishing grounds in a competitive manner.

Over the roar of the wind and the engine, Deen shouts that we're headed about fifteen kilometers (roughly nine miles) out, near one of the shipping lanes, where Abdul wants to set his nets. There are two main methods of fishing here: laying out nets, as we're going to do, and stringing out long lines with baited lures attached. Either way requires knowing where you hope the fish are, getting there before your friends do, and then waiting to see if any fish can be caught.

As we get farther offshore, the vessel traffic in the Strait increases. Abdul keeps an eye on the seaway, maneuvering the *perahu* around a couple of big freighters that are making little more than 10 knots, inbound to Port Dickson. After fifteen minutes of dodging the commercial traffic, Abdul slows the boat and stands to check the waters. He throws the *perahu* into a tight turn, then cuts the engine, leaving the boat bobbing in the silence.

Abdul places a hand on my shoulder as he makes his way forward to join Deen, getting the net ready to go into the sea. Though

I offer to help, both men politely tell me to relax, which is just as well since I wouldn't have the foggiest idea of what to do.

With surprising speed, the two men take what appears to be a tangled mess of nylon and begin feeding it overboard. Weights on the bottom drop it into the Strait, while flotation buoys draw it taut from the top. Abdul motors the *perahu* slowly forward to play out the net that Deen is feeding out over the port side. Once the tail end of the net is in the sea, a marker buoy is thrown over and then all that's left is to wait for the fish to come.

With a few hours to kill, Abdul decides to show me a nearby island he says I might find interesting. We motor south, toward Melaka and a small island that has what looks like a resort built on it. Abdul makes for a wharf jutting from the leeward side. As we get closer, everything appears deserted and run-down, which is indeed the case, as I discover after the two have tied the *perahu* to the wharf and we climb ashore. They call out to see if anyone's about, saying the island was off-limits to locals before it was abandoned a few years ago. With no guards in sight, they lead me to what had been a Malaysian government retreat, with a series of empty hotel buildings, conference halls, and dining rooms. The dense foliage has taken over the island and Abdul and Deen have to hack our way through the vines as we explore.

They show me a rocky beach where sea turtles come to lay their eggs, but we see nothing but garbage tossed up by the sea. There's really not much to see of interest on the island, except for the resort's swimming pool that is now filled to bursting with phenomenally beautiful purple-flowered water hyacinths. The two fishermen decide to take a smoke break here, idly swatting at the mosquitoes that have found us, so I ask how far Indonesian waters are. Abdul grunts in disgust as he lights up a cigarette; Deen is more forthcoming and figures that the demarcation line is about six to ten miles to the west.

"Fish good there," the young man says. "Better [than] here. But we no go there. Very bad can happen. Many times, the fisherman go to those places, to catch the fish, see? Indonesian fisherman do not like, and become angry. They attack us with the parang and beat us, steal our fish, sometime the *perahu*. Sometime they throw the fisherman into the sea. Not even police can help: we think the Indonesian police just as bad. This why we no fish there now. This why we have parang with us. Very dangerous."

I suppose it's understandable if the Indonesian fishermen get angry when their Malaysian cousins wander across the international border to engage in what is, really, a little poaching. Fishing disputes have been going on across the globe for centuries: Britain and Iceland have famously "fought" three cod wars since the 1950s, with vessels rammed, nets cut, and armed ships facing off against one another. Canada found itself embroiled in what became known as the Turbot War of 1995, when the issue of overfishing on the Grand Banks led to a Canadian patrol boat chasing a Spanish trawler into international waters, firing rounds from its machine gun across the bow of the fishing boat, and boarding her.

For thousands of years, the bounty of the sea has been a vital part of human society, sustaining and enriching many, though often at the expense of others. Since the most abundant fishing grounds are those found in shallow seas, control of these waters is paramount. Nations have rarely fought wars over livestock but have often come to blows over seafood, such is the importance of regional fisheries. And though the Strait of Malacca is shallow and rich in seafood, geography has given the best sites to the Indonesians. This is why the fishermen across the Strait are so protective of anyone entering their waters. It's also why they've taken to stealing the boats from villages like Tanjung Kling. When I asked the fishermen why their boats were targeted, they almost always answered, "Tsunami."

When the December 26, 2004, tsunami washed ashore along Sumatra's northern coasts, it devastated the local fishing fleets, as well as countless littoral communities (Malaysia was largely spared any impact from the event). The little boats were smashed to bits and cast inland by the waves, leaving thousands of Indonesian fishermen with no way of making a living. In the aftermath, foreign aid poured into the region and the hard-hit province of Bandah Aceh, over on the other side of the Strait, was able to avoid a horrendous humanitarian crisis. But the aid is now drying up and while many of the villages have been rebuilt, the fishing boats have not all been replaced.

This is why the Malaysians believe their boats are being stolen: because the Indonesian fishermen are desperate for vessels. It might also explain why incidents of piracy are beginning to appear again in the Strait of Malacca after a short hiatus, as many of the boats used by Indonesian pirates were also destroyed in the tsunami of 2004.

Abdul's been keeping an eye trained on the sea as Deen and I talk, and suddenly butts out his cigarette and says we must leave. He hurriedly leads us back along the overgrown path to the pier and we get the *perahu* untied. A trio of boats speed by us, the fishermen waving as we get under way. I finally understand the reason for Abdul's haste when I peer toward the western horizon and see a dark mass of clouds signaling a storm front coming our way.

We make it back to the net in record time. I can already feel a numbing pain in my lower back from the incessant crashing of the hull on the choppy seas, reminding me of how physically taxing fishing is. Abdul stops beside his net, and the two men begin to haul it aboard as we wallow in the Strait. I mainly try to keep out of the way, stumbling a few times as the *perahu* rocks from side to side. Deen cautions me not to fall overboard, saying that the current here is quite strong and would take me to Singapore by morning. He doesn't appear to be joking.

There aren't a lot of fish to be seen as the net had not been in the water that long, but concerns about the approaching storm outweigh thoughts of keeping it down any longer. They have it aboard in less than fifteen minutes, after which Abdul fires up the outboard for the short trip home and our dramatic beaching.

The storm that arrives that night turns out to be quite severe. It hammers the coast with high winds and driving rain that doesn't let up throughout the day, essentially trapping me in my little hut. An attempt to head out at midday for some lunch proves disastrous; I'm soaked to the skin in minutes, having stupidly forgotten to pack an umbrella, and forced to beat a hasty retreat back to my shelter, where I munch on a packet of peanuts and listen to the *BBC World News* on my shortwave radio. Periodically I hear a thud as a coconut falls from the palm trees outside, but by dusk the weather gets calmer and by sundown the skies have cleared and things are back to normal.

Famished from being stuck inside all day, I wander down the road to an outdoor restaurant I'd discovered on my first day here. The woman who runs it recognizes me and soon brings me some skewers of chicken *satay,* rice, and bottled water, all of which costs but a few dollars. The place is about half-full but appears to have a steady stream of customers coming and going, none of whom pays me any attention until I hear a voice calling out to me, "Hallo! Hallo!"

A short man in flip-flops, baggy pants, and a blue windbreaker, topped off with the ubiquitous baseball cap, approaches. He's grinning at me, though I've no idea who he is. Maybe he's from the village?

"Hallo, friend!" he says, extending his hand. "Food good, yes? Very good place. You like food of Malaysia, yes? Very good. Where you from?"

If there's one thing I know about Malaysians, it is that they are a friendly and generous people, courteous and respectful of others. They rarely interrupt someone who is eating, and when they do come up to talk to you they introduce themselves. This man has broken both those rules.

"I friend," he tells me while pulling up a chair to sit opposite me. "You American, yes?"

"Canadian," I respond cautiously.

"Canada . . . like America, yes?"

"Well, nooo . . . not as wealthy." I figure he must be getting ready to sell me something and hope it's not a young girl. There's something distinctly sleazy about him: He has a bad complexion, wiry bristles of hair that he must think are a moustache, and ugly yellow teeth, a few of which are missing. He pulls out a pack of cigarettes and offers me one, but I shake my head and try to finish the *satay*.

"Hmmm, I see you. In village. You talk with fisherman, go in boat, yes? Is fun?"

"Yes, I'm a tourist interested in these kinds of adventurous things," I respond while trying to figure out how to get away from the annoying man.

He leans closer and sucks on the clove-scented cigarette. "Maybe you talk with me, heh?" Great, someone else who wants to be interviewed. "You like know about pirate, heh?" Shit. "Many pirate in sea, long time. I know; I fish."

"Where do you live?"

"Other village, other place, not here. You come, I show you. People say you want know about pirate. I tell you, come. I have motorbike." He gestures at a rusty motorcycle.

Now, much as I am here to learn more about piracy and hear firsthand accounts of the problem, there's something about this situation that just doesn't seem right. Beyond the fact that the guy still hasn't told me his name or where he lives, the idea of jumping on a motorbike and heading off into the night in a foreign country should give anyone pause. I know I've got little of value on me—maybe 150 Malaysian ringgit, twenty American dollars, and some expired credit cards I carry for just these types of events—so I'm not worried about being robbed blind. But being beaten up in a laneway for these meager holdings, that's another issue.

I politely decline his invitation and say I am waiting for a friend, as bald-faced a lie as I can muster.

"How long you stay?"

"A few more days," which is another lie, as I depart tomorrow.

He stares at me with his gap-toothed grin, trying to appear friendly. "You worry is trouble? I know you no police, you tourist, heh? I am no harm, okay? You come, we talk. You like drink? I have Tiger beer, is okay. You smoke?" He means dope. "I get you, is no trouble. Meet my friends. They know pirate. You talk. No problem."

"No trouble." "No problem." He keeps repeating these words again and again. And then, as if to reassure me, he leans back, glances quickly around, and opens his windbreaker. There's a small revolver jammed into the waist of his pants.

Compared to some of the places I've visited in various parts of the globe, Malaysia is pretty safe, and this part of the country per-haps more so. However, a gun is a gun wherever you are, and people don't wander around with them hidden beneath their jacket unless they have a reason. All of this runs through my mind as the guy starts yammering away, though I hear nothing of what he says. Instead, I focus on the remaining bits of chicken *satay* on the bamboo skewer as my brain does a slow-motion playback of what's going on: Strange man knows where I've been, whom I've spoken to, and what I'm doing here. Man says he knows something about pirates. Says I should go with him to someplace where there's booze and drugs to meet his "friends." Strange man has a gun.

As near as I can figure, he doesn't know where I staying, which is a good thing. Unfortunately, my hut is about a mile away down a darkened road. It doesn't take a brain surgeon to realize that this is not a good situation to be in.

I look up to see the gunman glaring at me. He's waiting for me to make a decision, obviously to go with him, and I'm running out of options here. And then my savior arrives, in the form of a Malaysian transvestite.

She/he goes by the name Michelle and works for the family that owns the hut I am staying in. I spy her buying some vegetables from a seller next door to the restaurant and try to get her attention. Mercifully, she sees me and strides over. The guy with the gun relaxes and sits back in his chair.

"Hallo, Daneeyel," Michelle says. "Why you eat here?" Then she peers at my new friend, looking him up and down with distinct disdain. Michelle is large person, perhaps not the most attractive transvestite in Malaysia but certainly the most appealing on this particular evening. The guy sitting opposite me verily shrinks in her presence. Michelle speaks to him in Malay, obviously questioning him. By his responses and gestures, I could figure out he was saying something like, "This is my new friend and we're just talking together."

Michelle flicks her hand as though swatting a fly, dismissing the guy's response. Turning back to me, she takes control of the situation. "Okay, honey, you finish. I take you home."

This is one of those odd times when you ponder the surreal nature of what life offers you. In this case my options are to leave the restaurant with a gunman or a transvestite. I choose the transvestite without blinking, grabbing my coat and following Michelle to her car as the gunman shouts, "You come tomorrow, yes?"

As we drive away, I can't help glancing back to see if the man is following us; however, we seem to be alone. Michelle says nothing until we near where I'm staying. Staring at the road, she begins scolding me: "That man not good," she says while wagging her finger. "He not from here, okay? What you thinking? You must be crazy talk with that man." I can only nod dumbly. Dropping me off, Michelle wishes me a pleasant evening. "You be careful, okay, honey?"

I lock the door to my hut and try to calm down, keeping only one small light on as I listen to every sound I hear outside. About an hour later, I hear someone on the porch outside the door and tense up. There's a knock on the door. I turn the light off, which immediately strikes me as a silly thing to do. Whoever's out there now knows I'm inside, and what will darkness do? It's not like I can hide in the shadows.

"Daniel, you there?" a voice quietly asks. It's Kamarudeen. I unlock the door and see him looking concerned. Michelle lives in the village and once she got home spread the word about what she'd discovered. Deen's come to check up on me and sit with me awhile. He doesn't say it, but I can tell he's standing guard.

Deen asks me what happened and I recount the run-in with the gunman. He asks me to describe the guy, which I do as best I can. Deen takes this all in and, after a few moments, says the man was Indonesian—Michelle recognized his accent. He figures the guy was probably one of the spies the pirates use to reconnoiter the area, maybe the person who helped in the theft of the boats and engines. It was a good thing Michelle showed up, Deen tells me. It would have been dangerous to go with the guy.

We walk down to the pebbly beach and sit staring out at the lights of the passing ships on the Strait. The Moon above is waning, and I ask Deen if he saw the eclipse last week.

"Eclipse we call *bulan mengambang*. I not see this time, but I see before. We have story about this, the eclipse. Before, the people think that a spirit it is eating the Moon, swallow it. The people they not go out when this is happen. Keep children in the house, they think it bad time."

Deen doesn't believe these old superstitions but knows them intimately, and the traditional stories are still a part of his culture.

"The pirate who take our *perahu* I sometime think are like *puntianak*, what we call ghosts. They come when dark, no one see, then *perahu* gone. Like big mystery, yes?"

The young man falls into silent thought, staring at the sea. "You know, some people they think our problem today is because of the history, because the pirate is part of our culture. Fishermen here sometime are pirate, back in the history. Not just here, all over, heh? So maybe the bad things from the history are reason is pirate today?"

I wonder if he means something like karma, with the bad deeds from the past being paid for by the fishermen of today. "The 'karma' is with the Buddhist person, yes?"

Deen answers, "No, I am Muslim; we not have karma. This different, maybe . . ." Deen struggles to find the words in English to describe what he's thinking, finally telling me a traditional story that has been handed down over the generations:

A long time ago, two brothers set out on the sea to go fishing. They were far out in the Strait and night fell, so they decided to sleep in their boat. Sometime in the evening, a storm struck and the boat was overturned, throwing the brothers into the water. As they strug-

gled to keep from drowning, the brothers spied a piece of wood floating nearby and swam toward it. It wasn't much, barely big enough to
support one of them, so the older brother said to his sibling, "I have
a wife and children, dear brother, while you are single. It is better if
I stay with the wood and live, while you take your chances in the sea
alone."

So with tears in his eyes, the older brother pushed his kin away,
even as the younger man pleaded for his life. As the boy began to
be pulled by the current, an apparition appeared from beneath
the waves. It was a sea ghost—*hantu laut*—and it swallowed up the
younger brother in its mouth and disappeared back into the depths.

The older brother eventually made it to shore, but whenever he
would go fishing he would catch a glimpse of the *hantu laut* in the
waters, knowing the beast had eaten his brother because of his
selfishness.

"You see," says Deen, "the pirate today it remind us of the pirate
before, of the bad things that happen. The pirate, I think, never go
away. He always somewhere on the sea, just like *hantu laut*."

3

PIRACY, INC.

Crime, like virtue, has its degrees.

—JEAN RACINE, *PHÈDRE* (1677), ACT 4, SCENE 2

AS THE YOUNG Malaysian fisherman told me with such simplicity on the shores of the Strait of Malacca, pirates never go away. Indeed, they are one of the most enduring aspects of maritime life, more permanent than sail ships, steel hulls, steam power, and seafaring kingdoms great and small. For more than three thousand years these nautical marauders have been the scourge of every sea man has ventured out upon; they have enveloped coastal communities on every continent but Antarctica with panic and terror throughout the millennia; and their attacks have brought rulers to the brink of desperation.

But piracy has ebbed and flowed over time as those driven to dealing with the issue forcefully combated it. Statutes were drawn up to outlaw it, navies have been sent forth to face down the threat, soldiers landed on foreign lands to destroy pirate havens, fortresses were built to protect against further attacks, and everyone hoped the problem had been dealt with once and for all. Piracy has also been marginalized as a matter of public scrutiny, because it is represented as either something from the past or, if it is considered a current affair, something that affects only a minority of people and can be somehow dealt with swiftly.

All of which has led us to forget a crucial aspect of piracy: This is a business. A big business.

The reason piracy has endured over the years is that it is a hugely profitable enterprise, albeit one fraught with deadly risks. Analysts looking at the issue of modern-day maritime crime often peg the annual losses to the global economy somewhere in the range of $50 billion (U.S.), with piracy itself accounting for about a third of the figure. Even the lowball estimates of piracy losses hover around $10 billion every year, from ransoms paid, cargoes lost, higher insurance premiums, and delays and interruptions to shipping schedules. Ten billion dollars annually is a figure well above the gross domestic product of numerous nations, virtually unprecedented in our global economic history. And if piracy in days gone by generated but a mere fraction of today's figures, that was still sufficient incentive to becoming involved in this nefarious business.

Fundamentally, maritime crimes like piracy are all about a means of seeking wealth through illegal or quasi-legal acts on and around the seas. And if you're so inclined to engage in such an activity, it certainly makes sense to hope it will be both profitable and long running. From a business perspective, the risks entailed in embarking on a life of nautical crime are great: You must overcome whatever moral qualms you might have about a life of crime, recruit individuals willing to aid and abet in attacking mariners, acquire vessels to carry out these attacks, develop a base from which to operate those vessels, outfit the craft with suitable weaponry and sundry supplies, foster sources of intelligence from within the shipping community, and find the ways to dispose of whatever booty is obtained, to say nothing of risking your life and freedom. So if you are going to go to all the trouble of setting yourself up in this business, it makes theoretical sense that the goal ought to be a stable enterprise that brings continued returns on the investment.

To make a crime like piracy profitable, one must develop a business plan that factors in all the risks and find a way to mitigate those threats, or at least reduce them sufficiently to assure success. And the best way to begin plotting a life of crime on the high seas is to look at the history that came before you, to learn from the mistakes—and successes—of those who have preceded you. As a business endeavor, piracy has remained surprisingly little changed in a thousand years. Pirate leaders have always sought to create organizations that would provide long-lasting incomes for themselves and their followers, albeit with varying success.

Some, like Blackbeard or Captain Kidd, had relatively brief careers, lasting but a few short years.[1] Others, though, were able to create enterprises that proved exceedingly resilient and robust. Perhaps the most successful was the leader of the Red Flag Fleet, a pirate navy that roamed the South China Sea in the early part of the nineteenth century. The fleet was supposed to have comprised some fifty thousand men sailing aboard hundreds of vessels and was commanded by a rarity in the world of piracy: a woman. Cheng I Sao (also known as Ching Shih, Zheng Yi Sao, or Mrs. Cheng), a former prostitute and the widow of the Red Fleet's founder, assumed command of the fleet after her husband died suddenly in November 1807. She managed the affairs of not only the Red Fleet but also a confederation of other Chinese pirate gangs, and a measure of how good a leader Cheng was may be gleaned by another rare event among pirates: she died peacefully in her bed around 1844.

Pirate commanders like Cheng I Sao were successful because they set out a business plan, focused on a goal, and managed their resources; they sought a base of operations (or multiple bases at times), trained and motivated their personnel, aimed for maximum profits, and knew how to deal with shareholders who needed to be placated for having invested their time, money, or personal lives in these enterprises.

"Shareholders" may seem an odd concept to consider in the context of piracy, yet it is one of the prime underlying precepts of this maritime enterprise. The very nature of leaving land to attack a ship makes this an expensive criminal endeavor to carry out: you need a boat, someone who knows how to operate it, and the ability to know your way around a vessel. This is not like walking into a shop with a handgun to rob the owner. Even at its most basic level a pirate requires a bit of help to get things going, be it someone to front the money to gets things started or individuals with the skills to carry out an attack. All involved will want a cut of the take, a portion of the profits, or a healthy return on their investments. Hence they become shareholders. But even someone from the lowest rungs of society could become an investor in a pirate ship merely by joining its crew and being willing to stake his very life on the chance to get rich. To make things more appealing for these new recruits, many pirate captains drew up one of the most famous elements from the so-called golden age of piracy: the articles under which a seafarer would agree to join a crew embarking "on account."

During this period, which lasted roughly from the 1680s to the 1720s, these articles varied from ship to ship but generally laid out what rewards a crewman could expect to receive if plunder was taken, the compensation offered for potential injuries received on the job, and the guidelines of daily behavior expected by the captain. In modern terms, these were simply employment agreements; in the context of the eighteenth century, they were nothing short of a revolutionary new form of business accountability, one that laid out the risks and rewards and obligations to those who agreed to them in clear and certain terms. Few other businesses in that era would be so candid and open in dealing with their workers, and it would be centuries before this practice became common in the workplace.

Consider the articles that pirate captain George Lowther offered his crew after effecting a mutiny off the coast of Gambia in 1721.[2] Having called the crew of the sixteen-gun Royal Africa Company ship *Gambia Castle* on deck, Lowther explained the punishment that awaited them should they return home to England—which was imprisonment and likely execution—and offered instead that they should all "seek their Fortunes upon the Seas, as other Adventurers had done before them." To that end, Captain Lowther—formerly the vessel's second mate—drew up a series of articles that the mutinous crew all duly signed, sworn upon a Bible. They read like any legal contract between two parties and stated:

1. The Captain is to have two full Shares, the Master is to have one Share and a half; the Doctor, Mate, Gunner, and Boatswain, one Share and a quarter.

2. He that shall be found guilty of taking up any unlawful weapon on board the Privateer, or any Prize, by us taken, so as to strike or abuse one another, in any regard, shall suffer what Punishment the Captain and Majority of the Company shall think fit.

3. He that shall be found Guilty of Cowardice, in the Time of Engagement, shall suffer what Punishment the Captain and Majority shall think fit.

4. If any Gold, Jewels, Silver, &c. be found on board of any Prize or Prizes, to a Value of a Piece of Eight, and the Finder do not deliver it to the Quarter-Master, in the Space of 24 Hours, [he] shall suffer what Punishment that Captain and Majority shall think fit.

5. He that is found Guilty of Gaming, or Defrauding another to the Value of a Shilling, shall suffer what Punishment that Captain and Majority of the Company shall think fit.

6. He that shall have the Misfortune to lose a Limb, in Time of Engagement, shall have the Sum of one hundred and fifty Pounds Sterling, and remain with the Company as long as he shall think fit.

7. Good Quarters to be given when call'd for.

8. He that sees a Sail first, shall have the best Pistol, or Small-Arms, on board her.

For an eighteen-year-old working-class lad from an English slum, this must have been an unimaginable offer. Compared to what the British Royal Navy or the merchant marine had to offer, what Lowther was proffering in 1721's employment terms was well beyond the norm. One hundred and fifty pounds for a lost limb works out to just under $40,000 (U.S.) today, and the ability to be a part of the decision-making process placed an amazing amount of democratic power within the hands of an individual who was used to being powerless. The navy and the commercial seafaring industry offered neither.

Of course this was all still a lottery, like investing in any other scheme that might—*might*—work. But human nature is suitably greedy enough that risks can be subsumed beneath potential rewards and blinders put in place to mitigate the dangers. Those who ran pirate operations were smart enough to understand this human weakness and use it to make their operations viable. They needed mariners to crew their vessels, not only for their knowledge of the sea and seamanship but also because they understood how to work as a team. Aboard a vessel there is a cohesiveness, a unity of individuals that is barely understood outside the seafaring community. So who better to mold into a cohesive battle unit than a group that knew how to take orders and wanted to get rich? This applies to British and European sailors in the eighteenth century, to Chinese mariners a century later; to North African seafarers, Phoenicians, Greeks, Arabians, and North Americans. They knew the sea, were poor at home, and had little to lose.

With all these elements available to those interested in piracy, the only really sticking point was the illegality of the business. While there will always be individuals willing to cross the line and commit acts that contravene laws and regulations, for an otherwise upstanding citizen to engage in criminal acts on the high seas requires something more. Such as, perhaps, the inducement of one's political leaders. Luckily for those so inclined, history has shown that governing bodies have been amply willing to give their citizens a degree of sanction to let one and all enrich themselves from the bounty of their neighbors.

The granting of letters of marque by European powers led to the possibly greatest period of state-sanctioned crime on the seas, attracting tens of thousands to attack and rob their fellow mariners. Greed overruled whatever moral qualms an individual might have harbored, as colonial powers such as England, France, Holland, and Spain fought proxy wars, or outright conflicts, especially throughout the seventeenth, eighteenth, and early nineteenth centuries. Armed with a letter of marque, one could fire a cannon at another ship, assault her crew, steal the cargo, and hijack the vessel if he so desired. The value of this document cannot be over-estimated, for a letter of marque is one of the very rare times that governments have allowed their citizens to engage in criminal acts without being held responsible for their actions.

I stumbled on just such a letter while taking in a piracy exhibit at the Maritime Museum of the Atlantic in Halifax, Nova Scotia. It was easily the most overlooked artifact on display; most of the families wandering through the exhibit preferred to gaze at mannequins dressed up in historical garb or depictions of Blackbeard's life. Yet this letter was the most relevant item to be seen, for it had been issued in Nova Scotia to a local ship, granting permission to attack Americans and their French allies during the War of 1812. The vessel was the *Liverpool Packet* and her letter of marque, dated November 19, 1812, reads, in part:

> . . . *a Letter of Marque and Reprisals to be issued out of the High Court of Admiralty unto Caleb Seely Commander of the Liverpool Packet Burthern of about sixty seven tons, mounted with five Carriage Guns carrying Shot of twelve, six & four Pounds Weight and navigated with Thirty men, whereas the said Caleb Seely is commander, to apprehend, seize, and take the Ships, Vessels and Goods Belonging to the United States of America, or to any persons being Subjects of France, according to His Majesty's Commission and Instruction aforesaid.*

Armed with this letter, to say nothing of her five cannons, the *Liverpool Packet* became probably the most successful privateer that sailed against the Americans during that war, credited with taking fifty prizes, as seized vessels were known. The United States alone issued some eleven hundred letters of marque during the conflict, so that by the time the war ended in 1815, thousands of men were sailing the Atlantic in search of prizes and not a few were disappointed to hear peace had broken out. Having let this evil genie out of its bottle, Britain and the United States watched with increasing alarm as groups of privateers migrated to the Caribbean, where they continued to prey on shipping, sometimes using dubious letters of marque issued by local authorities, sometimes simply turning to outright piracy.

With the Industrial Revolution increasing global commerce, it was imperative that something be done to curb the plight of these rogue privateers who would interfere with shipping. So it was that diplomats from around the world gathered in Paris in 1856 to sign a declaration outlawing privateering (though the United States refused to sign, which led to more privateering troubles during the American Civil War). As the first international treaty to look at maritime crime, it led the way for latter agreements, though it would not be until 1958 that piracy itself would be addressed, in the United Nations Convention on the High Seas.

Though piracy and privateering are now codified and banned through international agreements, one might assume there is some part of the United Nations keeping an eye on the situation, advising mariners of danger zones, and helping to safeguard their lives when in peril. Unfortunately, this is not the case. Though piracy is a transnational threat to security and commerce, the United Nations cannot prosecute a pirate for his actions; this can only be done in a sovereign nation's court of law. Nor can the United Nations authorize the naval equivalent of peacekeepers into an area where piracy is rampant, such as the Strait of Malacca or the waters off Somalia. Instead, it is left to individual states to police their territorial waters or dispatch warships to patrol the high seas, a hugely expensive undertaking at the best of times.

Deploying armed vessels into pirate waters is one of the most effective deterrents to the problem, but this cannot be done easily. Beyond the political will to carry out anti-piracy operations, there is also the difficult nature of actually finding out where these criminals are operating. For instance, it's one thing to say that groups are based in Somalia; it's another to consider the country's coastline is almost two thousand miles long. To effectively respond to the threat of piracy requires a sophisticated intelligence-gathering structure. But the hydralike nature of pirate operations would task the most powerful government agencies on the planet, which may be why so few of them address it.

All of which makes it interesting that the main source of intelligence about worldwide piracy today comes not from some high-tech command post in the Pentagon or NATO headquarters but from a tiny outfit hidden away in an office building in Southeast Asia.

After a two-hour drive from the Malaysian coastal village of Tanjung Kling, I find myself standing outside Kuala Lumpur's main train station on a cloudless late-summer afternoon. The heat of the tropics mixes with diesel fumes from idling buses to create a pungent smell that envelops me. Though I thought I was acclimatized to the environment here, sweat stains are in abundant supply on the only dress shirt I've packed for my trip, forcing me to remove the sport coat I'm wearing for my upcoming meeting. Add in the general cacophony of a teeming metropolis—motorcycles buzzing by, car horns tooting, crowds mingling about—and I'm beginning to feel slightly overwhelmed after my time spent in a relatively placid fishing village on the coast (even considering my incident with the gunman).

I keep thinking how I must look like a rube to all the locals, or at least a foreign tourist who is an easy mark for all the hustlers offering cut-rate taxi rides, cheap places to stay, and Lord knows what else. I try to ignore the incessant offers and get my bearings. The Malaysian capital is noisy, relentless, and vibrant; the place is awash in a display of national pride stemming from last weekend's Independence Day celebrations. There are flags hanging everywhere—from apartment balconies, draped across office towers, on cars, scooters, and even the backpacks of schoolkids. A group of Malaysian naval officers pass by me, resplendent in dress white uniforms, while a nearby cluster of young women dressed in Muslim *hijab* are busy text-messaging on their cell phones. I ask one of the women for directions to the nearest public transit station and she answers pleasantly in fluent English, telling me to cut through a nearby series of vendors' stalls.

Pushing through the crowds, I meander past hawkers selling everything from Western-style T-shirts to tourist trinkets to cell phones every few feet. My guidebook tells me the city was once a sultanate and there are remnants of British colonial architecture around, but all I'm seeing is the sort of atmosphere one finds in New York's Lower East Side, Toronto's Chinatown, and London's East End: lots of cheap knock-off goods for sale and lots of bland late-twentieth-century architecture. Kuala Lumpur, commonly referred to as KL, is far from the largest city in Southeast Asia—the population is only about one and a half million people—but it's been doing its best to keep up with the neighbors when it comes to creating a regional center of finance and business. And it's clear that money is the driving force here.

Though it all seems rather chaotic to me, what with all the small entrepreneurs working the passing crowds from every nook and cranny, the city core is actually well organized, with a strong dose of master planning at play. One of those creations is a monorail system that carries me to the city center area known as the Golden Triangle. This is where KL's most famous buildings are located, the immense Petronas Towers designed by Argentine-American architect César Pelli. Opened with great fanfare in 1998, the Towers are supposed to embody elements of Muslim influence, such as having five tiers to reflect the five pillars of Islamic faith, yet they mainly convey the financial prosperity Malaysia has enjoyed from its oil and gas reserves.[3]

Almost all of that oil and gas is exported from Malaysia on commercial ships—supertankers, smaller tankers, liquefied natural gas (LNG) carriers, and barges—and any pirate attacks on those vessels could have a drastic effect on the domestic economy of this country. Add in the heavy international vessel traffic that transits through the nearby Strait of Malacca and you would think that Malaysia would have been at the forefront of anti-piracy operations over the last decade. Such has, unfortunately, not been the case, though it has improved vastly in just the last few years. Marshaling the Malaysian government's interest—and that of many other nations—in this issue has required considerable effort from a variety of foreign governments and international shipping organizations, as well as a small group of dedicated piracy fighters based here in Kuala Lumpur.

In the shadows of the Petronas Towers sits a nondescript office building that houses the epicenter of the global battle against modern-day piracy. While the IMB is based in London, downtown Kuala Lumpur is the site of its Asia Regional Office, wherein is found the Piracy Reporting Centre, established in 1992. It is from here that daily situations are monitored and regular reports sent out to mariners around the world. This is where seafarers call when they're under attack, where naval forces turn when they want to know what's going on out on the high seas, and where anyone looking into the scourge of modern-day piracy tries to visit. The only place of its kind in the world, it's not easy to gain access to, owing to the sensitive nature of the Centre's work, and it took weeks to get the approval for my visit.

The PRC is located on the thirty-fifth floor of the building, behind doors that are kept locked twenty-fours hours a day, seven days a week. After being buzzed in, I'm met by the head of the Centre, Noel Choong, and given a quick tour of the facilities. "Quick" is the opportune word in this case, as the nerve center in this global war proves to be a somewhat Spartan space, smaller than a typical grade-school classroom. It consists of Choong's office, one small meeting room, a kitchenette, a storage area, a lot of filing cabinets, and a couple of desks crammed close together near the windows. There are several maps of the world and various regional seas on the walls, studded with pins marking recent attacks. Two men working in the monitoring area nod politely at me, then go back to scanning their computer screens while periodically leafing through piles of paperwork and faxes that litter their desks. My first impression is that the Centre has all the tension of an accountant's office.

Including Choong, there are a grand total of three people here keeping an eye on maritime crime incidents occurring throughout the world on a daily basis, and he smiles thinly when I comment on the seemingly low-tech small scale of operations at the PRC. He's obviously used to receiving visitors who expect to see some sort of war room with locations of recent pirate attacks marked on digital maps and a team of people bustling about like soldiers in a command post.

Choong tells me the reason the PRC seems so mundane is because "its role is not to deploy response teams—such as navy or coast guard vessels, or armed teams—nor to organize the rescue of anyone attacked. We have no authority to do that. We are not a government agency or anything like Interpol. What we are is very often a first point of contact for mariners in trouble. They will contact us when a situation arises and we then relay that information to the relevant resources available."

The head of the PRC points to a bulletin board on the wall, on which are scrawled the most recent events of concern that the Centre is tracking. Under the heading "Phantom/Missing Ships/Etc." are listed eleven incidents: the hijacking and release of five vessels, the pirate captivity of three, the disappearance and presumed sinking of two, and the disappearance with no news whatsoever of one.

He goes on to add that with the availability of satellite and mobile phones, fax machines, and the Internet, virtually any professional mariner out on the seas can get in touch with the PRC, if the need arises. Though the shipping industry is a truly global business, it often surprises people to find out there are only about fifty thousand merchant ships plying the waters of our planet, manned by just over a million seafarers.[4] In those terms, what the PRC does is much like a 911 emergency call center in a medium-sized North American city.

Organized and neatly dressed, Choong ushers me into the tiny meeting room to explain the history of the Centre and its functions, backed up with yet another set of statistical reports on recent incidents of piracy and armed robbery against ships. Unlike the rest of the PRC, this room feels more active, more like a wardroom on a warship, with its walls filled with numerous plaques and commendations from appreciative naval units and maps highlighting the various hot spots the Centre is tracking.

Choong wastes little time with small talk, instead launching quickly into an animated description of the Centre that has the words tumbling out of him. The Centre, I'm told, was set up in October of 1992, and Choong arrived here five years later to head up its operations. With the funding they receive, the PRC has now evolved into the preeminent piracy-tracking outfit in the world, even if it may appear otherwise.[5] A major aspect of the Centre's activities is to cajole and prod governments and the shipping industry into taking a more active position in the fight against modern-day piracy, something that forces Choong to walk a fine line between various economic stakeholders. Recently the Indonesian government took exception to some of the statistics the PRC released about acts committed in their territorial waters, a disagreement the director politely declines to comment on.

Instead, Choong points out the way things have improved in the decade since he's assumed his role here: "For many years, this was seen as a minor, regional issue, confined to small areas and best left to the national security elements of neighboring countries to address. While that is true on paper, it overlooks a broader picture in which greater cooperation between states is required, such as with the Strait of Malacca. With Malaysia, Singapore, and Indonesia now working together, the Strait has become far safer today than five or ten years back. Or look at the Horn of Africa and Somalia, where there is little in the way of a functioning government to deal with piracy. We feel strongly that one means of addressing the problem there is by increasing the international presence in the waters, filling the vacuum created by political instability ashore."

To help combat piracy around the globe, the Centre works in conjunction with the IMB head office in London to be a public information outlet and keep track of trends in global piracy, providing their data to whoever requests it. Indeed, it is the PRC that receives the bulk of the daily information that allows us to understand how serious the problem is today.

"We use two satellites to send out daily updates—'sit reps'—at zero hours GMT[6] every day," says Choong. "These can be accessed by anyone—mariners, naval forces, government agencies, journalists, anyone who wants to know what is going on." The Centre makes these reports easily accessible for perusal on the Internet, the main form of communication for mariners today (as opposed to the days when radio transmissions were used).[7]

I wonder if pirates might monitor these reports, too, and Choong smiles slyly. "Well, I think that most pirates do not care about what has already happened, and our reports only list reported incidents and provide alerts to piracy-prone waters. Yes, there are elements within this criminal community that most certainly read our reports, and some of the pirate groups are undeniably very sophisticated, with extensive organizations, which use every resource available to plan their attacks. But you cannot read our reports online and figure out if there are naval forces or the like waiting in such-and-such a place to pounce on pirates."

Choong explains that the Centre breaks down the piracy hierarchy into three groups, reiterating what Pottengal Mukundan had told me in London: They have identified large criminal cartels that are highly organized, smaller groups that are less structured and concern themselves with more localized areas, and "opportunists" who are often nothing more than a few men intent on boarding an anchored vessel and making off with whatever is not tied down or locked up.

The Strait of Malacca is an example of one area where these groups overlap. As identified by the PRC's intelligence, one can find three types of pirate attacks in the Strait over the last few years: In the north, the aim is to kidnap senior officers, such as the captain or chief engineer, and hold them for ransom. This requires pinpointing targets of opportunity—ships owned by firms that have the resources to pay the pirates' demands, as opposed to smaller players who might not care about the safety of their hired personnel—and having a knowledge of international banking and money transfers that speaks to a degree of organization and intelligence on the part of the criminals. These are the guys who watch ships in port and track their passage through the waterway.

In the middle region of the Strait, which includes Tanjung Kling, where I had previously visited, the Centre has identified gangs of armed robbers, slightly less sophisticated than their northern brethren, looking for any money they can find. The modus operandi here involves watching for vessels of suitable size, ones that should have enough money in the ship's safe to make it worth risking an attack. These are the bank robbers of the high seas, the ones who hope that arriving with some weapons will scare the crew into handing over the loot.

Finally, in the south around Singapore the pirates are small groups who work almost exclusively at night. These criminals aim for whatever they might find: the money in the safe, the DVD players or cell phones of the crew, even the buckets of paint stored on the deck. Given the vast number of ships that call upon Singapore, one of the world's busiest ports, these pirates are aiming for quantity over quality: there is little targeted planning to achieve a single result.

The IMB has been able to use these synopses of the types of pirate activity in the Malaccan Strait to look at other regions more effectively. For instance, with the major piracy hot spots now being Somalia and West Africa's Gulf of Guinea, Choong and his team can look at the reports of attacks coming in from these places and make educated guesses as to what trends may be forecast for the future.

"Somalia is a good example of a place we can apply lessons learned," he explains. "We see very little attacks there of the kind where pirates climb aboard to steal the ship's supplies or kidnap only the master and chief officer. Instead it is almost exclusively aimed at hijacking entire vessels in order to make ransom demands from the shipowners. These are not small sums, either; they can be in excess of a million dollars. As a result, we have been warning vessels to remain several hundred nautical miles to sea, where the risk of an attack is lessened.

"On the other hand, if you look at a place like Nigeria, with a variety of violent attacks being committed against those working in the oil and gas sectors, it is primarily aimed at kidnapping workers for ransom. Robbing ships is secondary, and random acts of theft—of things like deck stores [ships' supplies]—are at the bottom. And they rarely hijack entire vessels. Nigerian waters today are not unlike what the situation was off Indonesia ten to fifteen years ago."

The Gulf of Guinea is a part of the southern Atlantic Ocean that abuts such West African nations as Nigeria, Cameroon, Benin, Togo, Ghana, and Côte d'Ivoire, with the former war zones of Liberia and Sierra Leone nearby. The region is also a major oil and gas producer, with Nigeria leading the way as Africa's largest oil exporter and earning the nation some $40 billion in annual revenue.[8] As Nigeria is closer to North America than the Middle East and has fewer problems with extremist Islamist groups, its oil and gas resources are regarded as being of strategic importance to the United States (the African country is currently the United States' fifth-largest oil provider).

All of the exploration and production going on has led to an influx of foreign companies and thousands of well-paid workers who man drill ships, offshore rigs, supply vessels, tankers, refineries, and storage facilities. It is these workers who have become the targets of armed gangs trying to get in on the windfall, because though there are billions being made from oil and gas, little is making it into the pockets of ordinary Nigerians.

The situation there receives much less press than piracy off Somalia or elsewhere, though it has been the scene of some of the most violent attacks against mariners in the last half decade. With forty-two reported attacks in 2007—almost one a week—the waters off Nigeria have been the worst part of the Gulf, with the highest number of injuries and deaths to mostly foreign workers. A random sampling of recent events reveals incidents in which Blackbeard himself would have relished taking part. Pirates here are notoriously ruthless, threatening to cut off the ears of captives, beating their prisoners with rifle butts and clubs, smashing their heads with bottles, shooting unlucky mariners in the legs, kidnapping the young children of foreigners, and, of course, murdering.

Nigerian pirates often operate in large groups and are fearless in taking on well-equipped guards or Nigerian soldiers. Back in January of 2006, forty armed pirates swarmed aboard the pollution control vessel *Liberty Service* as she was sailing off the Nigerian coast. They overwhelmed the crew, vandalized the vessel's equipment, and made off with four foreign mariners, who were held hostage ashore for three weeks until ransoms were paid. This occurred even though there were fourteen Nigerian naval personnel on the vessel. Months later, in early October, another group of gunmen attacked barges carrying fuel and supplies to a Royal Dutch Shell facility in the Niger Delta. They killed three government soldiers assigned to protect the barges, abducted twenty-five Nigerian workers, and off-loaded the barges' cargo.

Given the violent nature of Nigerian maritime criminals and the frequency of their attacks, you would think this region would be as well known as Somalia or Southeast Asia. However, many of these attacks have been carried out by so-called militants who claim to support political movements seeking redress for economic disparities or some sort of regional autonomy from the federal government of Nigeria. That is, they say they're attacking and robbing for political ends, not financial, which can make the situation more confusing. It's easy to explain away piracy off the Horn of Africa as being all about the money; it's much harder to distill the political aspirations of yet another militant group in some far-flung corner of the globe to a Western audience. Once the simple story of a kidnapping becomes mired in politics, attention spans wane. However, Noel Choong, for one, does not buy this argument, saying it is a ploy to mask what is really just a criminal endeavor.

"You have groups such as MEND [the Movement for the Emancipation of the Niger Delta] who say they want a better share of the revenue for their people and whatnot, yet their attacks have created greater instability and led to a reduction in overall oil production. In reality, all these groups want is money for themselves, so they will head out in small craft and board vessels, rob the crews, even kidnap them. They say they are acting as political movements, but I dismiss their claims. They're just thieves and robbers."

MEND is a militant group based in the Niger Delta region of Nigeria that has taken exception to the relentless pace of oil extraction going on in the area and, more specifically, the environmental devastation that has resulted from this. MEND also feels that the local people are receiving few benefits while foreigners reap much from the region's natural resources. While MEND does have some valid concerns, it is the manner in which they have chosen to deal with these grievances that leads Noel Choong and others to question the veracity of their political ambitions. Kidnapping foreigners for ransom and attacking offshore oil installations and the vessels that service them, instead of engaging in a constructive dialogue with the oil companies or the Nigerian government, seems to suggest MEND is in it more for the money. And they wouldn't be the first group of criminals to hide their financial intentions behind a mask of political injustice. I ask Choong how he knows so much about the detailed workings of nautical criminals and he pauses to choose his words carefully: "We receive information from many sources—within the shipping industry, from naval forces, private security outfits, individual mariners, and even certain . . . I guess you would say 'covert' sources. We recently set up an anonymous hotline for tips, leads, and any other information relating to piracy, maritime crime, terrorism—anything."

Some of these tips relate to mariners and vessels that have been hijacked by pirates, which has forced Choong to venture into the dark business of negotiating with criminals. This aspect of his job is not without risks and explains why he dislikes being photographed or interviewed on television. Within the global seafaring community there are few people who know what he looks like, and that's just fine with him. As Choong cautiously relates, this lets him do his job more effectively, developing a number of relationships with informers who have helped the PRC to aid in the freeing of hostages.

"For example, sometime in the recent past I had to fly to Bangkok to meet with . . . informers about a certain incident," he says, weighing his words carefully. "There was an incident—a vessel had been hijacked and its crew was being held for ransom. So, we met at the airport; it was all prearranged. I wanted to hear what they knew about this case, because lives were involved. These individuals said they could guarantee the seafarers would be released if some moneys were paid. So I struck a deal, and things worked out okay."

Choong goes on to emphasize that they never just pay money for tips; there has to be concrete proof that a ship or its crew is rescued before funds are released. This opens a somewhat touchy subject, for he is talking about essentially acquiescing to the demands of criminals: pay us and we'll release our hostages. He doesn't say as much, but it is clearly cheaper to do this than engage in drawn-out negotiations that could risk human lives or a valuable commercial vessel.

"Our main concern is the safety and well-being of those crew who are attacked and, sometimes, taken hostage. Is it wrong to pay ransom? Absolutely. There should be no such thing occurring today. But this issue is much more complicated than that. You have seen the figures," Choong says, gesturing at the most recent piracy report before me. "We are dealing with thieves and robbers who have shown a ready willingness to kill. Paying informers is a short-term solution, and I am glad to do that to get these [seafarers] back. These few times we have paid money to do that do not, in my opinion, compound the problem. It does not make the pirates think, 'Okay, we can capture this crew and the IMB will pay us.' No, the real issue is the larger problem of reducing pirate attacks in the first place."

Choong refuses to tell me how many times informants have been paid or the sums of money involved. "That could jeopardize things if it became known. I will say that it does not happen frequently and does not involve large sums of money," he tells me coolly. He prefers to highlight the Centre's ongoing ability to source intelligence from elements in the criminal underworld through a variety of means, efforts that have consumed this man for years and made him a passionate advocate for all those who sail through pirate waters.

"You know, I grew up in Malaysia about seventy miles from the sea, and it has always fascinated me. From the time I went to sea, working my way up to becoming a master mariner, shipping out from Singapore and being a part of this world, it has been an important part of who I am. Piracy is one of the biggest threats a seafarer can face and it bothers me when it is not properly addressed."

Choong is clearly angry at shipowners whose cost management

policies are imperiling the lives of mariners and the safety of vessels. As he says from this office high above downtown Kuala Lumpur, there are ships out there in the nearby Strait of Malacca that are sailing with no anti-piracy actions in effect: "Right now, some vessel is taking a chance that nothing will happen in the Strait. In the end, it all comes down to dollars and cents, and sailors, unfortunately, are usually considered shit."

It's the only time I see Noel Choong show a flash of the emotions that must trouble him, but he quickly catches himself and puts his mood back in check. A glance at his wristwatch brings our meeting to an abrupt end, and Choong walks me to the Centre's locked front doors. He has to hurry through KL's afternoon rush hour and drive down to Port Kelang, on the Strait of Malacca, to attend a naval reception aboard a visiting American warship.

"The strength of what we do lies in our ability to inform and educate about the very real threat that piracy poses, and we are able to do that because of the unique contacts we have fostered within the shipping industry, with various governmental organizations, and, of course, from criminals. It has taken years to build up these contacts." Gesturing around the office, he adds, "This may not look like much, but looks can be deceiving. Everything we do here is about getting an edge on the criminals, on the pirates, and that is done by quiet, hard work. There's a lot still to be done; piracy never ends. I don't even know if it will ever end, if we can ever stop it completely."

"Piracy? No, it is not so bad now. Sometimes you hear about some small ship attacked, but not very often. The customers we deal with are not so concerned with pirates. I think maybe some people like to make this a big issue when it is not so important."

To say this perspective is a surprise would be an understatement, but the man sitting opposite me shifts his bulk in the chair and nods for emphasize. I put down my notepad to ponder this news about the current piracy situation in Southeast Asia as the man stares blankly at me with the perfect poker face, completely devoid of any sense of emotion. Apparently, the PRC's Noel Choong was wrong about the extent of maritime crime going on in his backyard. Hell, maybe I wasted my time trekking up to Kuala Lumpur to sit in the PRC's office for an afternoon and listen to someone with a vested interest justify his job. But, then again, "vested interest" is a subjective term.

I'm sitting in an anonymous office in Singapore, down by the city's sprawling Keppel Road containerport facilities, talking with someone who clearly has a different view about what's going on in the world today from that of the International Maritime Bureau and many others. A large man, he wears a crisp white shirt, conservative blue tie, and expensive-looking wristwatch, as befits someone who makes his livelihood from the profitable world of commercial shipping. He's a broker who, I'm told, has years of experience in the shipping industry in these parts. His name is Mr. Lee, I think.

After meeting with Noel Choong, I'd flown back to Singapore laden down with yet more official reports on recent incidents of piracy and maritime crime. Singapore is one of the most important business centers on the planet, home to an exceptionally busy port and numerous shipping companies, to say nothing of the financial sector based there, so I'd lined up a number of meetings to get a better picture of how people perceive piracy in the region.

In particular, I'm trying to find out more about the phenomenon known as "phantom ships." This phrase does not refer to any ghostly apparitions that haunt the high seas but, rather, to vessels that disappear completely, with their cargoes and, at times, crews, presumably at the hands of criminals. What sets this form of piracy apart from other activities is that ransoms are rarely sought from shipowners; these pirates want to keep the entire ship and its cargo for themselves.

Usually this sort of seajacking involves a vessel being taken over by pirates who then sail it off for parts unknown where they can unload the cargo and sell it for themselves. A new name may be painted on the vessel's hull and the official registration papers altered so that the entire ship can be sold, or they may just scuttle her to the bottom of some remote patch of the sea. As for the mariners caught up in these situations, their fates may vary: the luckier ones are set adrift in a lifeboat with a few meager provisions or even put ashore on some small isle; the unlucky ones are simply murdered.

Renaming a ship and changing her registration is a surprisingly easy thing to do. Vessels are legitimately bought and sold every day, changing hands as quickly as one buys a new home, and it's all done using the Internet, fax machines, numbered companies, and faceless lawyers. And though every vessel must be registered—or flagged—in an internationally recognized state, there are plenty of nations whose regulatory structures are open to question.

Known as "flag of convenience states," these are places that welcome the income derived from the registration process and do not even require a ship ever visit them. For instance, a shipowner can easily ask that their vessel be flagged in Mongolia or Bolivia, both of which are landlocked. There are many places where government scrutiny of the registration process is circumspect at best, making the reflagging of phantom ships an easy process for criminal elements. Southeast Asia has seen a lot ships go missing over the last decade, everything from tugboats to large freighters, with one of the most famous incidents involving the hijacking of the tanker MV *Petro Ranger* in April 1998. A few hours after leaving Singapore bound for Vietnam with a load of diesel and jet fuel, the vessel was boarded by a dozen pirates who made it clear with their machetes what they would do to her captain if he did not follow their instructions.

The pirates proceeded to order the crew to alter course and then brazenly set about erasing the identity of the *Petro Ranger*. In the middle of a busy waterway, a new name was painted on the hull— *Wilby*—and the Singaporean flag was hauled down and replaced with a Honduran ensign. Shortly thereafter, the *Wilby* rendezvoused with two other tankers in the Gulf of Thailand and most of its cargo was off-loaded, fuel worth $2.3 million. The pirates then set sail for southern China, so complete in their ruse that when Chinese coastguardsmen boarded the *Wilby* for a routine inspection, the vessel was allowed to proceed on its way. Eventually, though, the real identity of the tanker became known and the pirates were apprehended in the port of Haikou, on China's Hainan Island, and the crew was freed.

According to Noel Choong in Kuala Lumpur, many of the incidents of phantom ships that occurred in the 1990s are believed to have been the work of organized-crime syndicates, though he demurs to name them. The logistical aspects of selling cargo on the black market—or even legitimate markets—are simply too complex for a bunch of impoverished fishermen to carry out. It requires the collusion of corrupt maritime officials and businesspeople, and this was especially prevalent in southern China at the beginning of the decade, where it was reported that even rogue elements of the People's Liberation Army Navy took part in these acts. Whether these were really naval personnel or pirates dressed in uniforms has never been fully clarified; regardless, the Chinese government eventually cracked down on the piracy situation enough so that incidents declined dramatically along their coastline.

In the last few years, though, reports of phantom ship occurrences have resumed in the waters surrounding Malaysia, Indonesia, Singapore, Thailand, and the Philippines, with small freighters and tugboats with cargo barges becoming tempting prizes. Choong believes these attacks are likely carried out by smaller gangs who are much harder to control, such as the group that hijacked the Indonesian general cargo ship *Alfa Gemilang* on January 6, 2006. The ship was sailing in the Java Sea, south of Kalimantan (Borneo), heading for the Strait of Malacca, when five men armed with pistols and knives overwhelmed the crew and forced them to turn the *Alfa Gemilang* east and then north toward the Philippines. The pirates were soon joined by three confederates, and after a few days' travel they stopped the freighter, deposited most of the captive crew on the isolated Philippine island of Tawi-tawi, and then sailed away. Neither the ship nor her three remaining crew members have ever been heard from again.

Wondering how a vessel and its crew could simply disappear off the face of the globe is what led me to "Mr. Lee." A former shipping colleague of Lee's suggested I speak with the Singapore broker because he worked, at times, in the gray area of shipping. I'd been told Lee can get you an inexpensive crew on a moment's notice, clear up customs problems in certain Third World countries, reflag a vessel, set up an anonymous corporation or numbered company for a new shipowner, and find markets for any excess cargo that may be lying around in a ship's holds. Mr. Lee had agreed, via e-mail, to meet with me, based on the understanding that I was looking to speak with shipping insiders about the current economic state of the business. (I had also been told not to mention piracy or maritime crime in any of my communications with him, as it would not be looked upon favorably.)

However, upon arriving in Singapore I suddenly found that the broker was not answering my e-mails. For several days I left messages on the only telephone number I had for him but heard nothing in return. It appeared he had gotten cold feet about meeting with me, which was, perhaps, understandable given the seamier nature of some of Mr. Lee's supposed business affairs. I finally got in touch with Lee's former colleagues to see if they could do anything and a few hours later received an e-mail telling me to call a different number in Singapore as soon as possible. And it was recommended I make the call from a public phone, not my cell phone.

This was all getting just a little strange, but I walked around downtown Singapore until I found a pay phone and dialed the number. After a few rings, it was answered by a man with a Chinese accent—Mr. Lee—who apologized for not having gotten back to me earlier, saying he had been out of town on business. When I ask if it's still possible to meet in person, there is a long pause before he answers in the affirmative, telling me we can talk—briefly—but it will have to be now. I jot down the address Lee gives me and desperately search for a taxi to take me down near the containerport.

The office tower I arrive at is badly in need of renovations, but I can see that there are a number of shipping-related businesses listed in the lobby. Several floors up, I wander around trying to find the broker's office until I deduce that it must be the door with no number and no name. I ring a buzzer and a young East Indian man lets me in after I tell him why I'm here. He tells me to wait in the small lobby, which is adorned with a dusty model of a 1970s-style ocean freighter, some well-thumbed copies of old shipping magazines, and a sofa that has seen better days. There are no indications of a company name anywhere—no corporate logo, business cards, or mission statements—and the little receptionist's desk in the lobby is deserted; there are no mail trays, no telephone, not even a chair behind the desk.

After I cool my heels for a quarter hour, Mr. Lee appears. I hand him my business card in the manner normally done in these parts—with both hands extended—and wait as he reads it. He does not offer his own card in return, another oddity. Lee runs his fingers across my card as though to check its authenticity and mutters, "Mmm . . . Canada." I begin to explain how I am interested in finding out how the shipping industry works here, such as how vessels are registered, but he cuts me off. "Yes, yes, yes, I know. You have written a book on shipping, yes?" I nod, realizing that he's checked up on me. "So what do you want to know now?" My response—that this is my first trip to Singapore and I'm doing research about the general state of the business by speaking with anyone available—seems to satisfy Lee, though I can tell that he's clearly annoyed at my presence.

For the first of many times in our meeting, he checks his wristwatch, and then he agrees to give me ten minutes to speak about the world of shipping. Turning on his heels, he silently leads me through the office, past standard-issue cubicles where three or four other guys huddle over computers. Everyone stares at me as I follow Mr. Lee to a corner that offers some privacy, beside windows facing out toward the harbor. I comment that the office is rather barren, and the broker tells me that they have recently moved and have not finished getting settled in yet. While this might be true, I do notice a lack of packing boxes; the entire office has a rather hasty feel to it.

We begin by chatting about the general state of the shipping business in Southeast Asia, and Lee gives me stock answers about the changing value of the American dollar and the rise of the Chinese and Indian economies, speaking in a monotone, offhand manner. The shipping business is in the midst of a boom period and Lee says he's never been busier, though you wouldn't know it from his bored demeanor. While he does not own or operate any vessels, his firm provides "a series of integrated services to customers to assist maritime operations. Sometime it is crewing requirements, provisioning, customs documentation, many things."

I ask how he got into the shipping world, but all Lee will offer is he grew up "near the sea." He prefers not to talk about his personal life. When I shift the conversation back to his business, I'm told that the demands of the shipping industry are causing him some headaches, such as finding seafarers to man vessels. Lee works with agents in Thailand, the Philippines, Indonesia, and Myanmar (formerly Burma) to hire crews. "The Burmese are very good sailors," he says. They are, in Lee's words, "very cost-efficient."

Another function his tiny firm provides is helping with registration issues: "Vessels are bought and sold all the time on the open market, so sometimes a customer asks us to facilitate this. It is a very easy procedure, just like when you buy a car. You need a survey, insurance, and certificate of registry. We can do all this, all the time. With the fax and computer, we can transfer ownership in a matter of hours."

When I ask if he ever asks any questions about the buyers and sellers he brokers for, Lee stares at me blankly, as though he did not understand my query. "Customers are customers," is all he has to say, checking his watch. Trying to sound casual, I ask if there are still incidents of phantom ships in the region. He brushes this aside: "You mean when the vessel goes missing, changes names by the criminals, yes? I do not know about these things." In fact, though he has just told me his firm can change a ship's registration easily, Lee now advises that they haven't done any such work in some time. How long? He can't remember offhand.

Having been told his little company also brokers the movement of cargoes, I ask Mr. Lee how that end of the business works. He shifts in his seat and yet again checks his wristwatch. "Shipping is a very complex business and sometimes requires firms like mine to expedite matters. There may be cargo destined for a customer who changes their mind, so the owner needs to find a new end user. Or perhaps the terms of the arrangement have changed and the buyer does not require as much as originally requested. That is where we can help. We monitor the markets; we know who is coming and going and some such things. Intelligence is what is important."

Many businesses keep a close eye on what their competitors are up to, even using a little corporate espionage to give them an edge, and the shipping world is no different. Knowledge about markets worth watching can come from seemingly inconsequential sources, and the flow of information often begins in a port, with a stevedore or dockhand noticing a certain cargo being loaded aboard a ship and learning where it's bound. A conversation overheard in a bar, a quick call on a cell phone to a "friend," and that news can soon be relayed to someone interested in the tip in an office not unlike Mr. Lee's.

This is what likely happened in March of 2001, when the cargo ship *Inabukwa* was preparing to sail from the Indonesian island of Bangka to Singapore with a cargo of tin ingots, zinc, and white pepper valued at $2.1 million. As the freighter cast off her lines and headed out for a routine eighteen-hour voyage, word of the departure was passed along to someone, somewhere, who became keenly interested in the *Inabukwa*. About twelve hours after heading to sea, a speedboat pulled up along the freighter's port side, a grappling hook was tossed up, and a dozen pirates swarmed aboard. Wearing balaclavas and brandishing weapons, the attackers soon subdued the crew and took control of the *Inabukwa*.

After ransacking the ship for anything of value, the pirates ordered all twenty-one crewmen into the small boat, having first stripped them to their underwear and blindfolded them. While one group of pirates took over operation of the ship, the second group headed off with the terrified prisoners in the speedboat. After a bit, the boat's outboard engine was cut and the *Inabukwa* crew was ordered to jump into the water. The pirates were ordering the prisoners to walk the plank.[9]

As the crewmen leapt into the sea, still blindfolded, the desperation they must have felt can only be imagined. Luckily for the freighter's crew, the pirates were playing a cruel trick on the mariners, for the prisoners found themselves standing atop a remote coral reef while the speedboat disappeared.

Meanwhile, the pirates in control of the *Inabukwa* had painted a new name on the ship—*Chugsin*—and headed toward a small fishing town in the Philippines called Salomague, where they prepared to transfer the cargo to another ship. Only because the Philippine Coast Guard decided to do a random routine inspection of the *Chugsin* did the vessel's real identity become clear, for the pirates had not yet managed to finish the process required to reregister her. The pirates were arrested, and the *Inabukwa* crew was eventually rescued from the coral reef by passing fishing boats. But this was a rare instance of a hijacked vessel being recovered and her assailants being captured. Had it not been for a piece of missing paperwork, *Inabukwa/Chugsin* would have become another phantom ship.

Informed sources have told me that the cost of hijacking a vessel, renaming and reregistering her, and disposing of the cargo can be as much as $300,000. This may seem a large sum, but when you consider that a ship and whatever lies within her holds may be worth many millions, it is not such a bad investment. In the case of the *Inabukwa*, paying $300,000 to take a cargo valued at $2.1 million would have netted the pirates a sevenfold profit.

I wonder if Mr. Lee ever has doubts about the people he's dealing with. Might they be criminal elements looking to pawn off stolen merchandise?

"These things happen, yes, but I cannot say how much. My firm does not engage in these activities. If you asked me to do some such things, I would tell you to leave. We only act as a broker for legitimate businesses. A customer may have commodities to sell and I might be able to help them find a buyer, but I must know who both the parties are before getting involved."

I always get wary when I hear the phrase "legitimate businesses," since it implies knowledge of and comparisons to illegitimate businesses. As our brief interview winds down, I finally ask the broker just how bad piracy is in the region, which is how I discovered that things are just peachy now and that neither Mr. Lee nor his customers are particularly concerned about maritime crime.

Reassured that everything's under control out there in the Strait of Malacca, South China Sea, Gulf of Thailand, and elsewhere, I let the portly man escort me out. He politely tells me to feel free to e-mail him if I have further questions (though he never responds to any follow-ups I make), shakes my hand good-bye, and shoos me out of his office, making sure the door locks securely.

Standing in the hall outside the unmarked door, I remember what the person who arranged this meeting had told me weeks earlier: "The only thing I can tell is that [Lee] probably won't tell you the truth. He's a cagey one. You'll have to read between the lines of whatever he says. It's all very gray with him, though he's not a gangster or wanted criminal. But you'll find plenty of those where you're going."

4

THE DRAGON'S TEETH

An act of atrocious piracy having been committed on one of our trading ships by the inhabitants of a settlement on the west coast of Sumatra, a frigate was dispatched . . . to inflict such a chastisement as would deter them and others from like aggressions. This last was done, and the effect has been an increased respect for our flag in those distant seas and additional security for our commerce.

—U.S. PRESIDENT ANDREW JACKSON,
FOURTH STATE OF THE UNION ADDRESS,
DECEMBER 4, 1832

FRIDAY NIGHTS IN Singapore are like Friday nights in most other large cities, with bars, restaurants, and shops filled with people relaxing and unwinding. From the windows of my modest little hotel I can see that the streets are swarming with locals and tourists alike enjoying the pleasant late-summer weather. I watch as they move up and down the narrow roads, mingling but unconnected. Across the street, groups of twentysomething Australians laugh just a little too loudly at each other's jokes while drinking cans of lukewarm beer. They're oblivious to the middle-aged couples passing by, the ones clutching guidebooks and trying to give the noisy kids as wide a berth as possible. These tourists, in turn, are ignored by small clusters of South Asian men—foreign workers, perhaps—who meander past, clad in sarongs and flip-flops.

People-watching in an exotic foreign locale is always interesting and, tonight, provides a welcome diversion from the frustration I'm feeling here in Singapore. I should be packing to catch a flight in the morning, organizing the sprawling mess of notepads, books, research material, and clothing strewn about the room, but my mind keeps wandering. Where is he? Why hasn't he called? My focus is on the cell phone clutched in one hand and an open laptop sitting nearby. I keep checking every few minutes to see if there's a text message or e-mail from my local contact but am continually disappointed. Eight o'clock rolls around and still no word. Nine is no better and by ten I have to face facts: My chance to experience what a small group of others have been able to do is passing. My chance to talk to a real pirate has slipped through my hands.

"You want to know what *I* think about pirates? They're scum, dirtbags, goddamn thieves. They think we're rich 'cause we're Americans; they think we all have money. Hell, they think we just print more when we run out of the stuff, that's what makes us rich. And I can't get it through their fucked-up heads that if I was rich, I wouldn't be doing this. I can't tell you how pissed off these assholes make me."

Months before I ever set foot in Southeast Asia, these were the first comments I heard from someone who had firsthand experience with pirates. Dripping with anger, the words tumble out of the man in a torrent before he catches himself and slowly regains his composure. Joe Casalino is a fifty-two-year-old no-nonsense professional mariner whose accent betrays his childhood in Brooklyn's Bensonhurst neighborhood, though he now lives in Northern California. After two decades spent working on oceangoing vessels he's risen to be a bosun, in charge of deck crews, and for the last five years has been shipping out on vessels under contract to the U.S. government as part of its Maritime Security Program (MSP).

The MSP was established in 1996 by the federal government and is made up of privately owned merchant vessels flying the Stars and Stripes and crewed by American mariners hired to provide logistical support for overseas operations deemed to be of importance to national security. These are the ships that ferry the supplies to troops overseas, deliver equipment and material to help reconstruct the infrastructures of war-ravaged nations, and even transport entire coast guard patrol boats to the Middle East. Joe Casalino has seen his share of danger while working these contracts, having watched as rebels pointed rocket-propelled grenade launchers at him in Liberia and ducked gunfire from fighters in Somalia. But neither of those events would affect him as much as a trip to Iraq in late 2005, when Casalino found himself as close to death as he'd ever been.

It was almost midnight on October 18 as the heavy-lift vessel MV *Ocean Atlas* anchored in the Khawr 'Abd Allah, the waterway at the northern tip of the Persian Gulf that leads to the main Iraqi port of Umm Qasr.[1] Casalino's ship was carrying a load of pipes to be used in rebuilding a sewer system somewhere in Iraq and was due to dock and off-load in the morning. The crew had no illusions about the hazardous nature of these waters, riding at anchor just a few nautical miles off the shores of Iran, Iraq, and Kuwait and surrounded by what their sea charts marked as a "Mine Danger Area" (a reference to the numerous sea mines sown by Saddam Hussein's regime during the years of fighting here). Still, they'd all been here before and, as Casalino dryly remarked to me, "We all knew we were going into a bad-ass area—I mean, it's Iraq, right? But none of us figured we'd run into pirates."

Being so heavily laden with cargo, the vessel's main deck was less than ten feet above the waterline, an easy height for anyone to scale with a grappling hook and a rope. Standard shipboard procedure on the *Ocean Atlas* required the crew to lock down the vessel against any intruders while in the region. This involved securing all entrance-ways into the ship's house—where the accommodations, bridge, and other compartments are—and also making safe the storage lockers on deck and the forward working spaces. Casalino and the ship's chief officer had almost finished securing all those forward compartments when the bosun found a trio of unwelcome intruders climbing aboard his ship.

"I walked over to the port side to do a final check on things and suddenly there are three guys standing there, pointing AK-47s at me. They ordered me to put my hands in the air, grabbed my radio, and then the chief mate showed up and they got him, too. They said a few words in bad English, like, 'You go bridge! Captain! Captain!' and then marched us back to the wheelhouse. So we walk in and I just say, 'Uh, Cap'n, we got company.' Then they had us sit down with our hands on our heads while they decided what to do next.

"These guys, shit, they could barely speak English. They looked probably in their forties, late thirties. They didn't look too comfortable; they looked nervous. Because they looked nervous, we just shut up. Except one of our guys who just wouldn't shut up. He was . . . well, I mean, people in these situations react in different ways, I understand that. He was just pleading and begging and whimpering the whole time they were on board. So one of the pirates finally just got fed up and kicked him in the chest, knocked him down to the floor."

Including Casalino, there were five Americans on the bridge that night looking at three armed pirates (the rest of the crew were in their quarters on lower decks, unaware of what was transpiring in the wheelhouse). Two of the attackers then forced the captain to go below and empty the ship's safe of $10,000 in cash before the trio ordered everyone to head to the main deck. Reaching a doorway leading outside, one of the gunmen gestured for Casalino to unlock it.

"They told me to open up the door, but apparently I didn't move fast enough, 'cause this one of them had his AK sticking right by my head and he fires it, right beside my ear. Luckily it didn't ricochet off anything and hurt the others, but the sound from the shot fucked up my hearing.

"I wasn't scared—yet. I was more pissed off that they had taken advantage of us. But when we eventually went outside and down to the stern and they had us all line up against the bulkhead, that's when I got scared. They had the five of us lined up there, and I thought they were going to shoot us, to execute us. There was this moment: their heads and eyes were darting about; it's dark; there's no one else around. I dunno, but they couldn't do it; maybe they thought the rest of our crew would come running or something. So they just told us to get lost and we started to run away as they begin climbing over the rail. I managed to peer over the railing down the side of the ship, to where the pirates had this little boat. They were shimmying down a line to it, but one of them saw me and fired off another round my way. So I didn't stick around."

Years later, Casalino remains partially deaf in his left ear from the incident, which lasted about half an hour, and he is still clearly angry about it all. The fact that the *Ocean Atlas* was anchored in an area where there were a lot of American and coalition naval vessels and patrol boats should have offered some protection against the attack. Instead, Casalino and the rest of the *Ocean Atlas* crew were left to fend for themselves.

"So get this," Casalino relates. "After the robbers left, we got on the radio and called up to the coalition forces to come around. And the coalition forces come back with, 'Be advised you are in waters that are prone to pirate attacks. Do what you have to do to defend yourself.' Right . . . what are we supposed to do? We got no weapons on board, no guards or soldiers—it was just bullshit. And those fucking guys never came around. Never. No one came on board when we finally anchored in Umm Qasr; no one came out to investigate the problem. Nothing. And you know what? By the time we tied up in port, everyone knew [about the attack]. The Iraqis ashore, they all knew. So that tells you the pirates were local guys."

What Casalino didn't know was there had already been a half-dozen other attacks reported in the area in the preceding six months.[2] Barely two months earlier, a Panamanian liquid propane gas tanker had been robbed at the same anchorage as the *Ocean Atlas*, leading the LPG tanker's master to advise other ships "not to anchor in this area during night hours." In every case but one, the attacks were carried out by small teams armed with automatic weapons who were successful in robbing the civilian crews. And at no point did any of the nearby naval forces come to the aid of these attacked mariners, something else that sticks in Casalino's craw.

"Looking back, it makes me feel pissed off. I mean, here we are trying to help out the rebuilding [of Iraq] and our own military just blows us off. Why? Because we don't rate? What kind of bullshit is that? We risk our lives like everybody else does out there and we got attacked and were just left high and dry. You know, there are a lot a people who don't think attacks like the one that happened to me are a big deal. The coalition forces certainly didn't. You hear about these hijackings and kidnappings and ransoms going on, and stealing ten grand and leaving me partially deaf might seem less important. But these motherfuckers are all the same, all cut from the same cloth. I have no sympathy for them. Not one bit. They just . . . they just make you want to hate them."

Joe Casalino's strong words stayed with me as I set out on my travels, not only because they were an early introduction to piracy on an intimate level but also because of the emotional reaction the event still caused him. The bosun's anger is the anger of all mariners who have been beset by pirates, and his lack of sympathy is obviously warranted. An attack on a ship is an attack on an individual's place of work and where he lives while at sea. It's a combination of robbing a bank, breaking into a warehouse, stealing your car, and invading your home. People make choices in their lives about how they will live, and that includes deciding to embark on a life of crime. It doesn't take a genius to realize that, for some, basic human greed leads to the open desire to rob and steal and threaten and kill. Opportunistic, morally shallow, and cold-blooded in their thirst for wealth, some individuals require little analysis to understand what drives them to become pirates.

Yet for others, like the Iraqis who attacked Casalino, becoming maritime criminals does not appear to have been a childhood dream fulfilled. It's true that the devastation and turmoil that have engulfed Iraq for decades have made it one of the most dangerous places on the planet, both on land and on water. Maybe the pirates who left Joe partially deaf were schoolyard bullies as children; maybe they worked for Saddam Hussein's secret police as adults; maybe they have always been brutes. But somehow I think not, if only given Casalino's description of their appearance and nervousness.

"They just looked scraggly; they didn't look well kept at all," he recalled. "They looked like bums, to tell you the truth; they were dressed like paupers: they had no shoes; they had raggedy clothes. Actually, they looked more scared than dangerous. They weren't big, burly guys who had things under control, you know? They looked like they were winging it."

No matter how amateurish or novice the pirates were who boarded the *Ocean Atlas*, they were still heavily armed and managed to inflict a serious injury on Casalino. This makes me wonder how I would react in a situation like his. Would I be brave? Afraid? Cautious? Timid? It's hard to say, having never encountered a pirate up close. Besides, as the American bosun saw himself that night off Iraq, people respond in different ways to these things, so there's really no telling how one will act.

Not long after arriving in Singapore and meeting with the mysterious shipping broker Mr. Lee, I find myself sitting in an outdoor food court in the city's Little India district replaying the audio recording of the interview I'd done with Joe months earlier. Listening to him talk in his broad accent makes me hope I'd be able to muster his sense of bravado in such a situation, especially when he quips, "I remember getting back to Houston after the trip ended and someone asking me if I needed counseling or anything. Chrissakes, counseling? I just said to the guy, 'You know, getting shot at is nothing new coming from Brooklyn.'"

"Yo, Brooklyn!" a man calls out from behind me, having overheard the tape, and I turn to see a welcoming face looming over my shoulder. It's my dinner companion, Peter Chin,[3] a friend of mine who lives and works in Singapore, though he was born in

Kuching, in the eastern Malaysian state of Sarawak. For years he worked in the shipping industry in Hong Kong and Singapore before landing a better-paying job in the IT department of a large financial firm. Though we've known each other for years, it's been quite a while since we've chatted one-on-one. He leads me around the hawkers' stalls that line the food court and expertly assembles a small feast for us, which we devour at a quiet table off in the corner while catching up on our families, careers, and lives in general.

Peter tells me he has been thinking about leaving Asia to work in the U.S. office of his current employer, because he finds Singapore a very expensive place to live and doesn't mind venturing off to new places. To his parents' unending displeasure, Peter remains unmarried in his early forties (preferring to say he's "waiting, not wanting"). For as long as I've known him, he's always displayed an independent streak at odds with his traditional Chinese family. Instead of going to work at his father's successful business in Kuching, Peter wanted to run away to sea and become a mariner. Somewhat reluctantly he chose to go into the business side of shipping so that he wouldn't be completely disowned, which, for me, was propitious, as he has been a great source of information and contacts.

He peppers me with questions about piracy and I tell him about my recent travels, leading him to say that he thinks I was lucky to avoid any harm up in Tanjung Kling with the gunman I met. As to the mysterious Mr. Lee, my friend says he's never heard of him but will make a few discreet inquiries to see what else he can discover about the guy. We finish up our dinners and order a couple of bottles of cold beer, and after they've been delivered Peter glances around at the other tables before leaning toward me in a conspiratorial manner.

"So, you still really want to meet a pirate?"

"Well, I guess I need to if I'm going to write a book about them," I mumble, "though my desire to actually meet a pirate has always been mitigated by a strong degree of personal cowardice." Peter laughs at this and says he's been looking into some leads since I first broached the subject with him a couple of months earlier.

Peter's exceedingly well connected with the shipping world in Southeast Asia, and though my friend does not engage in any illegal activity that I know of, he says he's seen enough of it by virtue of working with various shipping firms. In fact, it was the distaste he found in dealing with some of the shadier aspects of the maritime world that drove him to his current job in the financial sector.

"When you called me about this, I began to ask around. Quietly, of course," Peter explains. "There are a lot of people around here with shady backgrounds, especially over in Johor," he says, referring to the Malaysian state just across the water from Singapore Island. "Through the old 'friend of a friend of a friend' scenario I have got a guy who has pretty much agreed to talk with you. Says he knows about how things work, with the piracy. Hopefully in the next day or two he will meet with us."

Peter says he needs just a bit more time, which worries me because I've only got about a week open to stay in Singapore, and I hope he's not taking this all too lightly. Asking someone to poke around for you in the world of maritime crime is a delicate proposition, more so when it's a friend you've known a long time. The last thing I want to do is expose Peter to anything that might endanger him, but he quickly dismisses this while ordering another round of beer.

"You have no idea how cutthroat the shipping business is. Well, maybe you do, but my experience was much more immediate. Look, Southeast Asia is a cesspool of corruption and crime masquerading as the normal way things are done. At a certain level, you see or hear about a lot of things. It'll be fine."

Not many people deliberately set out to meet pirates, mostly because of the obvious danger involved. You must put your trust in individuals who can gain you access to criminals, to say nothing of the pirates themselves. Wandering around a Third World country asking strangers to find you a real pirate to talk to is strongly discouraged. However, if you do go in search of such individuals, you also need to be patient, as these types of meetings don't happen overnight.

This had been made clear to me before I ever set foot in Southeast Asia, with some of the best advice coming from American journalist Donovan Webster. Webster has done his fair share of trekking to far-flung locales while writing for the likes of *National Geographic Magazine*, *Vanity Fair*, and *The New York Times* and was one of the first journalists to look at modern-day piracy, with an in-depth feature article that was published in *Outside* magazine back in 1994.[4] At a time when few were paying much attention to the issue, even within the shipping community, Webster managed to gain the confidence of a group of Filipino pirates living in the central part of Luzon Island.

"It took me months and months of work to find the people I wanted to meet and begin to set things up," says the Virginia-based journalist. "You have to do this legwork first, before heading out, or else you'll end up wasting all your time sitting in a hotel room somewhere. When I got there, I'd already found local people to help me, who could explain to these pirate guys who I was. 'Cause they want to check you out, make sure you're not a cop, that sort of thing, so you need someone local to vouch for you. But I really felt it was vital that I talk to someone firsthand about this, not just report secondhand news. I just really wanted to talk to a pirate."

In some respects, Webster thinks it was easier to find pirates when he was there (in 1994), because there wasn't as much attention being focused on the problem. His hard work eventually paid off when he was introduced to a young man from a fishing village near Cavite City, south of Manila. The small community on the shores of the South China Sea had a long history of engaging in piracy, as a supplement to the meager income made from fishing, and Webster convinced the man to talk about what went on.

According to Webster, "He called himself Rande, Rande Victorio, and he claimed to be a 'reluctant pirate.' He was about twenty-six and desperately wanted to go to school and get a better education. He didn't want to hang out in this village, eking out a living as a fisherman with his father. And he certainly didn't want to carry on the family tradition of robbing passing ships. This idea—of wanting out of piracy—was fairly common in that part of the Philippines, because these guys were not making a lot of money doing it. This was not like the more organized gangs in places like the Strait [of Malacca]."

Piracy in the Philippines goes back centuries and Victorio's family had been doing it themselves for generations—even his mother took part in attacks—and he was introduced to the life while still a youngster. Webster shakes his head while recalling this. "The guy's parents took him out [to sea, on attacks] when he was, like, six. Can you believe that? The kid's six! I remember him telling me that when he found out what his family did, he broke down, crying all night. So this little boy then asks his parents how they can do this, because he knows the difference between good and bad, right? And all his dad says is, 'You just close your eyes.' That's it, kid; welcome to the family business."

Rande Victorio had, apparently, become quite good at piracy by the time Webster met him, claiming to have participated in dozens of attacks over the course of eighteen years. Whatever moral quandaries these posed for the young man, he had also learned to close his eyes, telling the American journalist that he had personally killed eleven men.

"I remember when he told me this—that he had murdered people—he was ashamed. He said it gave him nightmares. That's the thing that fascinated me about Victorio, how he balanced robbing and murdering with the understanding that what he was doing was wrong. Actually, he didn't do a good job balancing things, because being a pirate was eating away at him. But he couldn't escape it; he was caught up in this vicious cycle where there was a boss who more or less controlled the family's piracy operations. They were like indentured serfs, constantly in debt to the boss. Once you get drawn into piracy, it's really difficult to get out."

Having gained Victorio's trust, Webster was eventually invited to accompany the man on a pirate raid, something the journalist remembers as a hairy experience from the get-go. Setting out in a small fishing boat at four in the morning, the crew was soon fighting their way through a typhoon that was churning the South China Sea into a fury as they tried to get into the main shipping lanes where their prey lay.

"With the weather being like that, no one would expect a pirate attack on their ship, so it made for good cover to get in close. The boat—they called it a *banca*—was being hammered by these seas and driving rain, but these guys just kept going. We could see the big cargo ships out ahead, and as we got closer, Victorio and the others got ready: they were all armed, with guns and knives, and they started putting on masks. And I remember thinking, 'Here we are in the tropics, it's hot, and these guys are wearing knitted ski hats.' That's how you know they're real pirates—no one else would wear a balaclava in the tropics."

As the storm intensified, the *banca* was being tossed around like a toy and, with their targets within sight, the pirates were forced to give up the chase that day and hightail it back to the safety of shore, something that Webster doesn't regret.

"Yeah, I'd seen enough, no question. If the attack had gone ahead . . . I dunno. I went there to find out why someone would become a pirate. I didn't need to see them prove how ruthless they were." When I tell him about the offer from the gunman in Tanjung Kling to "introduce me to his friends," Webster laughs. "Alone at night, in the middle of Malaysia? I'd say you made the right decision not to go with the guy. My advice to you is talk to them, if you can, but avoid going out with them. There's nothing really mysterious about how they do it. The mystery, such as it is, is why."

Webster has his own views on what motivates someone like Rande Victorio to become a pirate: "For one, I think the cold war nations—like the U.S. and the Soviet Union—had a responsibility in creating this problem, because they had been essentially policing the high seas for decades, enforcing regional control in places like Southeast Asia. Once the cold war ended and you no longer had, like, the U.S. fleet making its presence known in the South China Sea, piracy began to take off. Let's face it, there was less maritime crime going on when you had the iron rule of Marcos in the Philippines or Suharto in Indonesia. So to a degree, we in the West helped create this modern problem. But then there's the simple issue of poverty. First World–Third World, north-south, whatever you want to call it, it's the economic disparity between nations that I think continues to drive it. This guy in the Philippines would gladly—gladly—do something else rather than head out to sea with a pistol and a balaclava. That's what he told me, and I believed him."

The American's last comment raises one of the thorniest issues about talking to pirates: how much can you really believe? In Webster's case, he feels there wasn't any reason for Victorio to lie about his true feelings or his family history: "Victorio did not have any sense of bravado about what he did or express any pride about his heritage as a pirate. If he had, then I would have questioned what he said, definitely. So that was a nightmare story, 'cause you could never quite be certain what was real and what was being faked. Did he really kill eleven people? I think so. Was the trip out in the storm staged for me? No, I don't think so. With the weather like what it was, these guys weren't going to go out just to show my dumb ass how it's done. No way. But the problem with pirates is that they're thugs, so you can never be certain they're telling you the truth or not. You have to remain skeptical at all times and don't close your eyes."

I ask if Webster has kept in touch with Victorio in the years since they first met, but the journalist just shakes his head. "I've no idea what ever became of him, whether he finished high school, got married, gave up pirating. For all I know, he could be dead by now, which is not unlikely. I'd say the odds are like sixty-forty against these guys making it to old age, if not worse. Violent death is kind of an occupational hazard of being a pirate."

Another American who has had the opportunity to talk to pirates provides a similar and equally bleak perspective on the life expectancy of modern-day buccaneers. Michael Rawlins is a professional mariner with over fifteen years' experience shipping out on a wide variety of U.S.-flagged merchant vessels, beginning as a deckhand and rising to his current rank of second officer. Except for Antarctica, he's been pretty much anywhere a cargo ship can go and has seen enough of the planet's oceans and seas that he now makes his home in the middle of the desert, in Las Vegas, Nevada.

A laconic man who speaks in measured tones, Rawlins hadn't had much personal experience with piracy while seafaring. Most of his early career had been spent working in U.S. waters, which haven't been known for being pirate prone in well over 150 years. More recent work contracts have taken him places where the threat is prevalent, so he became aware of the issue. Like his fellow seafarer Joe Casalino, Rawlins paid little attention to the reality of the situation, telling me, "We'd see these notices to mariners about piracy when I was working, the faxes and e-mails that come in, but I never really thought much about it. Sounded like guys trying to steal ropes and stuff, nothing that serious. I honestly never expected I'd ever meet a pirate in my life."

A few years back, though, Rawlins began to think more seriously about piracy after visiting Southeast Asia. Because of the way shipping contracts work for professional mariners, it's not uncommon for them to have three or four months of downtime after working at sea, and many keep busy during these periods by taking up a hobby or running a small business. Mike Rawlins decided he might try his hand at making a documentary about piracy.

"Before I ever became a mariner," he explains, "I wanted to be a journalist. That's what I went to school for, though I got sidetracked going to sea 'cause it paid well. But it was always at the back of my mind to return to it at some point, and by the summer of 2006 I was ready to take the plunge and see if could get some footage together to make something. The idea was simple: wander around small villages along the Strait of Malacca and see if I couldn't meet real pirates who'd let me film them. Looking back, I'd say I was lucky. In more ways than one."

Armed with a small digital camcorder, Rawlins and two friends spent weeks trekking around coastal communities in Malaysia and Indonesia trying to meet pirates, but finding little success. With time and money quickly running out, the team eventually decided to head for perhaps the most dangerous part of the region: the troubled Indonesian province of Aceh (properly called the Special Region of Aceh, Nanggroe Aceh Darussalam). Located at the northern tip of Sumatra, Aceh is perhaps best known as the scene of horrific devastation caused by the Indian Ocean tsunami of December 26, 2004. Before the tsunami struck, though, Aceh had been a stronghold of pirates who preyed on shipping big and small, mainly in the Strait of Malacca, which abuts its eastern shores.

"I knew that attacks in the Strait had gone way down after the tsunami," says Rawlins, "because the waves destroyed the boats the pirates used. I think there were only about a dozen attacks the year after the tsunami, and when we got there [in 2006] I think it was like half that again.[5] Still, I figured there had to be people around who knew about piracy and might be willing to talk, even to an American."

Rawlins was aware that Aceh was also home to a well-organized group of Islamist separatists who have been fighting the central government in Jakarta for decades. Though there was a peace treaty signed between the separatists and the Indonesian government in the aftermath of the tsunami disaster, he was still unsure how he would be received in this decidedly conservative Muslim province.

To be fair, the Acehnese people have never espoused an extremist anti-American bent like that of Al Qaeda. Instead, they have a long history of armed struggle against all kinds of outsiders, with the fighting often centered on domination of the shipping routes through the Strait of Malacca. For hundreds of years the Sultanate of Aceh was a major producer of spices, most notably pepper, and its ability to control these exports led it into conflict with the Malayan rulers across the Strait in Melaka and Johor and later the European colonizers. By 1873 the Dutch, who were in control of much of present-day Indonesia, found themselves embroiled in a nasty war against the Acehnese that descended into a guerilla conflict that lasted until 1908.

Being an American, Rawlins was arriving in Aceh bearing the baggage of his government's actions here, not since 9/11 but going back over a century and a half. For Aceh is also the site of the first armed intervention by the United States in Asia, way back in the 1830s. And the reason? Acehnese pirates.

In February 1831, the American merchantman *Friendship* was anchored off Kuala Batu on northern Sumatra's Pedir coast. It just so happened that the ill-named *Friendship* had once been a privateer out of New England, though now she was working the spice trade and looking to fill her holds with Sumatran pepper. For reasons unknown, pirates from Kuala Batu decided the ship looked enticing, so they boarded her, murdered her crew, and ransacked the vessel. When word got back to the United States of the incident, President Andrew Jackson spoke of it in his third State of the Union address (December 6, 1831), calling it a "daring outrage" committed by "piratical perpetrators belonging to tribes in such a state of society that the usual course of proceedings between civilized nations could not be pursued." His response was to dispatch a naval frigate with orders to "require immediate satisfaction for the injury."

It took a year for the frigate USS *Potomac* to make the lengthy journey from New York to Sumatra, armed with forty-two cannons and over three hundred sailors and marines. To assure their mission against the Acehnese pirates would be successful, the warship was disguised as a Danish merchant trader as she arrived near Kuala Batu in February 1832. Anchoring off the coast, the frigate's commander dispatched landing teams of marines and sailors who proceeded to fight pitched battles with the pirates, supposedly killing over 150 (while the Americans lost just two in the battles). The landing parties then returned to the frigate, which bombarded the pirate village with her cannons, killing another 300 Acehnese. Then, satisfaction for the injury having been achieved, the USS *Potomac* set off for home.[6]

To Rawlins's relief, there were no lingering animosities among the Acehnese whom he met about these American incursions. Instead, he found the people warm and friendly, though no one was offering up any pirate contacts. At least not immediately.

After a day of venturing around the eastern side of the province, beside the Strait of Malacca, Rawlins and his companions were advised to stay the night in a small town instead of risking the drive back on the only road out of the province. Like many Third World places, Sumatran highways have a reputation for the number of accidents and fatalities that occur there on an almost daily basis. Daylight hours are bad enough; the evenings can be even more deadly. So the Americans checked themselves into a small guesthouse and settled in for the evening. A few curious locals dropped by to meet Rawlins and his friends, and the conversation soon turned to life on the water.

"We were talking to a couple of local guys about this and I mentioned that I was a mariner and had been to Bandah Aceh before. I guess they liked that because a lot of them are fishermen. In the course of all this, I just kind of asked, 'What about pirates? Are there any around here?' And, well . . . that's when things got interesting."

One of the Indonesians sitting with the Americans began to

talk about piracy although, as Rawlins remembers, it was in a circumspect manner: "He said it had gone on here for a long time, there was a history of it, that kind of thing. Like it was completely normal. He wasn't, like, hiding that it went on or anything. Somehow out of all this talk I sort of said it would be interesting to see what these guys were like. The pirates he was talking about. I never expected anything from it—it was just one of those things you blurt out in a conversation."

The next morning, though, Rawlins was awakened by the Indonesian guy at his door, asking the American to go for a short walk. They headed through the thick mangrove forests and made their way toward a small inlet. The brush was thick, almost confining, as they approached the water. Then the forest opened up to reveal a small landing where a boat was beached. There was an outboard engine on its transom, gas cans of fuel crammed aboard, and the entire craft was covered in black plastic sheeting, as a sort of camouflage. And there were four heavily armed men wearing balaclavas staring at Rawlins.

"I remember just thinking, 'Oh shit,' as I'm standing there. These guys have pump-action shotguns in their arms, one of them has a couple of grenades hanging off his shirt, I mean . . . what have I gotten myself into? I'm thinking I'll meet some guy—one person—who will talk to me about piracy and instead I've got a small SWAT team checking me out."

With the help of the Indonesian who'd led him here, Rawlins was able to briefly talk to the men, who all said they were pirates. Business had been slow, they said, but was getting busier now. They had a new boat and were picking up where the tsunami had interrupted. After letting Rawlins take their photos and briefly talk with them, the pirates asked the understandably nervous American if he'd like to come out with them.

"They wanted to know if I wanted to see how they work," remembers Rawlins. "Okay, I've got a bunch of guys with shotguns pointed my way. I know I should have said, 'Thanks, but no thanks,' but something in my brain just shut down. So they tell me to return that evening. And I did."

That night Rawlins returned to the mangrove forest and clambered aboard the pirate boat, trying not to think about what might happen. His main concern was the same as I'd had across the Strait in Tanjung Kling—that he'd be robbed. But there was also the prospect that the boat would be seen by the Indonesian authorities, the crew captured, and Rawlins would be sitting in a dingy prison cell somewhere, trying to explain his predicament to an American consular official.

"We headed out into the Strait and I'm just in a weird place, very calm while surrounded by all these guns. I've no idea where they're going, where they're taking me, what's going to happen. I'm essentially riding in the backseat while a bunch of thugs go for a joyride. It was surreal."

Somewhere out in the Strait, Rawlins noticed that the lights of passing merchant vessels were getting closer, and he began to pick out individual ships plying the shipping lanes. The boat slowed down so the pirates could get their bearings and choose a target, then accelerated toward a freighter. As Rawlins watched in horror, the men prepared to board her: weapons were checked, a rappeling line readied, and the pilot was making for the ship's stern when a spotlight lit up on the freighter and began sweeping the seas. In moments, the beam of light picked up the speedboat; if the plastic tarp covering it had been meant to reduce its visibility or mask its radar signature, it had failed. The helmsman put the boat into a hard turn away from the freighter, running for the darkness that would hide them.

The pirates' first weapon—surprise—has been lost. Radio chatter would soon be advising all commercial vessels in the area of the suspicious craft glimpsed by the searchlight, so Rawlins's pirates made for home. They told him there would be plenty more nights to try again. But the trip back to shore was just as harrowing, because now the pirates started to make jokes at the American's expense.

"One guy waves his revolver in my face, wondering how much money I have on me, and they all laugh. Like I'm going to make up for not robbing a ship. Now I'm really nervous, trying to figure out what to do. So I ask the guy who seemed to be in charge—at least I think he was in charge—I ask him how dangerous it is out there. For them. And he says, 'Very.' Has he killed anyone? 'Yes.' Great. Um, what about his friends? Have any of his friends been hurt? And now he opens up a bit; he starts counting on his fingers, counting off to thirteen. These are the people he knows who have died taking part in pirate attacks. In the last few years. Him talking of a dozen guys he knew who are now dead, from pirating, that seemed to sober things up for them, and they didn't bother me anymore. We got back to shore and I hightailed it out of there, let me tell you. In hindsight, that was one of the stupidest things I've ever done. Interesting experience, but, man, I learned that life is cheap for these guys."

Stripped of any lingering romantic notions, this is the harsh reality of what faces those wishing to embark on a life of piracy today. It is a world in which one's life must be considered expendable, with the prospect of being injured or maimed a very real possibility. Given these risks, it hardly seems an appealing choice of vocation, yet there are clearly people willing to give it a try, or who believe that they have no better option.

———

Talking with Michael Rawlins, Donovan Webster, and Joe Casalino about their experiences has given me insight into piracy and pirates, but I'd still like to ask my own questions of someone involved in all this, as far-fetched as that may seem. A couple of days after I met up with my friend Peter Chin, however, there's still no news as to whether he's been able to arrange anything. A day later things seem to be in place, but my hopes are dashed at the last moment when Peter has a work commitment that prevents him from leaving the office (we'd both already decided I wasn't going anywhere without my friend and his fluent knowledge of the local languages and customs). For the next two days I spend my time trolling through research material at the National Library and Singapore's National Museum, still waiting to hear from Peter.

As the weekend approaches and my departure date looms, Peter calls asking me to meet him for a drink down by Boat Quay, beside the Singapore River, and I have a sense that something's wrong. Sure enough, as tourists take evening bumboat cruises on the river and teeming crowds of office workers spill out of the central business district's many bars, my friend breaks the news to me that all is not well: the guy he'd been hoping we could meet has backed out. Peter's sense of disappointment is even worse than mine, and he keeps telling me how sorry he is for failing to arrange the meeting. Though my friend says he has a couple of other leads, it seems evident that the chance to speak with a pirate is rapidly fading, if not gone completely. True, I am planning to be back in Singapore in a few months' time, but only for a very brief stopover, and I doubt he'll have any more success by then. So as I sip my beer, I'm reconciled to thinking that maybe I'll have better luck somewhere else.

The next morning I return to the National Library, where I'd already spent hours browsing through the repository of piracy-related material in its stacks, but grow frustrated at reading about the experiences of others. Seeking some fresh air, I take Singapore's ultraefficient subway down to the harborfront and wander over to Labrador Park, an oasis of green near the bustling port.

Scattered throughout the park are relics from the Second World War, gun emplacements, machine-gun posts, and other fortifications built by the British to defend Singapore from Imperial Japanese forces. In the end, all of these proved insufficient in protecting "Fortress Singapore," which the Japanese invaded after marching down the Malayan peninsula, taking the city on February 15, 1942.[7] This led to easily the darkest period in the history of Singapore—renamed Syonan-to (Radiant South) by the occupying Japanese. Tens of thousands of its citizens were massacred over the next three years, with the Chinese community singled out for particularly harsh treatment.

Yet the violent history of this part of Singapore goes back much further than World War Two, as is explained by a historical marker I stumble upon down by the southeastern tip of the park. It's a plaque commemorating—what else?—the history of piracy here, stating: "One of the first sights that greeted William Farquhar, when he stepped ashore at Singapore in 1819, was a row of skulls—the trophies of piracy. The islands in the south facing Labrador Park were well known hideouts of pirates."

Along with Stamford Raffles, the visionary Englishman who expanded British influence in the region (and for whom the Raffles Hotel is named), Farquhar helped to create a British settlement in Singapore, becoming the first Resident, or administrator. Whether or not he was aware that piracy was entrenched in Temasek—as Singapore was then known—the macabre display of human heads should have made it clear to Farquhar that these were dangerous waters. As the historical marker puts it, "By the 1830s, the menace had become so serious that it was believed to threaten the Asian trade with 'total annihilation.' "

Those skulls had been meant as a warning to visitors that the cove behind the park was a pirate lair, a secluded place from which the locals could plan their attacks on passing vessels. There was also another sinister marker that once stood here, by what is now called Keppel Harbour: two giant stone outcroppings that lay on either side of the harbor's mouth. Clearly visible from the sea, they guided the pirates home from their marauding missions and were noted by the Chinese historian Wang Da Yuan in the mid-fourteenth century, who bestowed on them the appellation Long Ya Men, or Dragon's Teeth Gate. When he named these stone pinnacles, Wang could not have known how apt the moniker was to a Westerner, alluding as it does to an ancient Greek myth.

According to legend, the Phoenician prince Cadmus killed a dragon guarding a sacred spring near where he intended to found Cadmeia (later called Thebes). Afterward, the goddess Athena told Cadmus to remove the dragon's teeth and sow them in the earth, where he watched in fascination as they grew into a band of fierce warriors who battled one another to the death. One could say that pirates are not dissimilar, arising as they do from places where the soil—and the sea—allows them to flourish.

Perhaps the British who followed Farquhar and Raffles felt the stones carried too much mythical symbolism, for as they set about hunting down the pirates who lived nearby, they also decided to blow up the Dragon's Teeth in 1848. This was supposed to have been in order to make the harbor entrance wider, though I can't help but wonder if it wasn't also done to eradicate any signs of the pirate presence here.

This small corner of Singapore offers a unique confluence of the history of what is an island, a city, and a nation-state, and most of that history revolves around violence, robbery, and the sea. Looking south toward the Straits of Singapore from the park, I can imagine pirate raiders heading out in their *perahus*, clubs and knives at the ready. I can picture William Farquhar and his British crew gazing at that line of impaled skulls and wondering what they'd gotten themselves into.

But I can also see something much more immediate: dozens of merchant ships riding at anchor out there this day, any one of which may have been attacked in recent years or might yet face a pirate assault in the near future. Over to my right is a tugboat pulling a barge and steaming slowly northward toward the Strait of Malacca, plum pickings for pirates if ever there was one. As she disappears from view, I wish her crew well and sigh in resignation, for there's so much more I'd like to know about those who prey upon these vessels.

I walk over to look at the concrete replica of the Dragon's Teeth someone has built here beside Keppel Harbour. The structure is a somewhat gaudy reconstruction of the physical landmark eradicated by those fighting piracy in these waters a century and a half ago. Yet it's also a reminder of the problems I'm facing in my investigation into the world of maritime crime.

The ranks of modern-day piracy continue to be filled by individuals ready and willing to risk their lives for ill-gotten gains, and I know there must be many people living nearby with stories to tell. Having heard the secondhand recollections of others has been important, but I wish I'd been able to get closer to the perpetrators here. The only solace I can take is that Southeast Asia is not the only hotbed of piracy today. The time has come to leave behind the Dragon's Teeth and enter the dragon's den.

5

NEW LIBERTALIA

He told his Men, that this was an excellent Place for an Asylum . . . that they might have some Place to call their own; and a
Receptacle, when Age or Wounds had render'd them incapable
of Hardship, where they might enjoy the Fruits of their Labour,
and go to their Graves in Peace.
—Captain Charles Johnson, *The History of the Pyrates*, 1728

THOUGH WE LIKE to think of our planet as one big global village, with the ability to travel to virtually any corner of it at the drop
of a hat, it's still an awfully big place. I'm reminded of this while
trying to rearrange my body in an airplane seat that has taken on
all the comforting properties of a sack of lumpy coal. I'm in the
midst of a two-day, three-flight journey across five time zones after
having left Singapore, currently somewhere over the Indian Ocean
slowly approaching Madagascar.

Though perhaps not as famous as Jamaica, Tortuga, or New Prov-
idence, the island of Madagascar was an important pirate redoubt
in the late seventeenth and early eighteenth centuries. It was the perfect haven for the likes of Captain Kidd, Thomas Tew, Long Ben

Avery, and others making the Pirate Round, as the journey from the Atlantic to the Indian Oceans was called. At Madagascar, they could provision and repair their vessels, relax ashore, and then set out to attack merchantmen returning to Europe from the Far East and India.

Two and a half centuries ago, Madagascar and the smaller islands surrounding it took on a somewhat mythological status as a place where sea robbers could live by their own rules, citizens of their own pirate republic. According to Captain Charles Johnson, the author of *The History of the Pyrates*, a French buccaneer by the name of Misson bestowed a name on this paradise—Libertalia. It was to be a place where power and money were to be shared by all, where a new language would be created, where slavery would be abolished, where justice was to be equally distributed, and where all who called it home would become guardians of the liberties and rights of people (well, except for the rights and liberties of their victims). The lush tropical island off southern Africa's eastern coast was to be transformed into a revolutionary pirate utopia.

The idea of a place like Libertalia must have struck fear into the hearts of the ruling elites in the West. A rogue state established by criminals where they could live according to such radical concepts as equality for all while being able to continue attacking merchant vessels with impunity could never be allowed to flourish. In 1721, a few years before Johnson described it for his readers, the British Admiralty dispatched warships to the area to eradicate any sign of this Libertalia, and French warships patrolling the Persian Gulf and Dutch vessels in the Red Sea soon followed.

Unfortunately for all concerned, Libertalia was really nothing more than a fanciful ideal. While it is true that Madagascar served as a base for a short period, allowing pirates to raid throughout the Indian Ocean, no one ever managed to carve out a sustainable outlaw nation there. They bickered with one another, fought with the natives, and were harassed by the naval vessels. Libertalia never became anything near the utopian paradise that Johnson had Captain Misson espousing. In fact, there are serious doubts as to whether Misson actually existed, many scholars believing him to be a fictional character created by Johnson, and no trace of any Libertalian settlements has ever been found on Madagascar.[1] The notion of a pirate haven on the African coast, some sort of rogue state that would allow men to plunder and rob at will, had been consigned to the history books. Or at least until the cold war ended and this notion resurfaced in a manner that no one could have predicted.

Bedraggled and more than a little exhausted from days of traveling, I am eventually set down unceremoniously in the decaying concrete monolith that is Jomo Kenyatta International Airport in Nairobi.

A glum immigration official scans my passport, looks at the visa application, and then fingers the crisp American fifty-dollar bill attached. This is not a bribe intended to speed my entry, just the required sum for a foreigner visiting Kenya. He looks at the bill and then hands everything back to me. The paperwork's in order; the money isn't. I'm told the serial numbers on the bill are of the wrong series and it could be a counterfeit. As I head off to find a foreign exchange booth, I wonder how bad things really are here when the immigration officials are checking the serial numbers on foreign fifty-dollar bills.

Kenya has always prided itself on being an oasis of stability and democracy in Africa, not a place of nasty civil wars and brutal dictators. This perception glosses over a number of serious issues that have plagued the nation since it gained independence from

Britain in 1963, including the jailing of opposition leaders and dissidents, censorship of the press, and violence surrounding elections in 1992 and 1997.

For the most part it has managed to avoid the pitfalls that have bedeviled so much of the continent in the last fifty years, though a few months after my visit the country would erupt in violence sparked by political animosities, charges of electoral fraud, and anger at nepotism and corruption. But on the morning of my arrival in Nairobi, Kenya was still one of Africa's top tourist destinations, a safe, pleasant, and welcoming place. As to the nations that surround it, well, that's another story.

Within a thousand miles' radius of where I'm standing, the lives of untold millions have been scarred by some of the most inhumane acts anyone could be expected to face. The people of Rwanda, Burundi, Congo, Sudan, Uganda, Ethiopia, and Somalia have endured war, genocide, drought, and famine on a scale few of us can really comprehend. It seems that as soon as one crisis ends in this region of Africa, another one starts, kind of like the way piracy never ceases on the seas.

Actually, it is the combination of these two elements—East African crises and a resurgence of modern-day piracy—that has brought me to Kenya, for the waters off neighboring Somalia have become the most dangerous anywhere in the world. In the last decade, the IMB's annual reports catalogue a steadily increasing number of incidents in this part of the world. There were five actual or attempted attacks in Somali waters in 1997. By 2007 the figure had risen to thirty-one, and keep in mind that many attacks go unreported.

However, more disturbing is the audacious nature of these pirates, who have targeted containerships, fishing boats, LPG carriers, tankers, general cargo ships, passenger vessels, private yachts, and

UN-chartered aid vessels. From bases along the coast of their strife-ridden country, marauders have attacked mariners as far out as four hundred nautical miles off the coast. In one bizarre incident, Somali pirates in a boat even fired on a couple of U.S. Navy guided-missile warships, arguably matching audacity with stupidity.[2]

Still, there is a chilling efficiency to the manner in which Somali pirates operate. Reports indicate that they have matured from a small group of criminals conducting a few random attacks into a much larger web of gangs closely tied to the warlords who control much of Somalia. Hundreds of people are now engaged in these operations, with the prime motivation being to hijack ships and crews and negotiate ransoms for their releases, ransoms that are believed to amount to tens of millions of dollars in annual revenue for these maritime criminals.

Three hours after presenting an acceptable American fifty-dollar bill for my visa to the studious immigration official in Nairobi, I find myself back by the sea. While Kenya is primarily noted for its safaris and wild game attractions, many forget that it also has a 333-mile-long coastline on the Indian Ocean, dotted with resorts and holiday hotels. There is a different mood here, where the landscape is flatter and the weather warmer than in the inland highland. Even the airport in Mombasa is a much cheerier, airier place than Nairobi's, full of Israeli and Italian visitors ready for a week by the water. As the package-holiday tourists pile into their minivans, I find a taxi to drive me into town, eventually passing beneath two immense metal elephant tusks on Moi Avenue erected for a visit in 1956 by Britain's Princess Margaret.

On checking into my hotel, I find there's a message waiting for me, so I quickly shower and change into something clean for my upcoming appointment. I'm due to spend some time with the one person who knows more about the issue of piracy off East Africa than many of the world's most sophisticated naval intelligence agencies, the "go-to guy" for anyone wanting an up-to-the-minute perspective on the scope and severity of what's going on in nearby waters. He has spent a decade developing close contacts with seafarers, shipowners, labor organizations, journalists, government, and naval officials (both Kenyan and foreign), and even with nongovernmental groups like the IMB and various bodies within the United Nations. His official title is Program Coordinator for the East African Seafarers Assistance Programme (SAP), based here in Mombasa, so he's likely to be a busy person.

Any worries I may have had that the man would turn out to be some sort of harried bureaucrat are quickly dispelled when I meet up with Andrew Mwangura. A shy, soft-spoken Kenyan in his midthirties, Mwangura has a gentle smile and tired, almost sad eyes. However, as I quickly find out, his relaxed manner masks a deep passion for the plight of mariners in this part of the globe.

My asking if he'd prefer for us to get acquainted at his office prompts Mwangura to smile in a slightly embarrassed manner. "I have no office," he tells me. "I am not paid for what I do, not regularly. I do not even have a computer. I use Internet cafés and my mobile phone to do all my communication. I think you will find that things are a little different here in Africa for people like myself."

We grab a couple of plastic bottles of mineral water and sit beneath the fans that push the warm air around in the hotel's lobby as Mwangura explains how he came to head the SAP, which he describes as a very small organization. Born here on the coast, he went to sea as a nineteen-year-old seeking to make enough money to finish his schooling, starting his seafaring career by cleaning the toilets on salvage ships working up and down the coast. In 1997 he began working as a labor organizer, having experienced firsthand the terrible conditions many local mariners toil under. As pirate attacks off Somalia increased, Mwangura found himself more actively involved in publicizing to the outside world the hijackings and hostage takings that were occurring. Working on behalf of local seafarers and shining a light on the criminal activities of pirate gangs have made Mwangura some dangerous enemies.

"Mombasa has a reputation as a port where seafarers are sometimes 'dumped,'" he says. "It is not uncommon for a ship to arrive here and the crew is told they are no longer needed: 'Just grab your possessions and leave.' A cheaper crew is replacing them. So when I try to help these seafarers, some of the owners do not like it. And the pirate gangs in Somalia, they do not like me, either, because of my work. So, for me, sometimes things can be difficult. Maybe it is better that I do not have an office here."

When Mwangura said the SAP was small, he wasn't kidding. The Program is, in fact, a one-man operation, and he survives on whatever meager funds can be solicited from foreign donors, often other labor and seafaring-related groups. It's barely enough to support his wife and five-year-old daughter, but he sees no one else willing to do the work. This is partly due to the lack of resources, which make it almost impossible for someone like Mwangura to earn a decent income while keeping an eye on piracy. But he also tells me there are powerful elements in the region that profit greatly from the situation in Somalia, individuals and groups that would prefer as little was reported as possible.

"This makes people not want to get involved. For me, this is wrong, it is just wrong. The situation facing seafarers off Somalia is dire—very, very bad. It [piracy] has become entrenched there, with violence and corruption considered normal. So many of those attacked are from developing nations, the Third World, here in Kenya, that they do not receive any attention. You know, Somalia is the forgotten place; no one cares about it. The value of life in

Somalia? There is no value. Life is worthless there, for the Somali people and also those seafarers who are captured."

To emphasize this assessment, Mwangura has arranged for me to meet with a mariner in the morning who is one of the many forgotten victims of Somali piracy. This will turn out to be Hassan Abdalla, the former bosun who was held hostage for a hundred days, traumatized by the experience, and compensated with all of $100, a dollar for every day he was in captivity. As I would soon discover, what Abdalla endured up the coast was neither unique nor new, for Somali pirates have been honing their skills for hundreds of years.

> *Next morning the Captain resolved to send the Long-Boat towards the Land . . . to try to discover the Reason of our Men's being detained; and in case they found they kept them Prisoners, or intended them for Slaves to try by Means of the Mulatto Interpreter to treat them for their Ransom.*

Captain Charles Johnson wrote this almost three hundred years ago, recounting the journey of the British East India Company ship *Albemarle*, which left London in 1700 bound for the Indian port of Surat before being blown off course and ending up by the coast of present-day Somalia.[3] Her master, Captain William Beavis, had sent a landing party in search of freshwater, but the sailors were taken prisoner by the locals and never seen again. It is possibly the earliest recorded English-language description of the kidnapping of Western mariners in that region, though it didn't really involve pirates. The unfortunate prisoners were captured while ashore and their disappearance may have had more to do with a misunderstanding between *Albemarle*'s shore party and the local inhabitants than any organized kidnapping for ransom. Still, the incident played to the fears of Johnson's readers, occurring in a mysterious, far-off land about which little was known. Things haven't improved much since.

Home to nine and a half million people, Somalia straddles the Horn of Africa, with the Gulf of Aden to the north and the Indian Ocean on the east, encompassing an area slightly smaller than Texas.

From 1969 to 1991 Somalia had fallen under the sway of Moscow during the era of cold war geopolitics. The Soviets looked on the country as one more wedge in their efforts to undermine capitalism in Africa, but even the Kremlin considered Somalia to be a low priority during this period. No one in the West paid much attention to it, because it had few strategic interests of note, with no oil or gas reserves and no important economic role in the global community. With the collapse of communism, however, came the disintegration of the Somali government, which soon left a vacuum of power that expanded from the capital, Mogadishu, throughout the countryside. The country's infrastructure fell apart, and it has never recovered.

Attempts by the outside world to bring some stability to the country have all ended in failure. In 1992 the United States sent approximately twenty-five thousand military personnel to help safeguard relief efforts intended to alleviate a famine sweeping the nation. Soldiers from Canada, Italy, France, Belgium, Pakistan, and other nations joined in the efforts, but the combined foreign presence was soon caught up in renewed fighting between local clans. Dozens of foreign troops would die in the next two years, most famously remembered by Americans for the "Black Hawk Down" incident in October 1993.[4]

Without a clear political mandate from the United Nations or anyone else, the military forces deployed there were doomed in their attempts at restoring effective order and government. Eventually, the rest of the world grew weary of all the turmoil in Somalia and the foreign troops were withdrawn. Even the United Nations threw up its hands for a while, unable to deliver relief assistance and unwilling to put its personnel at risk. By 1995, the entire country had again descended into anarchy, leading to its being labeled a "failed state."

Imagine living in a land without rules or government: No police or army or officials, no one to stop anyone from doing whatever they wanted to do. A completely lawless environment. This has been Somalia for the last dozen years, a land where famine, drought, war, and corruption have led to the deaths of tens of thousands and where warlords have set up their own private fiefdoms using heavily armed gangs to enforce control. This is the environment that led to a modern-day Libertalia.

To be fair, Somalia wasn't always a pirate haven, and if you look at the statistics compiled by various groups, the waters off it are not at the top of the list in terms of the number of incidents of piracy and armed robbery. Technically speaking, Indonesia and Nigeria have been holding the first two spots in maritime crime for the last several years. In 2007 the IMB recorded forty-three "actual and attempted attacks" in Indonesian waters, forty-two off Nigeria, and thirty-one off Somalia.[5] Of these three regions, it is Somalia where the returns on the investment—the ransoms paid to pirate gangs—have been astronomical.

The ship that Hassan Abdalla was aboard—the MV *Semlow*—was eventually freed after its owners paid a ransom of $135,000. That may sound good, but it was actually a fairly modest ransom when compared to other incidents. Andrew Mwangura gave me a rundown of a half-dozen recent sums paid out by shipowners to Somali pirates, and it reads like the strangest shopping list I've ever seen: A freighter like the *Semlow*, carrying rice or grain? That's worth about $100–150,000 (U.S.) for the pirates. A small containership? Three-quarters of a million. A fishing trawler with a full catch in its holds? Anywhere from $800,000 to $1.2 million. The largest ransom Mwangura knows of was $2.5 million paid out for the release of a merchant ship earlier in 2007. By his own conservative reckoning, pirate gangs in Somalia have made about $5 million in the preceding twenty months, not bad in a place where the average Somali might be lucky to earn $600 a year.

Somalia is an example of how organized piracy operates, bearing all the elements required for this scourge to take seed, gestate, and flourish. Without anyone to deter them, the greed of the warlords in this lawless land caused some of them to look to the seas surrounding Somalia and realize that there were unarmed vessels out there just waiting to be plundered. From a handful of attacks in 2004 Somali piracy exploded the next year to thirty-five incidents. Sixteen of those attacks resulted in the successful hijacking of vessels and crews, with healthy ransoms extracted from shipowners. As a result, organizations like the IMB warned mariners to stay at least two hundred nautical miles off the coast.

Unfortunately, the pirates must have foreseen this possibility, for they soon began using "mother ships" to allow them to venture farther and farther out. Mother ships are larger vessels, sometimes commandeered fishing boats or small coastal traders that can be used as floating bases from which to launch attacks. They provide a place for pirates to rest and replenish and allow the gangs to patrol vast expanses of sea for days on end, increasing the odds of success.

While most modern sea robbers rarely venture out of sight of landfall, Somali pirates cruise far out to sea, scanning the horizon for victims before dispatching boarding teams in small boats stored aboard the mother ships. Any mariner unlucky enough to meet up with these men understood that they were dangerous and well-armed foes, for the tales of pirate attacks off Somalia soon circulated through the seafaring community. Most commonly, the attackers came brandishing AK-47s and rocket-propelled grenade launchers, and had few hesitations about using the weapons.

One incident in April of 2005 gives some idea of the ruthless-ness of Somali pirates, and it is by no means an isolated example. While steaming sixty miles off the east coast, the bulk carrier MV *Tim Buck* was approached by two speedboats just past noon, local time. At 531 feet (162 meters) in length, the *Tim Buck* was as long as one and a half football fields, much larger than the tiny pirate craft. The ship's captain immediately took evasive maneuvers, in-creasing his speed, sending out a distress call on the radio, and or-dering the vessel into a lockdown mode.

For the next ten minutes, the pirates circled around the *Tim Buck* and peppered the ship with rounds from their automatic weapons. When this failed to slow the vessel, they began firing grenades at the ship, hitting a lifeboat and destroying it. With a portable ladder, pirates climbed aboard from their speedboats and tried to enter the ship's accommodations, only to find all the en-tranceways locked. A group then targeted the wheelhouse from the main deck, firing round after round to where the captain and helms-man were crouching. After an hour of shooting up the ship, the pirates finally gave up trying to commandeer the *Tim Buck*, leav-ing her frightened crew to head as far out to sea as possible and limp away to a safe port.

As 2005 progressed, attacks by Somali pirates increased as they became bolder and bolder, culminating in the dramatic attack on a cruise liner on November 5. The *Seabourn Spirit*, a 440-foot-long ultra-luxury vessel that is part of the Carnival Corporation, was en route to Mombasa from Egypt, sailing about eighty-six nautical miles off the east coast of Somalia, when pirates targeted her. There were over three hundred passengers and crew aboard that morning, all of whom were in for a rude awakening.

Gord Chaplin, an easygoing retiree from Cambridge, Ontario, was one of the passengers. Around six that morning, Chaplin and his wife, Celia, were in their stateroom when the couple heard something they hadn't expected to hear on a vacation cruise: gunfire.

"We looked out the cabin window and could see a boat about a hundred yards off the starboard side," he recalls, "and they were shooting an AK-47 at the ship. All of a sudden, my wife Celia noticed that somebody had something bigger than an AK-47, which turned out to be a rocket-propelled grenade launcher, and just as she looked it went off and hit about two staterooms down from ours. Fortunately, it didn't go right in; it exploded off the side but sent shrapnel into the room, destroying it. The woman in there was sitting down at the time, or else she'd have been killed."

Vancouver businessman Mike Rogers was in his port-side cabin with his wife when the attack began: "We could hear this metallic pinging sound and I wondered what it could be. Then it dawns on me that it's machine-gun bullets striking the steel hull. Then a bit later I heard the rocket fire. I felt the liner lurch sharply to one side and thought it was from the rocket hitting until I realized the captain was swerving the ship. He then came on the intercom and told us all to head for the dining room, which was downstairs, where we'd be safer."

"The captain turned the ship very hard," Gord Chaplin remembers, "and tried to run over one of the boats and wash the other. I could hear the rounds pinging, so people were pretty scared. There was a bit of praying, some weeping, but they kept on shooting at us. We were down there for a couple of hours, I guess, and the real question became how did they get a hundred miles off the coast of Somalia? I mean these were probably twenty-foot fishing boats with outboard motors on them. Well, the answer lay in the fact that there was a mother ship, an old beat-up trawler or freighter, sitting on the horizon."

As the passengers huddled below, the pirates kept up their attempts to force the liner to stop, eventually coming alongside and preparing to board. It was then that the *Seabourn Spirit*'s captain deployed the only real weapon he had to defend his ship, a long-range acoustic device. This parabolic sonic blaster emits an ear-splitting sound meant to repel boarders, and it seemed to work, for the pirates finally gave up the chase and returned to their mother ship empty-handed while the *Seabourn Spirit* made haste for the Seychelles Islands, leaving passengers and crew shaken but unhurt.

"We were very lucky," says Mike Rogers. "If they'd stopped us, the pirates could have done anything they wanted to us. And you know, more than worrying about getting injured or even killed, my greatest fear was being taken hostage." Adds Gord Chaplin, "The worst thing—for me—was that the bastards were smiling. You could look out the window and see like three of the five guys [in the boat] who thought it was quite funny. We certainly didn't."

"Ah, the *Seabourn Spirit*. My phone was ringing off the hook for days as journalists scrambled to cover that one. Everyone wanted to know about Somalia: 'What is going on there? When did this start? Have any other ships been attacked?' Two dozen ships had already been attacked by [Somali] pirates at that time. This was just a month after the *Semlow* was released, but no one was really interested in those other events."

Andrew Mwangura sighs as he recounts the great interest shown by the foreign media about piracy off Somalia in late 2005, if only for a few days. He doesn't say it, but I understand what bothers him: somehow a single, isolated attack on vacationing Westerners— an unsuccessful attack, at that—is considered more newsworthy than the hijackings and threats that mariners have dealt with in those waters on pretty much a weekly basis.

We've just met with Hassan Abdalla in his tiny hovel in the Kisauni slum north of Mombasa and are heading down to the city port. I'm sympathetic to Mwangura's unspoken sentiment, especially having heard Abdalla describe what he endured in captivity. After all, didn't the *Seabourn Spirit* incident at least raise some awareness of the issue across the globe?

Mwangura nods his head for a moment, then says, "Yes, it is true that *Seabourn Spirit* was a lead news item that revealed what was going on. But only for a week or so; then it all died down and my phone stopped ringing. Now . . . nothing. Piracy off Somalia did not end after this. Did the *Seabourn Spirit* cause the international community to finally do something to stop this? Well, there have been at least twenty-five attacks this year, so I do not see much progress. Do you? I am happy that the passengers on that ship were not injured or hurt. They were able to go home after it was over, and I doubt they will ever return. Most seafarers do not have this option. I will show you."

Just over a half-million people live in this vibrant city beside the Indian Ocean, with the main part of Mombasa centered on an island that juts like a small thumb from the Kenyan mainland. It's been a trading center for over seven hundred years and is now one of the most important ports in East Africa. We cross the Nyali Bridge and cut across the north end of town, caught up in the stream of traffic that chokes the streets. Minivans known as *matatus* are the preferred form of transportation in Kenyan cities, but there are plenty of other cars, motorbikes, and the small motorized mini-taxis called *tuk-tuks*. As we slowly wind our way toward the port district, I see whitewashed mosques, churches, and Hindu temples, a reminder that Mombasa is a crossroad of influences, not unlike Melaka in Malaysia.

Actually, Mombasa bears many striking historical similarities to Melaka. For centuries both cities were invaded, controlled, ruled, or otherwise held under the sway of Arabian, Portuguese, and English powers. The Portuguese first arrived here in 1498; eleven years later they landed in Melaka. These first European invaders built a fortress called A Famosa in Melaka, of which only a small gateway remains, while their Mombasa citadel, Fort Jesus, still dominates the eastern harbor.

We eventually arrive at the Port of Mombasa's main gates, where three stony-faced policemen with automatic rifles stand guard. They appear ready to turn us back until they see Andrew Mwangura sitting in the front seat of the car. A few words are spoken, hands are shaken, and we are waved through the barrier. Out my window, I can see a row of warehouses hugging the dirty water, bearing the logo of the United Nations World Food Programme. Each is filled to the rafters with supplies intended for places like Somalia. Past the warehouses, Mwangura tells the driver to take a left over a small causeway that leads to the port's southern wharves. Things are quiet in the port today, with only four vessels tied up here in Mombasa's Kilindini Harbor. There's a large containership off-loading its cargo at one end of the pier, a deserted-looking coastal freighter in from Zanzibar at the other, and two small freighters moored in between at berths eleven and twelve. Mwangura has the driver pull up beside the two freighters.

"Well, there they are," Mwangura says quietly. "The famous ships. Do you want to go aboard?"

The vessels have blue hulls with white superstructures and are clearly sister ships. One look tells you each has seen better days; they're beaten and bruised from years of service, prime examples of what one would call rust buckets. Then I spy their names and realize why I've been brought here: the ships are the *Semlow* and *Miltzow*.

These two freighters are part of what has to be the unluckiest shipping company in the world, one with the dubious honor of having had each and every vessel in its fleet captured by pirates between 2005 and 2007. The firm's four freighters—the *Semlow*, *Miltzow*, *Torgelow*, and *Rozen*—have spent a combined total of almost seven months in captivity, each hijacked by Somali pirates after leaving Mombasa. The *Semlow* was the first to be taken; this was the ship that would carry Hassan Abdalla. The *Mitzlow*, moored just in front of the *Semlow*, was the second to be taken hostage, a mere six days after the latter freighter was released. There's activity on the pier beside the two ships, meaning the vessels are still working the nearby seas. Stevedores are busy loading the *Semlow* for departure, hefting large white sacks from a nearby shipping container onto wooden pallets that are then swung by a crane into the freigher's open cargo holds. There a trio of guys haul into place the fifty-kilogram sacks of sugar, each stevedore stripped to the waist and barefoot, their muscled bodies glistening sweat under the warm African sky as they manhandle the arriving pallets. A lighter boat hugs the *Semlow*'s starboard side, the barge being used to transfer fuel oil into the freighter's tanks for her upcoming voyage.

I follow Mwangura up the gangway aboard the *Semlow*, ducking beneath laundry hanging from a clothesline strung on the port-side afterdeck. Stepping through an open door into the ship's house—the main living and working spaces—I'm enveloped in stifling heat. Though there's a slight breeze blowing outside, barely a whisper makes it into the *Semlow*. The un-air-conditioned ship has a rank smell. The fair-sized cockroaches that I see on the deck and bulkheads seem too lethargic to bother skittering away when we enter the companionway. It's narrow and dark, barely a meter wide, so tight that two people meeting would have to press themselves against the bulkheads in order to pass.

Mwangura pops his head into the tiny galley, then the ship's mess, both of which are empty. He then leads me up a ladder to the freighter's wheelhouse, where we encounter a short, slight man with metal-framed glasses who is clad in a dirty white shirt and khaki shorts. He sports a baseball cap balanced precariously above tufts of gray hair, the cap embroidered with a lion on it and the phrase "Born Free."

Though you wouldn't know it to look at the man, he's actually a seasoned mariner. This, it turns out, is Sellathurai Mahalingam, the sixty-year-old Sri Lankan captain of the *Semlow* when she was hijacked in 2005. He greets Andrew Mwangura warmly, shakes my hand politely, and welcomes me aboard his ship, inviting me to "call me Lingam; that is what my friends call me." Then he shouts for the steward to bring up some cold bottles of soda pop before talking to me about his time in pirate captivity.

For the Somalis who captured the *Semlow*, Lingam was the most important hostage. Because he was the freighter's captain, he was the one the rest of the crew looked to for leadership. He was the only one who knew how to sail a vessel of its size through those waters. Only Lingam knew the combination to the ship's safe, wherein lay $8,500 (U.S.). And only the captain could make sure the ransom negotiations could commence with the *Semlow*'s owners in Mombasa.

"I knew as soon they come aboard that hijacking is their profession," the captain says. "They were ruthless. When they forced me to open the [ship's] safe, they did it by holding a gun to my head. I have sailed here in East Africa for three years before this, so I knew their reputation, though that trip was my first aboard *Semlow*."

One of the captain's initial fears was that the pirates would single him out for harsher treatment because he was not Muslim, like the rest of his crew. As it turned out, the Somalis cared little about the religions of their captives, treating everyone with the same brutality.

"Their leader, 'Captain Issa,' was a brute," Lingam remembers. "He actually said we were under arrest for all kinds of stupid charges: entering Somali waters without a permit, engaging in illegal fishing, ferrying arms to rival gangs. We were carrying *rice*, on behalf of the United Nations. Weapons? Fishing? It was all nonsense. This Issa, he would not believe us and grew angry, threatening us. He forced the chief officer to get the radio working, to contact the pirate bosses ashore, and when he was a little slow with the radio, that was when the pirates began to fire off their weapons here in the wheelhouse."

The ship still bears the scars from the pirates, a gaping bullet hole in the forward heating unit and other hastily patched reminders of when the Somalis' anger boiled over. Lingam runs his fingers across one of the holes and says some of the damage was caused later in their ordeal, when the pirates ran out of their supply of khat, which they had been chewing constantly while aboard. Without their narcotics, the Somalis became quite edgy.

Captain Mahalingam tells me that the men who captured his ship were highly organized. "They said they were 'Somali Marines' and Issa's boss was a short man who called himself General Gray. I do not know, maybe he was a warlord? He visited a few times while they held us, and I remember one time he said, 'The Indian Ocean is mine.' He knew exactly what he was doing, said he received information from accomplices in Nairobi and Mombasa. He knew he would get the money from the owners; he knew how the negotiations would occur; he knew everything. This was not some accident."

At one point during Lingam's time in captivity, negotiations seemed to be at a standstill between the Somali pirates and the *Semlow*'s Kenyan owners, so he and the ship's chief engineer were ordered to leave the vessel. At gunpoint, the two mariners were taken ashore in a small boat and then driven by Jeep inland through desert for a few hours, ending up at a village under the control of General Gray. They were kept there for four days while more satellite telephone calls ensued between captors and shipowners.

The captain goes to the navigation table and searches for a nautical chart to show me exactly where they were taken. The map he pulls out and references is an old Italian government one from 1940, printed while Mussolini's Fascist republic still controlled this part of East Africa, but Lingam says it's still perfectly good for navigation purposes. He runs his finger along the coast until he finds a small settlement marked as "El Dere" on the Italian chart, just inland from Meregh.

"They treated us well there, but everyone in the village knew what was going on. The elders, the villagers, they knew we were prisoners. Maybe they were afraid, but no one offered to help. I remember there was one man who was with them, with the pirates. A short guy, Mohammed or Ahmed. He talked about America, where he had relatives. Everyone, they all knew what was going on with the piracy. All the Somalis. They think it is something good or normal to do."

The *Semlow*'s chief engineer, Juma Mvita, a large man still wiping sleep from his eyes, joins us in the cramped wheelhouse. The Tanzanian-born mariner was Lingam's companion on the visit to El Dere, and he shakes his head in loathing when I ask what he thinks about Somali pirates.

"When the pirates first came aboard, they said we were carrying illegal arms in our holds. So we told them, go look, it is just rice, there are no weapons here. And we tried to explain that this is food for Somali people, but they did not care. They had no interest in that; they only wanted to get the money from the owners. They were just thieves."

"You know," adds the captain, "the only thing they were afraid of was other hijackers. They worried that some other [gang] would come and take us from them and get the ransom money. This bothered me, because I worried we would get caught up in a fight between two gangs. The whole experience . . . it left me mentally tortured."

I mention that I assume neither seafarer has any desire to return to Somalia soon, which causes the captain to begin giggling and the chief to grin broadly. Both have returned to the country many times since they were released, and Juma Mvita gestures out the forward windows toward the cargo being loaded into the *Semlow*'s holds.

"We leave for Somalia in less than forty-eight hours, as soon as everything is aboard."

Driving away, Andrew Mwangura explains that mariners like Sellathurai Mahalingam and Juma Mvita don't really have much choice about traveling to the pirate-infested waters of Somalia. Jobs are scarce here—he figures there are about three thousand seafarers looking for work in Mombasa alone—so any work contracts that come up are quickly grabbed, regardless of the destination. If the captain and chief engineer were to quit, their places would be taken by others more than willing to accept the risks.

It seems slightly bizarre that anyone whose ships have been repeatedly targeted by Somali pirates would continue to do business up there, but it's amazing what the lure of money can do. The history of maritime commerce is rife with the stories of shipowners willing to run blockades, defy international sanctions, or risk entering war zones in order to carry someone's cargo.

Just past the Kilindini Post Office, we pull up in front of a three-story white concrete building housing the headquarters of the *Semlow*'s owners, Motaku Shipping Agencies. If the firm is reaping huge profits from its operations, they certainly aren't spending it on fancy corporate offices, for the open space I'm ushered into could pass for someone's rec room. It's crammed with nautical knickknacks, photos of vessels, sea charts, and official documents, the walls paneled in fake wood and a bunch of desks pushed close to each other. On one wall is prominently displayed a framed photo of current Kenyan president Mwai Kibaki, while a print of the country's first leader, Jomo Kenyatta, hangs nearby. In front of these sits Karim Kudrati, managing director of Motaku Shipping.

Kudrati has salt-and-pepper hair, his beard more salt than pepper. He speaks with a deep voice and tends to drop his head to stare at me over the tops of his spectacles when answering my questions, cautious at first but becoming more animated as our discussion goes on. A former marine engineer, Kudrati has run Motaku since 1977 with his brother, who sits nearby and listens in while manning the phones, cocking a none-too-discreet ear my way when I ask how anyone can trade with a place like Somalia.

"There is always trading going on up there, even when the fighting has been bad," Kudrati says in his sonorous voice while glaring at me as if I am a simpleton. "People still require food, goods, all manner of merchandise. You may find this surprising, but it is true. The roads in Somalia are very bad and very few, and there are many roadblocks and armed men along the way. It is far safer to use ships to move things. And it is much simpler, I would add."

There are still dangers involved with venturing north from Mombasa, he adds, but Kudrati says his family has a better understanding of how to deal with them than many others.

"For us, this is a family business," Kudrati tells me, "one that goes back a hundred and fifty years here. My family left India for Africa and soon became involved in trading, something that Indians have done for a long time. My grandfather used sailing dhows for his business, the traditional ships in this part of the world. They were good ships, very sturdy. Then my father began to put motors in the dhows. Our family traded all up and down the coast, even to Somalia. You see, we have a long history with Somalia, going back to when our family first came to Africa. At that time, a relative landed in Somalia by accident—he was intending to come here [to Mombasa]—and this started our family's relationship up there. Until 1992, we had relatives living in Somalia, and I will tell you we always loved that place."

Kudrati remembers 1970s Somalia as being "a paradise," especially around Kisimayo, a couple of hundred kilometers north of the border with Kenya. He remembers visiting it often and even thinking he'd like to retire there when he got older, only to see the country descend into its current anarchistic state. He and his brother have since concentrated on using their family connections with Somalia to maintain a meager commercial lifeline to the country. He emphasizes to me that the one cargo they have never carried up there is weaponry, though it appears the firm has been approached about this.

"There are many opportunities [for these], but there are enough guns there already, don't you think? We preferred to take other cargoes. even during the worst of the fighting. We have worked with the United Nations, the World Food Programme, UNICEF, the ICRC [International Committee of the Red Cross], and others for years and years, as well as carrying commercial cargoes. And we never—never—had any problems until 2005. Before that? We'd never heard of piracy in Somalia. Maybe it happened, but we never encountered it. But when the *Semlow* was hijacked, I don't know, it just changed things."

I wonder why things changed, why the *Semlow* and then their other ships were hijacked, but Kudrati becomes somewhat evasive.

"Many ships were attacked at that time, not just ours. The . . . they were going for all manner of vessels. Why us? Well, better to ask why not. Piracy has affected everyone going there. I will say that we thought they would not touch us, because of our long history up there and the charters we were on at the time. This was a bad time for us, all of us."

Though he won't divulge anything more, something happened in 2005, something that made Kudrati's vessels the targets of pirates. Perhaps his family connections in Somalia finally fled the scene, or perhaps his luck finally ran out. Regardless, shipping charters started becoming scarce at that time, forcing him and his brother to accept whatever contracts were available.

When bosun Hassan Abdalla, Captain Mahalingam, Chief Mvita, and the rest of the *Semlow*'s crew were captured in June of 2005, they were carrying food to Somalia on behalf of the United Nations' World Food Programme (WFP), aid for those affected by the tsunami that had devastated much of the littoral areas of the Indian Ocean. Eight hundred and fifty tons of rice donated by Japan was in the freighter's holds when the pirate gang commandeered her. According to Kudrati, this made the ship an easy mark.

"We do not have weapons aboard our ships or armed guards, and they know that. There are many spies here in Mombasa who work for the Somalis. So they know when a vessel leaves, what it is carrying, all this information. Whenever one of my vessels has been hijacked, it is our firm that has to pay the ransom, sometimes over $100,000. When the pirates steal the money from the ship's safe, that comes out of my pocket. Yes, this is a business, whether we are delivering WFP cargo or commercial cargo. But, frankly, if I can find other charters, why would I bother with the UN?"

The shipping market here remains tight, so he admits the firm continues to send its vessels and crews north into Somali waters, though there have been no problems for six months. The ships have delivered their cargoes and returned safely. And as to the safety and well-being of the mariners employed by his firm, Kudrati offers a suitably managerial perspective.

"Everyone who works for us understands that there are . . . risks entailed in this business. The sea, the weather, yes, even pirates. But no one is forced to work, not like when the British had their press gangs, eh?[6] Anyone can choose not to go to, let us say, Somalia."

As to the *Semlow*'s impending journey back north, Karim Kudrati says he expects it to be an uneventful trip: "We have taken certain, ah, measures to ensure everything will be safe. The captain will be in constant contact with us, we will monitor things from here, and the crew are aware of the situation. We have learned from what has happened."

"He said they had learned from the other incidents and were taking measures to make sure things would be okay," says Andrew Mwangura with a slight grin. The man sitting opposite us listens to this and then shakes his head in disbelief.

"I'll bet he 'learned,'" the man says in a gentle British accent.

Reverend Michael Sparrow heads the local chapter of the Mission to Seafarers, part of the Anglican Church's international outreach program to assist mariners.[7] After a lengthy career as a professional mariner working in African waters, Sparrow felt a higher calling and became an ordained priest. He has longish gray hair and pale blue eyes and is turned out in a crisp white shirt replete with epaulettes that make him seem still like the merchant marine officer he once was. Surprisingly for someone who lives this close to the equator, he has pale English skin in lieu of a tan.

The Mombasa Mission is located near the port in what were once the offices of a shipping firm. It's a bright and airy place outfitted with a gymnasium, a pool, recreation areas, a convenience store, and a chapel, all to give seafarers a place to unwind. There's a somewhat genteel British feel to the Mission, harkening back to the colonial days, when I could imagine officers from a visiting freighter enjoying gin-and-tonics here by the garden, where an immense tortoise holds court. The place is empty today, save for three Russian sailors who are splashing about in the pool with bottles of beer in their hands.

Reverend Sparrow and Andrew Mwangura know each other well, having worked together for years helping seafarers in Mombasa. The good minister knows a lot about the pirate attacks off Somalia. I quickly realize he is not just some naïve missionary seeking to spread the word of God in a corner of East Africa but someone who has developed many contacts within the local shipping community.

"No one trades up there without paying bribes; it is what makes the difference between a safe voyage and a hijacking. You see, this is like a protection racket going on. If you want to take something to Somalia by ship—running shoes, building material, UN food aid, anything—there are warlords who control the ports who need to be paid. If you want to fish off the coast, because there are good [fishing] grounds there, you must pay them. Nothing gets into or out of Somalia, nothing passes by its coast, without money being paid. If you don't pay, that is when you are targeted. The pirates up there, they are the enforcers of this; they work for the warlords.

Mwangura picks up on Sparrow's views: "It is all about money, isn't it? Everything in Africa involves money—bribes—especially in a place like Somalia. The sugar in the *Semlow*? This is a valuable commodity in Somalia. Someone will sell it in his shop, making money. To get the sugar to the shop means people are bribed from the moment the ship leaves Mombasa. It is in their interest to assure it is delivered so everyone can make something when goods for sale are shipped and everyone is content. Nothing can move in or around without someone being bribed: the gangs, the officials, everyone. That is the system; that is how things work. Whenever we hear of a commercial ship being hijacked by pirates, we usually assume that not enough money was paid to the right people."

But as Mwangura goes on to explain, food aid is much less valuable because "fewer people make money from the United Nations [aid]. It is given away for free. The gunmen are smart, too. They know they cannot steal the food and sell it themselves. That would be dangerous." By this, Mwangura means that the Somali warlords understand the international community would not stand by as its donated assistance is stolen by armed gangs. The intervention of foreign troops safeguarding humanitarian aid could threaten the ability of the warlords to extort money from other parts of the economy. "So the one way Somalis can make money [from the aid deliveries] is to hijack the ships and the crews and hold them for ransom. The vessel and the seafarers become more important than the cargo, you see?"

Sparrow pulls out a recent copy of the British seafarers' newspaper, the Nautilus UK *Telegraph,* and opens it to a blurry photo of a suspected Somali pirate mother ship. The photo was taken by the crew of a British merchant ship that had been harassed by the mysterious vessel while sailing 2,410 nautical miles off the coast.

"You see this one? It looks like a long-liner [fishing boat]," Sparrow murmurs. "I saw a ship very similar to this one here in the port about two months ago."

"Somali pirates have come to Mombasa?" I ask.

"Well, not necessarily as 'pirates.' This is East Africa's busiest port, so there is a lot of traffic, even from Somalia. Could a ship come with a crew who had been pirating? Of course. How would you prove they were pirates? You can be a pirate one day and a fisherman the next. There is also a large Somali community here, so shipping goes on all the time, back and forth."

Reverend Sparrow points out that many of the Somalis living in Mombasa have fled the trauma of life in their homeland. But there are people within this community who aid the pirates, providing intelligence and tips about merchant traffic.

"If you go down to the bars or around the port, seafarers don't usually talk about where they're going. Remember that old phrase from the war? 'Loose lips sink ships'? It still applies today, here. This is a small community, seafaring I mean, and there are just too many informers. Not to be too dramatic, but how long are you here? A week? Okay, if you're nosing around about piracy, I guarantee that they'll know about you.

"The real issue, I think, is that piracy there is not just affecting mariners from Mombasa or wherever, as bad as that is. No, the real problem is that it impacts directly on the lives of ordinary Somalis. The warlords, the gangs, the pirates, all of them are starving their own people. People are dying up there because of this and it seems no one cares. That is the real issue."

Individuals like Reverend Sparrow and Andrew Mwangura have made it their business to work for the welfare of seafarers in

East Africa. While piracy is clearly something both are greatly concerned about, each man is also aware that combating it requires far greater resources than either can ever mobilize on his own. The best they can hope for is that by helping to publicize the hijackings, hostage takings, and corruption going on, larger organizations or governments will pay greater attention to the situation.

6

FEASTS AND FAMINES

There was a demon, a monster called Mukunga Mbura, that lived under the water. He could be glimpsed at night when he came to feast on the people and animals of a village, or see his reflection in the sky when it rained—that is the rainbow. He was very evil, but the village warriors discovered a way to defeat him: if they could surround the demon, they could throw their spears into a small area on the back of his neck. That is how they killed the monster.

—TRADITIONAL KIKUYU MYTH

FOR THOUSANDS OF years pirates have kept to a basic modus operandi, robbing unlucky vessels and mariners as well as periodically attacking coastal settlements. But there was one unwritten rule that all these maritime criminals rarely broke: you focused your pirate operations on foreigners, not your own people. Every pirate called some community a home, be it a bustling port, a backwater village, or a cluster of huts. No matter how little time one spent ashore, this community was a reminder that a sailor can only be at sea for so long before the desire to wander again among "landlubbers" surfaces.

The last thing a mariner wants is to be forsaken by his comrades; the second-to-last is to be shunned by his land-based kin. People ashore will usually put up with seafarers in their midst so long as this doesn't cause too many headaches or hardships, and any trickle-down economic benefits can only help to cement the relationships. This holds true for sea robbers as well as for law-abiding mariners. Hundreds of years ago, the citizens of cities like Jamaica's Port Royal or the Bahamas' Nassau were more than willing to turn a blind eye to the pirates wandering their streets, if only because the brothels, bars, shops, and flophouses in each city were doing brisk business whenever a ship arrived laden with plunder.

Besides any unwritten moral code against harming your own people, it was just plain common sense for pirates to not anger those they communed with ashore. After all, these were people who might force you from your refuge, turn you in to the authorities, or even kill you. This is what happened in Bangladesh a few years ago, near the country's main port. The city of Chittagong has long been notorious for sea robbers who mostly climb aboard anchored vessels to steal whatever supplies they can find on deck, though they are not above attacking local fishing boats or even terrorizing villages, murdering, looting, and raping at will.

By early December 2003, though, the Bangladeshi villagers had had enough and took things into their own hands. They headed out en masse one weekend, found twenty-eight suspected pirates, and promptly lynched them all (though they did hand another six over to the police). Two years later the villagers' frustrations would again boil over when remaining pirates resumed attacking local fishing boats. After one attempted sea robbery, the fishermen decided they weren't going to be victims any longer and fired warning flares, drawing the attention of other fishing boats. Four suspected pirates were beaten to death and then tossed into the Bay of Bengal by the angry sailors.

You don't really hear of many situations like these, though, because most pirates are a cautious lot, as odd a notion as that may seem. They've always known enough not to piss off the local populace too much and, more important, to only attack when they had a clear advantage over their victims.

Too bad no one told the Somali pirates about these simple precepts.

Pirates at the Horn of Africa have managed to flout many of the lessons learned by their criminal brethren over millennia. They have attacked vessels while being vastly outgunned, such as the American guided-missile cruiser USS *Cape St. George*. They have attacked ships with little chance of commandeering them, such as the luxury liner *Seabourn Spirit*. And they have attacked ships bringing much-needed humanitarian aid to their fellow Somalis, such as the *Semlow*. Their desperation has managed to elevate piracy in these waters to new heights of inhumanity, such that it affects not just mariners at sea but also men, women, and children ashore. Simply put, Somali pirates are killing their own.

The United Nations maintains two dozen various agencies and programs out of Nairobi, overseeing regional operations for everything from the Office of the High Commissioner for Refugees to the World Health Organization. One of the most important offices the United Nations has based here is the WFP office responsible for dealing with Somalia. Unable to maintain a permanent headquarters in Mogadishu because of the ongoing instability there, WFP personnel shuttle back and forth between Kenya and Somalia when required, something they've been doing for the better part of two decades.

In the wake of the civil war that erupted in Somalia in January

1991, the WFP and other aid organizations began to deliver humanitarian assistance to the people there, while literally dodging bullets. By 2000 over 113,000 metric tons of food had been distributed by the UN agency throughout Somalia, but as the fighting just went on and on and the people continued to starve, the outside world began to lose interest in the Horn of Africa. In the time since Somalia spiraled down into unending anarchy, the international community has had to deal with the collapse of communism, ethnic cleansing, genocide, terrorism, global warming, and a variety of wars large and small. Somalia? Well, it kind of got lost in the mix.

"Yeah, there is a certain 'fatigue' about Somalia, an exhaustion of sorts," says Peter Smerdon. We're sharing bottles of local beer beneath a cooling night sky in Nairobi. Smerdon is a senior public affairs officer with the WFP in Kenya, and like many who do this job, he is a former journalist. The wiry ex-pat Brit comes to the job with a passion for Africa and the media, his youthful complexion masking experiences as a foreign journalist covering such events as the Rwandan genocide. The former reporter understands how quickly news can slip from the front page, especially when there seems to be no end in sight to the problems.

"Since the 1990s, I think Somalia has frightened the West, it certainly frightened the Americans, and many countries are just fairly tired of it," he says. "You know, there's been civil war and civil conflict ongoing in the country, there's been famine, malnutrition, starvation, displaced people, and it can seem like a place where things never change. Plus you have Iraq, Afghanistan, and any number of other places vying for attention, from the media, from governments, and from aid groups. And because there aren't any good photo ops in Somalia—no foreign soldiers handing out food, no dying children, no celebrities—the situation there has slipped off the radar of most people. That's a cold, hard assessment of things, but I know that's how it works."

As Smerdon puts it, Somalia is a place just barely surviving, with little in the way of a functioning government, an economy in shambles, and health care essentially nonexistent. There is a shaky entity known as the Transitional Federal Government (TFG) that has been recognized as the "official government" of Somalia since 2004, but it's been able to do little in the way of actually governing. Somalia has become the forgotten corner of the continent, a failed nation-state receiving the barest minimum of palliative care from both the outside world and what passes for its government. Having recently returned from the country, Smerdon offers a bleak assessment of what things are like.

"The people there are feeling ground down. You may get by in the city—though in Mogadishu these days you might get killed—but in the countryside they've been weakened and ground down like you can't imagine. Plus, three hundred thousand people have been displaced by the fighting going on in and around Mogadishu, forced to find refuge anywhere they can."

Compounding the issues, 2007 would see the country's worst cereal harvests in thirteen years. Though most of Somalia is semi-desert or dry grassland, there are two districts in the south that have fertile farmland. These districts—the Middle and Lower Shabelle—were once known as Somalia's breadbasket, but the poor summer harvest left the regions unable to feed themselves, let alone having anything left over to export elsewhere in the country. Malnutrition was already exceeding emergency levels in many parts of Somalia, and Smerdon says aid workers were struggling to figure out how to feed 1.2 million people—up from a million the year before—in the coming months.

"Look, Somalia cannot ever feed itself; the land is simply not arable enough. So it has to rely on imported food, which, in the current situation, is where [the WFP] comes in. Just across the border from Kenya you have places where in a 'normal' year you get acute malnutrition rates of twenty to thirty percent. Twenty to thirty percent in a normal year, okay? Now, fifteen percent is considered the emergency level. In Somalia, life expectancy is about forty-six years and a quarter of all children die before they reach the age of five. Remember the hundred thousand tons of food we distributed [there] between 1991 and 1999? Well, we reckon we need to get thirty to thirty-five thousand metric tons of food into Somalia by the end of this year, within the next four months. The situation in Somalia right now is *exceedingly* serious."

In an era of general apathy about Somalia and skyrocketing prices for food, the WFP has been scrambling of late to find donors to contribute to its relief programs.[1] Supplies are running short in UN warehouses, such as the ones I saw down in Mombasa, so a few weeks earlier the WFP put out an urgent appeal to the international community for $22 million (U.S.) so that additional stocks of food could be purchased. Without new contributions, it's anticipated that the food will begin running out in October.

But beyond that problem was the issue of how to get the humanitarian aid into Somalia safely and consistently. Trucking the food overland from Kenya is difficult as the routes are often little more than rutted tracks and the convoys are invariably held up at roadblocks by armed militia groups or even members of the "governing" TFG itself.

"They don't care if you're carrying humanitarian assistance or not," says Smerdon. "Everyone makes money out of checkpoints. These are set up by various armed gangs who each control small bits of territory. To pass, drivers must pay, say, fifty dollars for each truck. Now that may not seem like much, but when you factor in the number of roadblocks that line the delivery routes, it becomes a huge impediment to our work. On one route we've used, from the Kenyan border to Wajid in the south, a distance of 125 kilometers [seventy-seven miles], there were twenty-nine checkpoints the last time I was there. Add it up. So delivering aid by truck is not very reliable. We've only relied on trucks to deliver about twenty percent of our aid."

He tells me of a recent conversation he had with a Somali woman in one of the refugee camps. The woman had been living there for several years and told Smerdon how angry she was about the delays of food caused by the checkpoints and how her children were going hungry as a result. But she also said her husband was manning one of those checkpoints, making money from the convoys while increasing the plight of his own family.

All of which brings Peter Smerdon to the issue of piracy. He sits back in his chair and sips his beer when I ask what the piracy situation has been like for the WFP.

"Pirates . . . I mean, I thought I'd seen a lot here in Africa, in terms of how badly people can treat each other. And, I want to emphasize, Africa does not have a monopoly on inhumanity; that's a misperception of outsiders. Anyway, the most efficient and cost-effective way to move the donor aid into the country has been to send it by ship from Mombasa. Or it was until the pirates started attacking."

Since the *Semlow* was attacked in June of 2005, WFP-contracted vessels have been hit by Somali pirates four more times. In late February of 2007, the Motaku Shipping Agencies' freighter MV *Rozen* was hijacked and held for forty days before a ransom was paid. Shortly after the *Rozen* was released, pirates opened fire with machine guns on another cargo ship under contract to the WFP—the MV

Victoria. Though the attack was repulsed, a Somali guard hired by the agency was killed.

The result of these attacks has been the temporary suspension of deliveries by the UN agency for the last three years. They were scared off by the threats to the crews and the interception of the food being shipped. Something must have been worked out to allow deliveries to resume, but Smerdon is adamant that the WFP did not strike any deals with the Somali warlords who control the pirates.

"We do not negotiate like that, absolutely not. Look, what we do is work with a Somali [shipping agent] who is responsible for the unloading and dispersal of the aid. Here [in Kenya] we contract with a shipper to deliver the cargo—such as Karim Kudrati, who you have already met [in Mombasa]. These two are then responsible for the rest. They are paid per a standard contract and expected to both agree to the terms and fulfill it. If a ship is held hostage and a ransom demanded, that is their responsibility. We do not pay ransoms. The UN does not pay ransoms. It would set a precedent if we did. Besides, if we had made some sort of arrangement with the pirate gangs, why would they continue attacking our ships?"[2]

Though the paying of bribes is unofficially standard practice for many aid organizations going into conflict zones, ransoms are another matter entirely. Should an organization like the WFP become involved in paying out sums that can total in the hundreds of thousands of dollars, this would make their contractors easy marks for the pirates and mariners and shipping companies might decline the jobs. Unfortunately, the WFP's policy of not paying the pirates has made little difference, for the agency is currently unable to find anyone willing to carry their food aid into Somalia.

According to Smerdon, "They say they're all busy carrying

commercial cargoes and, frankly, are afraid of the piracy situation. They just don't want to deal with it and would rather do something safer. We've tried to convince companies to work with us and recently thought we had a ship out of the [Persian] Gulf, but it fell through. So we're struggling to find a way to get the aid into Somalia in the next few months and, yes, we're a little concerned."

So while a humanitarian crisis increases in Somalia, the supplies of food donated to the WFP languish in warehouses, unable to be delivered by shipping firms afraid of pirate attacks on UN-contracted vessels—but not afraid of carrying commercial goods like sugar.

"Yeah, dealing with the Somali situation is very frustrating for me," admits Peter Smerdon. "We're trying to feed people in need, but logistics—delivering food—is not that sexy. There are no blue helmets, no white UN vehicles, no Western troops handing out food to dying people in a war zone. This is nuts-and-bolts work we're doing, but it is among the most vital things the United Nations can do. We must feed these people, because we're talking about millions of people—millions—who are going hungry, are susceptible to disease and unable to function. And, yes, one of the reasons the Somali people are in this situation is because of the actions of the pirates. Somali pirates are threatening the lifeline that feeds their own people."

If the WFP can find a vessel to go to Somalia soon—and it's a big "if" as we sit here in Nairobi—Smerdon knows the chance of it being targeted by the pirates is high.

"You said Kudrati has a ship heading to Somalia now? Makes sense. He's probably trying to get in and out before the monsoon season ends. The reason things have been quiet on the seas up there the last couple of months is mainly because of the winds, which have prevented the pirates from venturing out. But now that the monsoon season comes to a close in a few weeks, the pirates will return. You see, as the monsoon season ends the pirate season begins."

With armed gangs preparing for the new pirate season due to begin in a few weeks, it's inevitable to wonder whether there should be weapons aboard vessels that could deter attackers.

The arming of mariners is a controversial topic, with the vast majority of opinion weighing in against the idea. There is no maritime body that advocates the practice, not the International Maritime Organization (IMO), the IMB, shipowners, seafarers' unions—no one believes there should be guns aboard civilian vessels. Their thinking is quite simple: arming mariners increases the chances that they will be injured or killed in the course of an attack by pirates. Most mariners are not trained in the use of weapons, so giving a deckhand a shotgun or rifle may lead to an accident, especially in the confined spaces one finds aboard vessels. And pirates may be more trigger-happy if they think their victims have weapons.

A sad example of what can happen when weapons are used in self-defense is the case of Sir Peter Blake's encounter with South American pirates. One of the most remarkable yachtsmen of the modern era, the New Zealander had sailed around the world numerous times and led his country to winning two America's Cups. He then went on to become head of expeditions for the Cousteau Society before setting up his own organization to do research in Antarctica and becoming a special envoy for the United Nations Environment Programme (UNEP).

On December 5, 2001, Blake was aboard the *Seamaster*, a thirty-six-meter (118-foot) research vessel moored in the Amazon Delta of Brazil, preparing to continue an expedition looking into environmental issues in the region. A group of local thugs who called themselves the Water Rats boarded the *Seamaster* that night intending to rob the crew. Deciding to fight back against the intruders, Blake retrieved a rifle from below deck and managed to get off a shot that wounded one of the pirates. But then Blake's gun jammed and one of the boarders raised his own weapon and shot Blake in the back, killing him instantly. The pirates then robbed the remaining crew of watches and cameras and fled into the night.[3]

Despite the risks, there are cases where merchant ships have been known to carry weapons. Before the collapse of the Soviet Union, it was common practice for Russian vessels to be armed, and, possibly for this reason, these vessels were rarely targeted by sea robbers. Similarly, Israeli vessels are believed to routinely carry firearms aboard. Whether or not this is true, you'd be hard pressed to find a single incident of pirates attacking one of them.

These have been the exceptions among the worldwide fleets. Of all the mariners I have met, only one group has ever felt that weapons should be available when sailing into dangerous waters. It's been American mariners who have usually voiced this opinion, though the motivating factor is often the increased animosity shown toward them by some foreigners in the post-911/Iraq/Afghanistan era.

Joe Casalino, the Brooklyn bosun who was injured in an attack off Iraq, told me he most definitely thought there should be weapons on ships, discounting the idea that you can't trust a mariner with a weapon. "People say, 'Why would you give a gun to a drunken sailor?' And I say that there's no such thing as a drunken sailor on ships anymore. The work policies are way too stringent nowadays to allow that. In twenty years of going to sea, I've never seen that. Besides, many of the guys I know are, like me, trained in using small arms."

Even so, Casalino concedes that if he or the chief mate had been armed at the time of the attack, things would have likely ended badly, because "those pirates were really nervous. So . . . a gun would have added to the problem. Yeah, in hindsight it was probably better that we weren't armed."

Another idea is to put armed guards aboard vessels, personnel who have been trained in the use of firearms and are aware of the local situations. There are a small number of businesses that market this service to the shipping community, likening it to hiring security guards. For a time, some ships transiting the Strait of Malacca utilized these individuals, but it was quickly frowned upon by officials in the region, who worried that putting mercenaries aboard vessels would increase the overall risks. As well, the costs of putting armed guards aboard or arranging for a security escort by another vessel are expensive, anywhere from $20,000 to $100,000 just in the Strait of Malacca.

So if most mariners don't want weapons aboard their vessels and the use of armed guards is either frowned upon or considered cost prohibitive, then what about calling upon naval warships to help safeguard the seas and escort those WFP ships carrying food to Somalia? After all, it takes less than three days to sail from Mombasa to Mogadishu's seaport, a couple of days to off-load cargo, and then another three days to steam home. Surely someone could assign a warship to shadow the freighter during this brief journey, right? Everyone's seen images of peacekeepers securing airports in places like Sarajevo and then protecting the convoys that carry humanitarian assistance. Putting aside any academic questions about the actual effectiveness of those peacekeeping operations, at least there was a protective military force.

Indeed, warships from a variety of nations do already patrol the waters off the Somali coast. For instance, there is a multinational task force known as Combined Task Force 150 (CTF 150), variously made up of warships from the United States, Canada, the

United Kingdom, France, Germany, Spain, the Netherlands, and Pakistan. Established not long after the 9/11 attacks, CTF 150 falls under the coordination of the U.S. Navy's Fifth Fleet regional command headquarters in Bahrain and deploys warships throughout the Gulf of Oman, Arabian Sea, Gulf of Aden, Red Sea, and as far down in the Indian Ocean as the Kenyan coast. Though its main role has been related to the global war on terror, the task force's maritime security operations mandate also includes safeguarding the seas in general, which clearly includes dealing with piracy and attacks on vessels.

There have been a couple of cases of the task force responding to pirate attacks along the Somali coast, such as when the American guided-missile destroyer USS *Winston S. Churchill* captured a gang of Somali pirates in January of 2006. And a few months later, on March 4, two coalition vessels received a distress call from a South Korean fishing trawler that was under attack. The Dutch frigate HNLMS *Zeven Provincien* and the American destroyer USS *Roosevelt* responded but were unable to save the Korean fishermen. The reason that these warships could not help is central to why vessels carrying humanitarian aid keep getting hijacked.

When Somali pirates commandeered the Korean trawler the *Dong Won 628,* her captors forced her crew to make haste toward the coastline. The pirates knew there were warships in the area, though they seemed to worry little about this as the naval vessels had been mostly ineffective to date. But even if armed ships were to respond to the Korean master's Mayday—which, in this case, they did—the Somalis knew they could count on international maritime law to protect them. All they had to do was get the pirated trawler into Somali territorial waters, behind the imaginary line that extends twelve nautical miles offshore.[4] As soon as the pirates crossed that line, with the American and Dutch warships in hot pursuit, they were safe. The naval vessels had to call off the chase, because they had no permission to enter Somali waters.

Under international maritime law, a warship from one country cannot enter the sovereign waters of another without the latter government's express consent. But Somalia has, in the words of the CIA World Factbook, "no permanent national government," no one to allow the coalition warships into these waters. Lacking that permission, warships chasing down pirates become akin to sheriffs racing after the bad guys until they hit the county line and have to give up the pursuit.

So even if a warship had been shadowing the MV *Semlow* back in June of 2005 as she made her way from Mombasa with a cargo of WFP rice in her holds, the naval vessel could only protect the freighter while she was in international waters. As soon as the *Semlow* crossed the twelve-mile limit, they'd be on their own. And the Somali pirates know this. It may sound bizarre, but foreign warships have to follow the rules, even in a place like Somalia, where there do not appear to be any. It's a central tenet in the Western concept of law and order that nations are supposed to respect the inviolable sovereignty of others. To disregard this is to potentially undermine elements of international law (and is something that has been argued about in recent years with respect to the invasion of Iraq that toppled Saddam Hussein). Until someone gives warships permission to enter Somali territorial waters, the patrols will have to concentrate on making the international waters safer for shipping. That's a serious challenge when the area to be monitored covers several million square miles. The chances of running across a pirate boat are somewhat remote, though the mere presence of international warships might, at least, give the sea robbers some pause.

One of the vessels currently on patrol in the Indian Ocean is the Canadian frigate HMCS *Toronto*, and I managed to briefly reach her executive officer via satellite phone while they were cruising a hundred nautical miles northwest of the Seychelles, heading toward Somalia. Lieutenant Commander Angus Topshee and the rest of the frigate's crew left Halifax two months earlier to join a small flotilla of NATO vessels on a circumnavigation of the African continent. The mission is meant to increase NATO's global presence and test the ability to send Western warships to far-off places in response to potential international crises.

"We do not have a mandate, per se, to deter piracy," says Lieutenant Commander Topshee over the phone, "but the crew is very aware of piracy. We've adopted an unusually high force protection posture because we're going to be traveling in a known area of piracy. Every nation is required under the United Nations Convention on the Law of the Sea to repress piracy on the high seas and each one of us is prepared and is trained and ready to take action if there's a pirate attack. And I'll be honest, the ship's company would like nothing more right now than to come across a pirate attack and do something about it."

Lieutenant Commander Topshee is also aware that the pirates are smart and know the rules of the game, such as the inability of foreign ships like HMCS *Toronto* to enter Somali territorial waters. While he tries to be diplomatic about this situation, I sense the warrior's frustration at not being able to fully do what he's been trained to do.

"You hear the stories—of ships being hijacked and people detained, aid intercepted—and, yeah, it bothers you. If you'd asked me this question just four or five years ago, I'd have said, 'No, pirates don't exist; this is nonsense.' But the reality is the modern-day pirate is alive and well, with a keen economic sense and with a vicious determination to get whatever money they can out of people.

We find it very frustrating that the generosity of nations can't get through to the people who so desperately need it."

The World Food Programme knows that naval escorts of any kind would go a long way to help convincing shipping firms to resume delivering humanitarian aid. In July of 2007, the head of the WFP and the head of the United Nations' International Maritime Organization made a joint call for concerted and coordinated action to be taken against pirates off the coast of Somalia, leading to the Security Council encouraging Member States to be 'vigilant' about Somali piracy.[5] And a few weeks after I met with Peter Smerdon in Nairobi, French president Nicolas Sarkozy told the same Security Council that his country would offer naval protection for WFP shipments. Early signs are that the international community is now ready to do something more forceful in combating the lawlessness raging on seas off Somalia, which is a good thing, because piracy isn't the only problem out there.

Down by the Likoni ferry terminal, just across the Kilundini Harbor from Mombasa Island, there's a fair breeze blowing in from the sea, warm and dry. Perched in the shade of a scrawny tree at an outdoor café, Andrew Mwangura squints at the cloudless sky. "Yes, I think a few more weeks before the monsoon ends. And, yes, I think the pirates will begin attacking again then."

Though most people associate the word "monsoon" with rain, it really refers to a seasonal wind, and in this part of the world, at this time of the year, we're nearing the end of the Southwest Monsoon season. It began back in May and should be over by October, when the strong winds and hot temperatures abate. Mwangura traces a map of East Africa in the dirt and explains why the Southwest Monsoon causes a reduction in piracy here.

"The winds come from the south and can be very strong, especially up by the Gulf [of Aden, along the northern coast of Somalia]. And because they blow from the ocean toward the land, this makes for strong seas along the coast. Waves can be high, water rough, and this is a problem if you are in a small boat, like the speedboats the pirates use. There can also be fog on the waters, sand and dust on the land, so the pirates prefer to wait until the monsoon season ends and the sea becomes calmer."

Somewhere northeast of us, groups of men are likely waiting for the season to change, eagerly looking forward to the chance to set out upon the seas and resume plundering. They'll be awaiting the orders from their leaders, other men who have a larger picture of who should be targeted, when, and where. Intelligence from a variety of foreign and domestic sources, such as spies and members of the Somali community here in Mombasa, will help the pirate leaders plan how they should use their assets. Weapons, equipment, and boats are likely being readied, for Somali sea robbers are among the most well-prepared maritime criminals at work today.

Pirates in Somalia are just one element in a group of well-organized criminal organizations that are the business and political elites of the country. They control huge parts of the economy, with interests in the agricultural, telecommunications, retail, banking, transportation, and fishing industries. From the intimate knowledge of the region that Andrew Mwangura has developed and the investigative work done by the United Nations Monitoring Group on Somalia, it's believed that there are four main pirate groups operating from the country.[6]

Across the border from Kenya is a gang that likes to call themselves the National Volunteer Coast Guard (NVCG). Believed to be under the command of warlord Garaad Mohamed, the NVCG is based primarily out of Kisimayo and prefers to operate close to shore, where they can prey upon small boats and fishing vessels. Farther up the coast, near Mogadishu, can be found the Marka groups, so named because they are based around the town of Marka. They operate farther offshore than the NVCG and engage in piracy, sea robbery, and smuggling, using vessels that in some cases have deck-mounted guns, and are allied to Sheikh Yusuf Mohamed Siad—also known as Yusuf Indohaadde, or Inda'ade—a warlord in the Lower Shabelle district. (It should be noted that Yusuf Mohamed Siad has gone to the media to deny that he is personally involved with piracy operations.)

In the northeastern part of the country is found what are called the Puntland groups, named after the semi-autonomous state in which they live. Most of these sea bandits are older men, drawing upon a tradition of piracy and smuggling that goes back centuries. These seem to be the country's "pirate elders," for it is believed that they have provided training to their brethren, including the largest group operating in Somali waters: the Somali Marines.

The Somali Marines (the ones who hijacked the *Semlow*) are the most-feared gang in the region, with the most sophisticated organization. Their main operating base is the coastal town of Haradheere, though they have ranged up and down the seaside carrying out their attacks. The group also likes to style itself the Defenders of Somali Territorial Waters and is thought to be loyal to the powerful regional warlord Abdi Mohamed Afweyne. No one knows how many the gang employs pirating, but the warlord can call upon hundreds of willing men and the group has developed a highly ordered structure, with a fleet admiral, admiral, vice admiral, and head of financial affairs. (The vice admiral—and head of marine operations—is believed to be "General Gray," the same man who spirited the *Semlow*'s captain and chief engineer ashore for a few days.)

This is the group that has become so adept at hijacking vessels in the waters off Somalia, but along with their pirate comrades they, too, are expanding the scope of their maritime operations. In the vacuum created by a nonexistent central government, the warlords of Somalia have realized the potential to exploit all the resources within their ocean domains, including the offshore fishing industry.

"People have been coming to fish here for centuries," says Mwangura. "The fighting in Somalia has not stopped that. Instead, some people realized this could be an advantage. Somalis and foreign fishermen both understood this. Some fishermen, they think there are no rules there; they can just sail their boat there, catch whatever they want, and go home to sell it. They do not realize that the pirates are waiting for them."

Proportionally, a higher number of fishermen have been held hostage by Somali pirates than other mariners, attacked as far out as 210 nautical miles from shore. Because fishing vessels are slower and smaller, with a lower freeboard—the distance between the waterline and the deck—they make for easy victims. On a single day in 2005, Somali pirates managed to hijack three Taiwanese trawlers and hold their crews hostage. However, Mwangura tells me that he is emotionally torn when it comes to the attacks on fishermen.

"Most of these men are not well paid, such as the ones from Asia and Africa. Fishing is a very hard job, and piracy only makes it worse. So they are the most vulnerable." He pauses for a moment, choosing his words carefully. "But many of these boats are fishing illegally. Well, the majority are, okay? They bring this on themselves; they are a part of the problem."

Illegal fishing is a global problem of epic proportions. According to the world's oldest environmental network, the International Union for Conservation of Nature (IUCN), the annual worldwide value of illegal, unregulated, and unreported fishing is estimated at between $4.9 and 9.5 billion.[7] The Swiss-based organization also calculates that 30 percent of this fishing goes on in international waters, where national regulations do not apply. It occurs in every ocean, sea, lake, and river on the planet, and Africa has seen more than its fair share of it along its continental coasts. Yet few fishing grounds have been so lucrative as those off Somalia.

Those waters are rich in tuna, shark, shrimp, lobster, and swordfish, among other species, and draw boats from as far away as Western Europe and the Far East. Some of these just show up and hope that the pirates won't notice their presence. But others have made "arrangements" with the warlords, essentially paying security bribes to avoid the fishing boats' being attacked. The Somalis prefer to think of these fees as fishing permits, and charge anywhere from $50,000 to $150,000 to allow a single vessel the "right" to work the seas.[8] This collusion between pirate warlords and commercial fishing enterprises angers Mwangura.

"Right now there are fifty-two foreign vessels fishing the waters off Somalia, twenty of which are Spanish. Let us assume that a third of all those vessels . . . no, let us be cautious and assume a quarter of them have paid the Somalis for these 'fishing permits.' And let us say that each boat's owner—the fishing tycoons—paid the smallest amount possible, say $50,000. Okay, so that becomes over half a million dollars that the warlords are making this month so that someone can eat fish in Europe or Asia. Is that right?"

Of course it isn't. Lining the pockets of warlords and their cronies is never right. The rapacious nature of offshore fishing is well known in the developed world, where we have witnessed the collapse of viable fisheries in such places as the northwest Atlantic, the Mediterranean Sea, and the southeast Pacific. And these are waters where regulations and protection are in greater evidence than other areas, such as the Horn of Africa. With around eight hundred foreign fishing vessels working the seas off Somalia every year, according to Mwangura, the financial incentives for all concerned are immense.

"The way things are now," he says, "the profits from illegal fishing go to the warlords, the pirate gangs, and the militias on land. You have heard the term 'blood diamonds,' yes? For the diamonds that come from conflict zones, like Liberia or the Congos? Well, as far as I am concerned, when someone in Europe eats tuna from Somalia, they are eating 'blood fish.' Their meal is helping to maintain the way things are in Somalia. That [tuna] steak will help pay for weapons or ammunition, and increase the suffering of the people. This is wrong, but no one seems to care. The seas there are bloody, bloody waters for so many reasons."

After years of brutalizing their fellow Somalis, haranguing passing vessels, interrupting the delivery of aid shipments, and extorting vast sums from foreign shippers and fishing enterprises, you might think there would be little more left for the warlords' pirate gangs to capitalize upon. But of course, you'd be wrong.

For Somali gangs, the Indian Ocean is both a source of bounty and a vast expanse of emptiness. Or, rather, that emptiness is another potential region to be marketed to foreigners, exploited as an appealing garbage dump for Western waste. UNEP and several other nongovernmental groups had known that the seas off Somalia had become a dumping ground for waste as far back as the early 1990s, after the country slipped into anarchy. Reports filtered in that European companies were paying for the "right" to discard garbage in the seas, but there was little definitive proof since the evidence lay beneath fathoms of water.

But shortly after the December 2004 tsunami that ravaged the Indian Ocean, an unsettling result of illegally dumped waste washed up on the beaches of eastern Somalia. Hazardous-waste containers came ashore as a result of the tidal forces of the tsunami, spilling a toxic mess that no one expected. As the waves receded, they left behind steel drums and concrete containers filled with heavy metals and radioactive waste. Uranium, lead, cadmium, mercury, garbage from hospitals, it all splayed across the shoreline and soon began affecting local people. As UNEP discovered, hundreds of people became sick in the aftermath, with symptoms such as skin infections, mouth and abdominal bleeding, and other problems caused by the various wastes.[9] The effects of the release of such toxic waste on communities ashore are both an immediate problem and one that will linger for years to come, similar to the long-term impact created by chemical weapons.

For years, rumors have placed the source of much of this garbage as being Western Europe. In the early 1990s, Italian journalist Ilaria Alpi investigated what was going on in Somalia, trying to see if there was any basis to the whispers that Mafia-run firms were sending industrial waste to the Indian Ocean to be disposed of. Tragically, she was killed, along with her cameraman, while seeking the truth in Somalia, and so the questions remain ominously unanswered.

According to Andrew Mwangura, the warlords charge as little as $2.50 per ton for the "right" to dump waste off the Somali coast, while it costs about $250 to properly dispose of the same ton in Europe. At this bargain basement rate, it's not likely the dumping will cease anytime soon, and the prospects that anyone will step forward and offer to clean up the mess are currently nil.

"These ships that come from Europe, they are garbage cowboys," Mwangura tells me. "Clean up the ocean? Who? The Italian Mafia? NATO? They do not care about Somalia, about Africa, about anything, just like the fishing boats, with their blood fishing. The West has an interest in what is going on up there [in Somalia], but not the way most would think. There is no real effort to bring stability to Somalia, help the people there, or make the seas safe.

No, the real interest is in maintaining a source of inexpensive seafood and a good place to dump garbage."

Andrew Mwangura is a patient and thoughtful man, but while we wait for the ferry in Likoni a flash of anger crosses his face. Yes, he understands that it is Somalis themselves who have torn their country apart through greed and violence. But they have had a lot of help from the outside world. The weapons the pirates brandish— those Kalashnikovs and rocket-propelled grenades—are not manufactured in Somalia. Nor are the speedboats and engines and radios. The money to purchase weapons and supplies can come from foreign fishing fleets willing to pay off the warlords, transferring the sums through international banking systems. And the decision to toss hazardous waste into those same waters is only partially made by the Somali warlords.

It's easy to discount the situation off Somalia because it occurs in a region most of us consider far-off. Yet the way that piracy has developed in Somalia is another reason that we should all be concerned about maritime crime. Unchecked, it has the ability to evolve from small-scale petty theft into a well-organized entity that affects political, environmental, and economic control on national and international levels, becoming a prominent threat to state security.

A recurring problem in recent years for the United States, Great Britain, Canada, and other coalition forces has been how to deal with insurgency movements in Iraq and Afghanistan. Trying to combat these groups has swallowed up billions of dollars and the lives of tens of thousands, civilian and military. With Iraq, no one appeared to foresee the growth of these armed groups in the wake of the invasion that toppled Saddam Hussein, but there has been a lot of thought put into the problem since then.

One of the most incisive analyses of this comes from Dr. Max Manwaring, a professor of military strategy at the U.S. Army War College at Carlisle Barracks Garrison in southern Pennsylvania. Picking up the work done by several other academics, the retired army colonel began looking at the growth of insurgent groups and noted that they often followed a pattern that was similar to the ways street gangs evolved in places like the United States and Latin America.

Dr. Manwaring has observed three distinct evolutionary phases that gangs mature through in their criminal lives. Most begin as turf-oriented petty thieves, the type of gangsters who might control a neighborhood and provide "insurance" to local business. If you pay the protection money, your windows don't get smashed and your store doesn't get robbed. After a time, these opportunistic gangs begin to realize they can expand their local operations, extorting money from the next neighborhood over or getting involved with other lucrative ventures such as drugs and prostitution.

These second-generation gangs become more business oriented, seeking greater financial gain for themselves. They may forge alliances with other groups, like drug traffickers or organized-crime syndicates, becoming enforcers or de facto mercenaries in the pay of these other entities until such time that the gang believes they do not need to play second fiddle anymore.

"The third-generation gang is the most politically astute," says Manwaring, "with a clear and implicit political agenda. They want to control specific pieces of territory or even the entire government of a country. They don't necessarily want to replace the government, but they want to have greater control so that their criminal enterprises can operate without interference. This is often where people begin to take gangs seriously, for they often usurp the powers of the state. Depending on the evolutionary development of the insurgent or the gang, the intent is to control territory and the people in it, which is the definition of sovereignty. So if an insurgent group, a warlord, whatever, exercises sovereign powers of the state within the territories he controls, he's impinging upon the sovereignty of the state."

It's easy to see how Manwaring's definitions of generational gangs can be applied to Somali pirates, with the largest—the Somali Marines—now wielding what amounts to political control over vast expanses of water. Those pirates who steal from a ship and then go off to sell whatever they get their hands on, they're really first-generation gangs. As they go further—stealing the whole ship, for instance—that's an expansion into a second-generation gang. And when they begin handing out fishing licenses and negotiating with foreigners for the right to dump waste in "their waters," they have morphed into the last category.

According to Dr. Manwaring, pirates like the ones in Somalia need to be looked at in the same way we look at insurgents in Iraq—as a potential threat to our national security. Sooner or later, a failed state has got to be dealt with. Failure to do so can lead to it developing into a military dictatorship, criminal state, or narco-state.

"Piracy can most definitely be a form of unconventional, non-state war, which can lead to the deposing of governments," argues Manwaring. "People misuse a term: they call places 'lawless' or 'ungovernable.' That's not true. They're not lawless or ungoverned; they're just not governed by the democratic state, if it has such a thing. They're governed by the warlord or drug baron or the insurgent leader. These are the ones who fill whatever void has been created by political instability and who then thrive. Warlords today have the same power as a baron in 1300s Europe. Gangs, such as pirate gangs, have the ability to bend politicians and governments to their will through coercion, intimidation, and bribery."

This has certainly been the case in Somalia—with one notably brief exception. In 2006 there was a dramatic decrease in pirate incidents along the coast that was directly related to the rise of the Islamic Courts Union (ICU, also known as the Union of Islamic Courts and the Council of Islamic Courts). Fed up with the country's endemic corruption and infighting, this loose coalition of clerics, Islamic militias, and other concerned Somalis managed to toss the warlords out of Mogadishu in June 2006 and force the internationally recognized TFG to flee south. The ICU expanded its control over almost half the country, seeking to reimpose a sense of order in the areas they controlled (which included the imposition of Sharia law). They banned the use and sale of khat, the popular drug, and sought to crack down on corruption.

One of the ICU's goals was to stamp out piracy along the Somali coastline, and they made it quite clear that anyone engaging in the practice would face severe repercussions. With their warlord bosses on the run and facing the prospect of certain death at the hands of the ICU, Somali pirates gave up their marauding ways; there were only a couple of reported incidents while the ICU was in control. The clerics had managed to do what no one else had and address a serious criminal endeavor, rather like the way the Taliban tackled opium production in Afghanistan.

In the post-911 environment, the prospect of a conservative Islamic government in Somalia did not sit well with many in the West. Though the ICU managed to bring some stability to parts of the country, the shadow of Afghanistan under the Taliban loomed within the minds of strategic thinkers in foreign cities. There were fears that some factions with the ICU had ties to Al Qaeda, and many did not want to see Somalia become an Islamist state. So in December of 2006 TFG forces, aided by the Ethiopian military (and with the tacit approval of most Western countries), managed to overpower the ICU and return Somalia to . . . lawlessness. Within weeks of the defeat of the ICU, pirate attacks resumed.

So how, then, do we deal with piracy in a place like Somalia? Clearly we can't rely on the current "government" to curtail it, nor should we expect the warlords to undergo a magical moral transformation anytime soon. We know that fighting crime is like fighting a forest fire, always easier to combat in its early stages. Putting the first-generation pirate genie back in the bottle is exceedingly difficult when it has transformed into a third-generation colossus.

"This is an issue that governments in general don't want to deal with," says Dr. Manwaring, referring to the lack of response to gangs in their nascent phases. "We are not equipped to deal with asymmetrical war, nontraditional in tone. Many of our leaders are still thinking in terms of a Westphalian concept of sovereignty and aggression, wherein uniformed members of a state military force cross the inviolate borders of another state's. Gangs—including pirates—do not operate that way."

Pirates in Somalia are really maritime guerrillas, and to truly combat their threat requires a new way of looking at them. Warships patrolling up and down the coastline are only effective in international waters, so perhaps the time has come to redefine the limits of national maritime sovereignty. The presence of foreign fishing boats, operating with or without "licenses," only enriches the warlords, so perhaps the time has come for a moratorium on all fishing off Somalia. The pirate bases ashore are known and pose a threat, so perhaps the TFG needs to be pressured to eradicate them.

"Will the United States intervene in Somalia?" wonders Manwaring. "I'd say it's not likely. I know President Bush made a statement about piracy, but I'm not sure whether you could say it signaled a change in strategy and I don't know whether it even mentioned Somalia.[10] And if the U.S. doesn't do it [intervene in Somalia], neither will anyone else. If the U.S. can't deal with gangs on its own territory, how can it be expected to deal with insurgents or gangs—or pirates—in a foreign nation? 'Not very well' is the answer. The United States has no real credibility in this regard. In my view, the gang problem, the piracy problem, reverts down to questions of poverty, disease, and all kinds of stuff that creates unrest and the willingness for young people to do this sort of thing because the alternatives are so limited."

And then there's the "Iraq factor." Iraq has had a huge effect on the way the United States and many other nations look at crisis situations in places like Somalia. As Manwaring puts it, "I think it's going to be a long time before the United States does something like this again, intervening in another nation's sovereignty—that's an act of war. Unless it's a really, really serious situation, we'll just let it pass."

Will it take another attack on a WFP vessel or a passenger ship to mobilize the concerted efforts of the industrialized world to stamp out Somali piracy once and for all? It's doubtful, because piracy off Somalia is just not important enough. Instead, vessels will continue to be attacked, shipowners will continue to pay ransoms and security bribes, fishermen will buy illegal licenses, and waste management firms will maintain their relationships with the warlords, since none of these are considered to be a threat to anyone's national security, regardless of what you may think. In the West's current global mind-set, there's really only one thing that will cause leaders to sit up and pay attention. And as the ICU's rise and fall confirmed, that's the threat of terrorism.

7

SIX DEGREES OF SEPARATION

By God, the youths of God are preparing for you things that would fill your hearts with terror and target your economic lifeline until you stop your oppression and aggression.

—OSAMA BIN LADEN, OCTOBER 2002

THE HEAT OF Mombasa is not oppressive, certainly not like other parts of Africa, but it can still be uncomfortable here on the coast as the Southwest Monsoon season wanes. Normally one's hotel room would provide some refuge as long as the air conditioner functions. My unit does, but it's about as quiet as a trash compactor, so I invariably shut the thing off when I go to sleep and rely on the small ceiling fan and an open window to cool me down at night.

On this particular morning I rise from a fitful sleep around 4:00 A.M., covered in a clammy layer of sweat with the sheets thrown aside. The power's gone out and neither the fan nor the cranky air conditioner is working. There's a slight breeze coming from outside, cool and inviting, though laced with a slightly mechanical smell to it. Still, as I stand before the window the air is as refreshing as the coolest drink on the hottest day and the gentle breeze dries the sweat off my body.

There is no sound outside the open window, no tooting horns or revving engines from the street below. Deciding sleep is unlikely, I pull on some clothes and head downstairs to go for a walk. Mombasa is quiet at this hour, with hardly anyone on the streets as I go along Nkrumah Road down toward Fort Jesus to watch the sun rise over the Indian Ocean. The early-morning silence seems delicate and I walk as lightly as possible in case I might awaken those still slumbering, feeling like someone tiptoeing through another's home.

The Portuguese fortress commands the entrance to the old harbor, its thick coral walls awaiting yet another daybreak just as they have for over four hundred years. Through a small portico I end up beside the mouth of the harbor, with nary a soul in sight. It may not be the best vantage point to observe day breaking, but as I sit on a rock with my back to the fortress's battlements the early-morning air is cool and peaceful. I'm just beginning to nod off when the moment is interrupted by the gentle sounds of the day's first calls to prayers coming from a nearby mosque.

Through the predawn darkness, I follow the muezzin's recorded call to a narrow street and a tiny white stucco building where a couple of men in long white robes and skullcaps greet one another and go inside. If it weren't for its small tower and the speakers atop broadcasting the call, you would think the mosque was just a residence or shop of some sort. As I stand outside the mosque, a young man scurries up the street, nods my way with a shy smile, and hurries to prayer.

Leaving the faithful to their worship, I meander through the peaceful laneways of the Old Town. Many of the buildings have been painted in pleasant pastel shades of pink, yellow, green, or cream, with timbered second-floor balconies overhead and ornately carved wooden doors below. Down by Sir Mbarak Hinawy Road, there's a strange little shrine erected on a telephone pole that catches my eye. It consists of an old clock, a one-legged doll, some plastic flowers, and a hand-painted sign reading: "Liverpool You'll never walk alone." This is the anthem for the soccer team from the hometown of the Beatles, and the shrine is a testament to the popularity of professional sports here, especially of foreign clubs like Liverpool.

Arriving back on Digo Road, I'm met by a city already awakened and anxious, with people heading to and fro to begin their days. The sun's first rays are creeping ever westward, illuminating crowds of students making their way to the university and office workers heading for the various commercial and government buildings in the downtown core. At a corner of Moi Avenue, one of Mombasa's main thoroughfares, I hear a noise and look down a side street to see a row of minivans rushing toward me like stampeding wild animals. Three abreast, the minivans—called *matatus* here—toot and honk as their drivers gesture for pedestrians to get out of the way. It takes less than thirty seconds for the herd to dissolve into the flow of traffic on Moi Avenue and then they're gone.

Street sellers have already set up their displays of wares on the sidewalks, carefully arranging prepaid calling cards, ballpoint pens, and cigarettes with brand names like Rooster and Sportsman. A kiosk offers magazines and newspapers, and among the various headlines I spy repeated references to Al Qaeda. Intrigued, I buy a copy of the local English-language paper to read over breakfast. Before making it back to the hotel, though, I've digested the article and realized today is the anniversary of that notorious attack on America by Osama bin Laden. Today is September 11.

While we in the West tend to think that Al Qaeda's campaign of terror has been aimed primarily at Europe and North America, Kenya has been the scene of at least three incidents by the shadowy group since 1998, two of which were here on the coast. The most devastating was the destruction of the U.S. embassy in Nairobi by a truck bomb on August 7, 1998, killing over two hundred people and injuring something like four thousand others, mainly Kenyans. (This attack coincided with a similar bombing of the American embassy in Dar es Salaam, Tanzania, which killed eleven and injured eighty-five.) Then, in late November 2002, suicide bombers drove their car into the front doors of a hotel just north of Mombasa, killing thirteen, while accomplices fired missiles at an Israeli passenger jet taking off from the airport, narrowly missing the target.

The attacks had a serious impact on the Kenyan economy, scaring off the tourists who spend so much money here. They did come back eventually, but the terrorists shattered the image of Kenya as a peaceful oasis in Africa. In the wake of the attacks, security forces from Kenya, the United States, and other nations sought to determine the strength of Al Qaeda in the country, which has a large Muslim population that lives mainly along the Indian Ocean coast. However, few Kenyan Muslims share the extremist views of Osama bin Laden and most analysts believe that the terrorists who carried out the attacks were foreigners who slipped into the country, likely from Somalia. There are only two ways the terrorists and their explosives could have been transported to Kenya. Driving overland from Somalia was possible and the border between the two countries is known to be quite porous, but there is still the risk that Kenyan border guards or the military might be present. The second way Al Qaeda could have moved their operatives and matériel into Kenya was by ship, and the likely entry point would have been Mombasa. A fishing boat could have made port, ostensibly to replenish her stores, and a couple of terrorists could have easily made their way ashore and disappeared, along with their explosives. From my own experience down at the docks, no one ever searched small vehicles leaving the port, and after nightfall the security was less than strict. So there's a distinct possibility that Islamist terrorists made their way here by ship in order to carry out their deadly attacks.

They may have walked down the street in front of me, visited a nearby mosque, bought a soda from one of the kiosks set up by my hotel. And that's the fear that gestates within me while standing on Moi Avenue in Mombasa this sunny morning: Terrorists have come calling once. Could they come again?

Undoubtedly, the boogeyman of the West—since 9/11—has been the terrorist, that amorphous entity previously thought to practice his dark crafts in foreign parts but who now appears to menace our very homelands. With the hijacking of four airliners on a warm Tuesday morning in September, a global war on terror or, more correctly, a global war against terrorism began in earnest. Led by the United States, it soon involved Canada, Great Britain, Germany, Spain, and dozens of other nations. Whether correct or not, many felt that their world had suddenly become a much more dangerous place thanks to the likes of Osama bin Laden and that a new peril had appeared out of nowhere.

Terrorists have existed in one form or another for centuries, in all parts of the globe, and their historical activities have become a part of our modern lexicon: Zealots were Jewish rebel groups who harassed the Romans in biblical times; Assassins was the name given to a sect of eleventh-century Shia Muslims who targeted political leaders for death; Thugees—who gave us the word "thug"—were members of a Hindu cult that engaged in ritual murders with the intent of terrifying their victims. And it was the French who bequeathed the very term "terrorism" to us, as a result of the revolutionary *régime de la terreur* that saw forty thousand people guillotined in 1793–1794.

Anarchists, extremists, fundamentalists, and rebels have killed presidents, kings, and tsars, ignited a world war, and terrorized billions over the course of thousands of years. Even the United States has had some of its own terrorist problems to deal with, such as the Ku Klux Klan and the Oklahoma City bombers, though none created quite the psychological impact Al Qaeda did in September of 2001. Because of the global nature of Al Qaeda's attacks, Americans were no longer immune to the threat that had plagued so many other nations. In today's world, it is a simple reality that whatever affects the United States very often concerns much of the rest of the planet. Like it or hate it, air travel has never been the same since September 2001 as a direct consequence of Al Qaeda's actions against the United States.

Though the 9/11 attacks did not mark the start of Al Qaeda's operational efforts against its perceived enemies, it did force Western nations to reassess the threat in a new light. With the bombings in Kenya and Tanzania, followed by those in the United States, Madrid (March 2004), London (July 2005), and Bali (October 2002 and then October 2005), among other places, it has become impossible to say where the next attack will occur. We know terrorists have attacked airplanes, hotels, commuter trains, buses, subways, and office buildings, but forgotten by many is the way ships have fallen prey to these criminals.

Lost amid the worries about airport security or the vulnerability of public transit systems is the fact that terrorist groups have, since the early 1990s, engaged in numerous attacks on shipping and used vessels as strike platforms on numerous occasions. The last decade alone has seen maritime terrorism increase to levels never before seen, with dozens of assaults being staged by known groups. Palestinian radicals, Tamil separatists, fanatical Indonesian and Filipino Islamists, and Al Qaeda have all used the seas to spread fear. They have attacked supertankers, cargo ships, oceangoing ferries, fishing boats, and naval vessels, killing hundreds.

Just as the existence of modern-day piracy is unknown to most people, so, too, is the extent to which terrorist groups are using the world's waterways to further their various agendas. The scope of maritime terrorist activity is an extremely touchy subject for many in the seafaring and security communities: in some quarters it is dismissed as an overblown, media-hyped red herring, while in others it is considered the next threat to national security. The arguments inevitably center on assessing the degree to which maritime terrorists pose a real and present danger and what responses are suitable to deal with the problem. But it's not like it's a new problem.

Modern terrorist groups have been using the sea to further political agendas since 1961, when a Portuguese cruise ship was hijacked in the Caribbean. Now a mere footnote in the history of maritime terror, that incident involved the liner *Santa Maria*, whose six hundred passengers had just embarked from the port of La Guaira in Venezuela when a group of Portuguese and Spanish exiles commandeered the vessel. These self-styled rebels were seeking to promote the overthrow of dictatorships in their homelands and held the liner and her passengers and crew hostage for eleven days before surrendering to the Brazilian navy. (A more memorable incident was the 1985 hijacking of the cruise ship *Achille Lauro* in the eastern Mediterranean Sea by members of the Palestine Liberation Front, in which the terrorists killed an elderly wheelchair-bound passenger and dumped his body overboard.)

About the only thing that most experts, analysts, and informed observers can agree on today is that there is a wide variety of ways that terrorists *could* use the seas. They might commandeer an oil tanker and sink her in a major shipping lane or place a bomb in a container bound for some Western port; a passenger vessel could be hijacked in order to hold the passengers hostage or suicide bombers may use small boats laden with explosives to attack a ship. The central argument of those who say the issue is overblown is that terrorists do not have the operational capability to carry out seaborne attacks. These analysts feel that the degree of seafaring proficiency required to mount an attack on the oceans, let alone pilot a vessel, is simply beyond the scope of most terror groups. While that may be true of the Taliban in landlocked Afghanistan or insurgents in urban Iraqi centers, this overlooks the fact that there are at least half a dozen other factions of terrorist organizations currently engaged in maritime actions, groups with both the seagoing expertise and the will to use those skills ruthlessly to further their political goals.

At least superficially, there may be a nexus between piracy and terrorism. Could it be that while we've been watching the skies for the next attack, terrorists have been looking to the seas?

In a coffee shop not far from London's Houses of Parliament, I put the question to an international security expert: "Just how big a threat is seaborne terrorism?"

"It's a fifty-fifty proposition," he answers. "By that I mean that it has equal parts of credibility and distortion."

The man is a former military officer who would prefer to remain anonymous for a variety of professional reasons, but I know that his perspectives are considered important by many.

"Trying to assess the reality of maritime terrorism has not been easy, for a variety of reasons. There are a lot of people trying to ramp up the threat of this, if I can be frank. People who play on the fears of things. For a period [after 9/11], some would have had us believe that bin Laden was about to strike at any moment from the sea. He or Al Qaeda were supposed to have control of a number of freighters that could deliver the next horrific attack. This [conclusion] came from looking at ownership records of various ships, and, yes, there were ships that fell under the mantle of companies that the bin Laden family controlled. Were they 'Al Qaeda's navy'? Not likely. Were they potential assets [to the terrorists]? Absolutely."

The problem as he sees it is that a *potential* threat easily morphed into a *real* threat in the months and years following 9/11, but the difference between the two is crucial.

"The reaction to terror attacks since 2001 has been fueled by fear," says the security analyst, and he doesn't just mean among the civilian population. "Everyone in the intelligence community was worried they might miss the next one. You know, the story went that no one saw the attacks coming, though we now know there was credible intelligence indicating otherwise.[1] Regardless, every possibility, every potential threat, had to be looked at in the immediate aftermath. That's what intelligence agencies are supposed to do. But there was so much disorganization and mismanagement of resources going on at the time that instead of filtering the information and focusing on the important, probable threats, a hugely wide net was cast. Land, sea, and air. Foreign and domestic. This is why we call it a global war on terror."

As he explains it, government agencies and military branches in dozens of countries were suddenly ramped up into a state of activity unheard of in decades and everyone had to look engaged. Now that the threats to various nations appeared very real, money was no longer a problem for organizations that had seen their funding reduced through the 1990s. New equipment, new weapons, increased manpower, active missions, covert missions—the months and years after September 11, 2001, were a busy time for anyone involved in national security issues in the United States, the United Kingdom, and many other countries.

By October of 2001, the United States and Great Britain were bombing Afghanistan, and it wasn't long before Special Forces units from the United States, the United Kingdom, and Canada were scouring the area for Al Qaeda.[2] In March of 2002, Operation Anaconda began, the invasion of Afghanistan by U.S. and coalition forces. If you were a soldier or airman or commando or spy, this was your shining moment of glory. If you were a sailor? Well, things were just a bit less dramatic.

"Naval and maritime elements were the 'poor cousins' during this period," says the British security expert. "It was the forces on the ground [in Afghanistan] and the pilots in the air who were getting all the attention. So there was a certain, um, pressure for them to show their effectiveness in the war on terror, their utility. It didn't take a genius to realize that terrorists could attack from the sea, so while others were slogging it through the mountains of Afghanistan, maritime-concerned people emphasized the seaborne threat. And they had good reasons for this, given the attacks on the *Cole* and the *Limburg*."

He refers to two of Al Qaeda's now often forgotten, but treacherously successful, marine operations that bookended the 9/11 incidents. Al Qaeda's first major attack on the water happened in 2000, when an American guided-missile destroyer was targeted. With a crew of 338 officers and men, the USS *Cole* was among the most modern vessels in the American fleet, a billion-dollar fighting platform that had been launched less than five years earlier. As she was refueling in the Yemeni port of Aden on October 12, a speedboat was seen approaching her port side. Unbeknownst to the *Cole*'s crew, the small craft was packed with 270 kilograms of C-4 explosives and piloted by two Saudi suicide terrorists. The impact of the explosion blew a forty-foot hole in the destroyer's hull and killed seventeen American sailors, a stunning attack on a warship in peacetime that was without precedent.

Osama bin Laden was apparently so pleased with the attack on the USS *Cole* that he sat down and put pen to paper to compose a poem about the incident, reciting it at his son's wedding in early 2001:

> *A destroyer: even brave fear its might.*
> *It inspires horror in the harbor and in the open sea.*
> *She sails into the waves*
> *Flanked by arrogance, haughtiness and false power.*
> *To her doom she moves slowly.*
> *A dinghy awaits her, riding the waves.*[3]

Less than a year after the attack on the USS *Cole*, bin Laden's fanatical followers were piloting passenger planes on suicide missions against targets in New York and Washington, leading to increased surveillance of the skies. But the Al Qaeda leader had not forgotten about the seas, and sometime after September 11, 2001, he again turned his attention to Western shipping interests in the same region where the USS *Cole* had been bombed.

The attack on the American destroyer was the brainchild of bin Laden's associate Abd al-Rahim al-Nashiri, a Saudi national who became known as the Prince of the Sea and was Al Qaeda's chief of operations for the Arabian Peninsula. Tasked by bin Laden to attack U.S. or other Western interests in the waters off the peninsula, al-Nashiri had been looking to strike at oil tankers when the USS *Cole* stumbled into his lap. The success of the attack on the USS *Cole* brought al-Nashiri an elevated status within Al Qaeda and he then began to develop some even more audacious plans of attack, including striking at shipping in the Persian Gulf's strategic Strait of Hormuz and in the seas off Gibraltar.

In the late summer of 2002, as his Afghan base of operations lay in ruins, bin Laden gave al-Nashiri the go-ahead to mount a second terror attack against Western maritime targets. It was October of that year when Al Qaeda operatives set their sights on the French super-tanker MV *Limburg* as she approached the Ash Shihr oil terminal outside the port of Mukalla, 350 miles east of Aden. This immense vessel was carrying four hundred thousand barrels of crude oil in her tanks when another pair of suicide attackers rammed their small boat into the *Limburg*. The attack killed one mariner on the tanker (and both Yemeni terrorists), injured twenty-five other crew and spilled about ninety thousand barrels of crude into the Gulf of Aden. In the immediate aftermath of the *Limburg* attack, Yemen saw port calls by merchant vessels virtually cease, creating an economic impact on the small Arabian nation that was measured in the billions of dollars.[4]

Unfortunately for the so-called Prince of the Sea, his campaign of terror was short-lived: a month after the *Limburg* attack, al-Nashiri was captured in Aden and handed over to American officials who transferred him to their detention facilities in Guantánamo Bay, where he remains as this book is being written.

These two marine attacks became known within the maritime security community as "their 9/11." While far fewer victims died in the Aden attacks than had perished on September 11, the events were considered visible examples of an expanded campaign by Al Qaeda against the West that needed to be addressed.

As the British security expert puts it, "The question became, 'Where would the next attack occur? And how can we prevent it?' I'm speaking here not only of maritime threats. Remember, it was a chaotic time: There were threat assessments coming in from everywhere and reassessments of prior incidents being scrutinized. Planes, ships, trains—everything could be a weapon for terrorists, or so it seemed. So a great amount of effort was expended to prevent [bin Laden] from striking against America or Britain by sea. New initiatives were put in place to increase port security; information was gathered on vessels and crews arriving and leaving ports; armed patrol boats could be seen patrolling harbors. It was all about us showing that our defenses were up."

One of the things that created some anxiety in the world of security analysis around this time involved the hijacking of the *Dewi Madrim*. The thirty-nine-hundred-ton tanker was commandeered by ten attackers while sailing through the Strait of Malacca in March of 2003. For about an hour, the boarders had complete control of the tanker. They made no ransom demands of the crew of the vessel, no threats to remove anyone, and no contact with any confederates. Instead, they appeared to want to sail the tanker through the busy waterway for a bit and then leave, taking with them some money, equipment, and technical manuals.

To a number of observers, this sounded an awful lot like terrorists masquerading as pirates, using the *Dewi Madrim* to make a test run and see what their seamanship skills were like. It appeared somewhat reminiscent of the way the 9/11 terrorists had practiced their flight skills in Florida before attacking New York and Washington.

So what, I wonder, is the British expert's take on the *Dewi Madrim* incident? He sighs, having clearly been asked this question before.

"Well, how many reports, analyses, and conjectures came out of that one? Dozens. And, to be fair, at the time it had certain signs that something was different about the incident. Or so we thought. As presented in the media and in some 'informed sources,' it looked like a bunch of guys interested in only steering a ship through a major waterway, with no intent on docking it or hijacking it. So people wondered if [the attackers] wanted to use the ship as a platform, you know, aim it at another ship or blow her up in the middle of the shipping lane, blocking a major trade route. But looking at it now, I think it's safe to say they were just pirates, not terrorists. I base that not on the actual incident but on the fact that since then—since 2003—there has *not* been an attack carried out by anyone, in the Malacca Strait or elsewhere, that has shown these people used any lessons from the *Dewi Madrim* to then execute a successful terror attack on the sea."

The man takes a moment to sip his coffee, stare at the tourists milling about outside the café, and think about what he's seen over the last half-dozen years.

"Americans like big ideas: if there's an attack by four guys on a target, they assume there must be a vast network behind them. So, by extension, the [*Dewi Madrim*] must have been a harbinger of worse to come, the tip of the iceberg. We in the U.K. like smaller ideas: if four guys are up to something, there must be only two more out there. The reality is somewhere in between. And the reality is that the maritime terror threat is not Al Qaeda. It's other groups."

He gestures at the tourists outside the coffee shop and says, "Ask any of them about Abu Sayyaf or the Sea Tigers and see what they have to say, see if they've even heard of them. If someone from the West—from Britain or America or Canada—isn't being threatened, it's not seen as an issue. Since the *Limburg* attack [in 2002], Al Qaeda has not mounted a single verified attack against any major [maritime] target. Does that mean our defensive posture is working? Perhaps . . . probably. But has maritime terrorism gone down since the attacks [of 9/11]? Not at all."

I realize he's right on all counts. While we've been obsessed with worrying about Al Qaeda, Osama bin Laden, and where they'll strike at us next, we've forgotten the other terror groups who lurk out there. They rarely impact our Western world, leaving a sense that maybe the seas are safe from the threat. However, since this century began there have been more incidents on the seas carried out by known terror groups than ever before. Hundreds have died. Just not Westerners.

Manila's commercial waterfront can be a confusing place at the best of times, with its many wharves busy loading and unloading all kinds of commercial vessels day and night. On a warm evening in late February of 2004, the scene at Pier Four, in the North Harbor, was even more chaotic than usual as hundreds of people milled about, preparing for the departure of the overnight ferry to the islands of Bacolod and Davao. The ferry systems in the Philippines are the lifeblood of a nation that is composed of over seven thousand islands, moving millions of people back and forth every year.

The vessel tied up alongside the pier that night was the *Super-Ferry 14*, a modern ship built in 2001 that could carry a thousand passengers and three hundred vehicles. She was 155 meters (550 feet) long, painted bright white, and offered restaurants, a karaoke bar, a business center, and other amenities to keep passengers busy as she made her way to the southern islands of the archipelago. In the hours before her scheduled 11:00 P.M. departure, port officials and the ferry's crew were working to get all the passengers aboard, almost nine hundred of them for this particular trip. As families and friends were saying their good-byes on the pier and excited children were racing about, the officials struggled to maintain some semblance of order on the quayside. Among other things, this involved checking each individual's ticket and identification as they embarked, though it was nowhere as stringent a system as one finds at most airports.

Had a better screening process been in place, maybe someone would have stopped to question the young man with a ticket for Berth 51 on the *SuperFerry* who clutched a cardboard box containing a TV set in his arms. Passenger 51, as he would come to be called by authorities, gave his name as Arnulfo Alvardo when he purchased his ticket, a somewhat odd choice as that was the known identity of a member of the Abu Sayyaf terrorist group. Since the early 1990s, Abu Sayyaf (the name can be translated into English as either "Father of the Swordsman" or "Bearer of the Sword") has been engaged in a violent struggle with the government in Manila as they sought to create a theocratic Islamic state in the southern Philippines. The terrorist group has a history of assassinating opponents, extorting money from businesses, attacking hospitals, and kidnapping foreigners and is notorious for beheading their hostages.

Claiming outright to be a known member of Abu Sayyaf should have raised a red flag somewhere about Passenger 51, even if the real Arnulfo Alvardo was dead. But as the crowds of passengers surged aboard the *SuperFerry 14* that evening, Passenger 51 was ignored by the port officials and made his way to his assigned berth while still clutching the television in its cardboard box. Then, not long before the vessel's mooring lines were cast off, Arnulfo Alvardo—without his TV box—made his way through the crowds and back onto the wharf, disappearing into the Manila night like a ghost.

Leaving the capital city behind, the *SuperFerry*'s captain set a westerly course for the mouth of Manila Harbor, whereupon they would make a turn and head south through the Verde Island Passage into the Visayan Sea. The crew had done this run hundreds of times before, so a quiet routine settled over the ship as they motored into the bay. There were watches to be kept, engines to be checked, and passengers to be made comfortable. About an hour after departure the ferry approached Corregidor Island, the fortress to which

General Douglas MacArthur had retreated during the Japanese invasion of the Philippines in the Second World War, and any passengers on deck might have caught a glimpse of the island off the starboard side. Most, though, were bedding down for the night unaware of the catastrophe that was about to unfold, for within the television nestled in Berth 51 lay three and one-half kilograms of TNT and a timer prepared to detonate the explosives.

"Improvised explosive devices" is a term familiar from reports of the fighting in Iraq and Afghanistan, where roadside bombs have been used with deadly results against foreigners and locals alike. An IED is essentially a homemade bomb, and this is what Passenger 51 had left behind. As the ferry passed Corregidor, the weapon detonated, shaking the ship and engulfing the berths surrounding the bomb in a blast that immediately killed a few nearby passengers before creating panic among the rest. With fires spreading on the lower decks and alarms sounding throughout the ship, her captain stopped the engines, dispatched emergency teams to assess the damage and calm the passengers, and then radioed his first Mayday.

But the carnage was just beginning. Men, women, and children raced to escape the flames in the enclosed spaces of the ferry, trampling one another in the ensuing panic. Firefighting teams had difficulty containing the onboard fires amid the melee and the vessel began to list dramatically to starboard. By dawn, the ship had keeled over completely on her side, with smoke billowing across Manila Harbor from the fires still burning. Rescue craft eventually arrived to help take off the survivors but over a hundred lives were lost aboard the *SuperFerry 14* that night, with untold more injured. Abu Sayyaf had just carried out the most deadly maritime attack in modern terrorism's history.

As horrific as the attacks were on the *SuperFerry 14*, USS *Cole*, and tanker *Limburg*, they failed to let Abu Sayyaf or Al Qaeda claim the title of most fearsome maritime terrorists operating today. For that honor you must look not to the Middle East or the Far East but to a group operating from a tropical island that some have thought of as a paradise. Or a paradise lost.

Just off the southeast coast of India lies Sri Lanka, an island the size of West Virginia that is home to just under 20 million people. Since the early 1980s, it has been the scene of a particularly vicious civil war that has pitted the minority Hindu Tamils against the majority Buddhist Sinhalese people. Leading the Tamil fight in this brutal conflict is a group with the longest tradition of maritime terrorism, albeit one that most in the West have rarely heard about. They are known as the Liberation Tigers of Tamil Eelam (LTTE) and have been fighting for an independent homeland in the northern part of Sri Lanka (Eelam means "Precious Land" and the tiger is a historical symbol for the Tamil people). The Tigers were one of the first modern groups to widely utilize suicide bombers and they have effectively mounted such attacks on land, in the air, and at sea. Many Western nations, including Canada, the United States, and Great Britain, officially label the LTTE as a foreign terrorist organization.

The reasons for the civil war in Sri Lanka between the Tamil minority and the Sinhalese majority are, on one level, complex and go back centuries (there have been tensions between the groups since at least the fifth or sixth century A.D.). But today's troubles are often traced to the years after the island nation gained independence from Great Britain in 1948, when the Sinhalese-dominated government began limiting the rights of the Tamils. As relations between the two groups soured, vocal opposition to the Sinhalese on the part of the Tamils began to turn violent, finally erupting in

1983. Hundreds, perhaps thousands, of Tamils and Sinhalese died in days of ethnic rioting.

The violence of 1983 marked the first time many outside Sri Lanka had ever heard of the LTTE, a group formed in 1976 by Velupillai Prabhakaran that had, until then, been waging a low-level campaign for independence. Since then, the Tamil Tigers have become a politico-military organization feared throughout the island and beyond. They have assassinated political leaders (including Indian prime minister Rajiv Gandhi in 1991 and Sri Lankan president Ranasinghe Premadasa in 1993), mounted large-scale attacks on government military bases, and maintained control over the island's north through intimidation and brute strength.

To understand the effectiveness of the Tigers and the situation in Sri Lanka, I make contact with someone who has an intimate knowledge of the civil war that still simmers, a Tamil journalist who has been forced into exile because of articles he had written there that were critical of the LTTE and the Sri Lankan government. His moderate views did not sit well with extremists on either side of the Tamil–Sinhalese divide, leading to death threats against him. After a series of cautious e-mails on his part, he agrees to meet with me when some business brings him to Toronto.

On a cool summer evening there's a light fog hanging over the city's streets after a couple of hours of incessant rain. Damp hair and damp clothes cling to me as I make my way to a small coffee shop in the west end of town to meet with the man. Yet again I've been asked to protect someone's identity, so I will call him Ratnam.

Ratnam is in his early forties, a short man with a quiet voice and gentle demeanor that masks a life spent amid violence and conflict. Grabbing a couple of cups of tea, I watch as he scans the nearly empty café and takes a seat that keeps his back to the wall and provides a clear view of the front door. Talking to a foreigner about the

Tigers is not something that a Tamil does lightly, and Ratnam will frequently lower his voice or cover his mouth when someone sits nearby, his eyes constantly darting about the café. The reason for his cautiousness comes from having worked as a journalist in a place where this is considered a particularly dangerous occupation.

"Would I still be alive if I had stayed in Sri Lanka? Well, I never know," he says while sipping his tea. "The Tigers do not like independent-minded people like journalists, especially if they are Tamil. The Tamils in the north say they open their mouths to do two things: to eat and to yawn. You know, terrible things happened there in the eighties, caused by both the Tigers and the government forces. But when the newspaper I was working for in Jaffna was bombed by the Tigers, I didn't feel safe anymore. I so desperately wanted to leave Sri Lanka and I'm glad I got out."

Having fled his homeland, Ratnam ended up in Europe, where he was able to resume his career as a journalist while maintaining his contacts back in Sri Lanka. He describes how the fighting escalated throughout the 1990s as the Tigers broadened their operations and the Sri Lankan government forcefully responded. In 1995, government forces had mounted a military campaign in the north that sent the LTTE into the jungles. The Tigers responded by regrouping and then attacking targets in the capital, Colombo, with truck bombs, followed by a successful full-scale military assault to regain their northern strongholds. However, the Tigers weren't just fighting on land at this time, and Ratnam had begun to tell me how the group began their seaborne ventures when two policemen entered the café to get their evening caffeine fix and he paused in mid-sentence. After a moment, he looked at me and grinned with embarrassment.

Once the police leave the coffee shop, Ratnam finally relaxed and continued his story: "Back in 1991, the Tigers suffered a very bad defeat from government forces. The Sri Lankan army had surprised the Tigers by landing troops on a beach and marching inland. So in response, the Tiger leadership decided they needed to do something to prevent this from happening again. You see, the Tamils are good fishermen, good sailors, and the Tigers had already been making short trips to India to smuggle in weapons. So they had expert sailors and knew every inch of the sea, and began to slowly build up their so-called navy."

By 1994, the LTTE's maritime branch—known as the Sea Tigers—began attacking commercial vessels in the waters around northern Sri Lanka. Their initial goal was to gain control of the seas surrounding Tiger-controlled territory and undermine the movement of "enemy" shipping. To do this, the LTTE leadership initiated a campaign of terror against any vessels they did not control, targeting coastal trading craft, small freighters, bulk carriers, passenger ferries, and fishing vessels. Using small boats with outboard engines, just like the ones favored by pirates elsewhere today, the Sea Tigers would swarm around ships at anchor or at sea, blasting at them with automatic weapons and grenade launchers.

As Ratnam explains, the Tigers were maturing as a terrorist group by expanding their operations beyond hit-and-run attacks or the assassinations of government officials: they were opening up new fronts in their battle for political autonomy. "The LTTE want a separate state and so are prepared to do almost anything to gain that. The Tigers were really organized and they maintained their grip through sheer terror. And they were always kind of secretive. You never knew when they were going to attack."

To fund their operations against the Sri Lankan authorities, the LTTE created an efficient network of friendly allies in various countries to convince Tamils living overseas to support the movement with donations of money. For instance, Ratnam tells me that in the Toronto area the group has managed to access electoral lists and pinpoint where Tamil Canadians are living. Teams of LTTE supporters then go door-to-door or call up people asking for donations. The system is so comprehensive that should a Tamil Canadian refuse to pony up here but then decide to pay a visit to the homeland, it's quite likely these individuals will receive a visit from the LTTE while in Sri Lanka. "The Tigers keep track of thousands of people on their databases. So they pay a visit to you when you go home and say, 'We see from our records you did not offer to donate while in Canada. Why? Perhaps you would reconsider now?' It is very hard to hide from them."

Throughout the early 2000s, the Sea Tigers were exceedingly successful in their brutal campaign and northern Sri Lankan waters gained a reputation as among the most dangerous in the world. Mariners gave the island a wide berth when sailing in the Bay of Bengal for fear of being attacked, and their fears were justified as the attacks became more violent and reports of murders began appearing. As Ratnam tells me, the region reached an apex, of sorts, when a Chinese fishing trawler was working the seas near the northeastern tip of the island on March 20, 2003. With a crew of twenty-six, the *Fu Yuan Yu 225* was sailing some seventeen nautical miles off the coast, which put her in international waters. Legalities mattered little to the attackers, who ventured out from the island in three or four speedboats, surrounded the trawler, and without warning opened fire on the trawler with automatic weapons.

For a moment, just imagine the plight of the fishermen: It's four in the morning; you're far from home and are toiling away to haul in nets and empty the catch. This is a brutal job at the best of times, involving hard labor, long hours, the stench of rotting fish, and vessels that are not generally noted for their cleanliness. Now they're faced with a group of speedboats circling around them like sharks and there's that moment when the fishing crew and the bandits eye one another, with the Chinese wondering just what's going on here. Suddenly the attackers point automatic weapons at the trawler and open fire. For the next half hour the *Fu Yuan Yu 225* resounds with the thud of bullets slamming into the steel hull and wooden frame, filling the night air with sharp splinters and ricocheting metal. Then several explosions ring out and the trawler begins to sink, trapping several of the crew inside. In a panic, the rest of the fishermen jump into the sea, clinging to whatever debris they can find.

That's when this particular incident becomes even more horrific, as the shipwrecked survivors of the trawler were gunned down in the water. By the time the sun rose over the Bay of Bengal that day in 2003, there were only nine left alive to tell the tale of this massacre at sea. (It should be noted that the Tigers denied responsibility for the attack, as did the Sri Lankan government. However, the *Fu Yuan Yu 225* was trawling the waters near the town of Mullaittivu, which has long been a major Sea Tiger base.)

But most of these events went unreported outside the region, something that Ratnam explains by telling me, "By this time, the war had caused the deaths of tens of thousands of people—Tamil and Sinhalese—and displaced hundreds of thousands more. So these events with the ships, they seemed unimportant in comparison. The Tigers are very careful not to target people from the West, from Europe or America, only locals or sometimes people from Third World countries. So when they kill some Chinese fishermen, well, it does not make the front page here. And then, of course, we had the tsunami, which overshadowed everything, and everyone thought peace would come."

The tsunami of December 26, 2004, in the Indian Ocean killed 170,000 people in twelve coastal nations, over 30,000 in Sri Lanka alone. In its aftermath, both the LTTE and the Sri Lankan government put down their guns and turned their energies toward helping those affected by the disaster, and for a time it seemed as though a lasting peace accord might be reached and the civil war and pirate attacks would end. It was not unlike the situation three centuries earlier when an earthquake destroyed Port Royal, Jamaica, on June 7, 1692. Known as the wickedest city in the New World, Port Royal was a pirate base from which buccaneers such as Henry Morgan sailed forth to terrorize shipping in the Caribbean. Once Port Royal had been flattened by the quake, many hoped that the port's demise would put an end to piracy in the nearby waters. However, it would take more than a natural disaster to stop either the pirates of the Caribbean or the Tamil Sea Tigers.

During 2005 maritime attacks by the LTTE ceased. The Tigers were too busy caring for their own people to bother targeting anyone on land or at sea. This was similar to the situation in the Strait of Malacca at the same time, when Indonesian pirates ceased their own attacks because their vessels had been destroyed by the tsunami. And, as in the Strait, it was only a matter of time before old habits resurfaced.

The Sea Tigers resumed their operations in 2006, battling Sri Lankan naval forces in several deadly engagements that year. In May about fifteen Sea Tiger boats attacked a troop transport carrying 710 government soldiers as she sailed off the northeastern coast of the island. Sri Lankan navy fast-attack boats shadowing the troop transport engaged the rebel fleet, destroying five of the Tiger vessels and preventing damage to the larger ship.

Intelligence sources pegged the Sea Tigers as having about two thousand personnel, with another one to two hundred being considered "suicide bombers."[5] In late January of 2007, the Sea Tigers sent an explosive-laden boat to ram the Sri Lankan–chartered cargo ship *City of Liverpool* near Jaffna Harbor. This area was ostensibly under the control of the Sri Lankan government, though the LTTE exerted considerable influence in the port. The attack on the *City of Liverpool* damaged the ship, which had to be towed back to Jaffna, and announced that the Sea Tigers were definitively back in business.

Barely a month earlier, the group had shown their opportunistic colors with an attack on a freighter that had the misfortune to encounter engine problems off the northeastern Tamil-controlled part of the island. The MV *Farah 3* had left Kakinada, India, on December 15, 2006, bound for Durban, South Africa, with fourteen thousand metric tons of rice. She was just shy of 150 meters (about 490 feet) in length and had been built back in 1981, which may have explained why her power plant failed.

After wallowing in the seas of the Bay of Bengal for four days as her engineers tried to repair the malfunction, the *Farah 3* found herself drifting perilously close to a rocky shoal northeast of the Mullaittivu Lighthouse. It was Friday, December 22, when the freighter's captain, Ramaz Abdul Jabbar, gave the order to let go the anchor. Captain Jabbar knew there were no other vessels in the area that might offer assistance, so the Iraqi-born mariner got on the radio and requested a salvage tug be sent from Colombo, on the southwestern part of the island. Told that the tug wouldn't arrive for another two days, the captain had the crew settle in to wait, though everyone aboard knew these waters had been the scene of numerous attacks by the Sea Tigers. Given the recent cease-fire, though, it was likely that the crew hoped they faced nothing more than a couple of days of boredom and routine watches.

Throughout the following day, the crew of *Farah 3* went about their business within sight of the island. The nearby beach was long and sandy, bordered by a few straggly palm trees dotted here and there. It had the look of a weather-beaten, deserted isle, having been hard hit by the tsunami two years earlier, but looks can be deceiving.

From well-concealed hiding places onshore, the Tamil Tigers had been patiently watching their quarry since she first appeared on the horizon, waiting for the right moment to attack. Their leader recognized the merchant ship as a suitable prize and knew she would be no match for the Sea Tigers' weapons. Throughout the day they kept an eye on the *Farah*, gathering information about the crew's movements, how she was riding, and where best to board her. As the sun set that day, the LTTE leader ashore must have seen enough and gathered his men to go over the plan with an efficiency borne from dozens of prior assaults. With no sign of bad weather in the offing, they'd wait for cover of darkness and use their small boats to sneak up on the ship.

By midnight the crew of the freighter was on edge, and the stifling tropical heat inside their quarters certainly didn't help. The rescue tug was due to arrive sometime in the next twelve hours, giving hope to some of the men that maybe things would work out for the better. But over on the island, six small boats began motoring from a secluded inlet toward the freighter, each one filled with armed cadres methodically checking their weapons. Though the lookouts on the *Farah* couldn't see anything in the darkness, they might have heard the first telltale sounds of outboard engines somewhere out there.

Just before 0300 on December 23, the second officer had the watch on the bridge on the *Farah* when he noticed six echoes on the ship's radar screen. They were closing in on the freighter. He quickly called Captain Jabbar to the bridge, who ordered the outside lights turned on to illuminate the ship. As a series of shots rang out from the approaching boats, Captain Jabbar placed an urgent distress call to anyone who could hear, stating that the MV *Farah 3* was facing an armed attack by unknown individuals. It was the last message he was able to get off.

Within moments the ship was surrounded and the Sea Tigers were climbing aboard. They swarmed throughout the ship following their leader's instructions. One group began rounding up the crew, another set off for the wheelhouse, while a third group headed toward the forecastle near the bow, ready to blow the anchor chain with explosives. It took maybe thirty minutes for the pirates to secure the ship and make her theirs. On the bridge, the boarders burst in with weapons at the ready. They smashed the radio and hustled Jabbar and the wheelhouse crew outside to join the other prisoners. Standing on the deck, arms behind his head, Captain Jabbar could hear the anchor chain being cut, meaning his ship would soon begin drifting toward the shoals and her demise.

The looting had already begun, the pillaging of laptop computers, DVD players, and personal effects, but the *Farah*'s crew was helpless. Standing on the deck with their arms behind their heads, they were told they would be "guests" of the Tigers and ordered to jump into the small boats. Some refused. There was shouting and threats of violence until the prisoners realized the alternative and leapt, one by one, into the boats and into captivity. Though there really was nothing more he could have done, one can only imagine how Captain Jabbar felt as the motorboats headed toward shore, for he'd lost his ship, he'd lost his cargo, and he might soon lose his crew and his life.

"This is the hallmark of terrorists like the Tigers," says Ratnam, "to subdue those they consider to 'not be with us.' The Tigers own the seas there. Call them pirates or terrorists, they control the place, attack when they want, and inflict damage when they can. Some consider the situation in Sri Lanka to not be important [in the global war on terror], because it does not affect someone in . . . I don't know, Ohio or Iowa. This is wrong. We are all connected. We are all affected."

News of the attacks by the LTTE on vessels trickled down to various nations through the mariners affected. The *Farah 3* had crew from Egypt and Jordan and Iraq whose tales of the incident would be passed along to family and friends. Some will get angry; some will blame the West for inaction. Whether rational or not on their part, it's not implausible that a relative of a deckhand on the freighter will think ill of India or the United States for not helping out in this situation, and that emotion will fester and bloom in the future. And the same might be said for those who knew the crew of *Fu Yuan Yu 225*.

Ratnam's emphatic plea to look at what's happening in his homeland is heartfelt and correct. He takes his leave of me, shaking his head at the way Sri Lanka's troubles are considered of less interest than other parts of the planet, though he's a smart enough journalist to understand what makes headlines and what does not. Ratnam knows he can never go back, not now, not in the near future, and that the seas around his island birthplace are fraught with dangers. But he remains troubled that many in the West really just don't care about the one place on the globe where maritime terrorism is running rampant.

So is there a direct connection between piracy and terrorism? The simple answer is yes, and it begs us to pay attention to what's going on out there on the water. And it all comes down to the "what if?" scenario.

Fundamentally, modern-day pirates have revealed weaknesses in the way developed nations operate, primarily because so much of the global economy is transported on the seas. They have shown that our international Achilles' heel is the 90 percent of world trade carried by largely unarmed merchant vessels across our planet's waters. Interrupt that flow of commerce and economies are impacted dramatically.

For example, in October 2002 a ten-day labor dispute closed twenty-nine ports along the U.S. West Coast, interrupting the loading and unloading of over two hundred vessels and roughly three hundred thousand shipping containers. By the time it was ended by presidential authority the White House estimated the stoppage had cost the American economy as much as $1 billion a day.[6] That was a simple labor dispute. Imagine if terrorists placing bombs in shipping containers had caused it. That's what keeps observers and analysts up at night worrying.

It may surprise many to know that while there are internationally agreed upon legal definitions of what constitutes piracy and maritime crime, there are no similar statutes defining terrorism. This may be because one person's terrorist is another's freedom fighter. Regardless, the lack of a clear delineation between piracy and maritime terrorism means that it can be easier for governments to put both groups into the same gray category. For instance, was the hijacking of the *Dewi Madrim* carried out by pirates or terrorists? Perhaps it was pirates morphing into terrorists, or terrorists trying their hand at piracy?

But there are several problems that arise when you try to find a nexus between terrorists and pirates. The first is that pirates and maritime terrorists are two completely different criminal animals who rarely see eye-to-eye. Terrorism's general characteristics are violence, the threat of violence, and a public display of this manifestation, with the idea being to coerce or intimidate governments and civilians. Pirates, however, are opportunistic criminals hoping to enrich themselves at someone else's cost. In simple terms, pirates and terrorists have diametrically opposed goals: the former want a steady supply of maritime traffic to exploit, while the latter seek the destruction of those same commercial interests.

The second problem is that history has shown that it requires a persistent level of attacks against Western interests before any threat is deemed necessary to be addressed. One attack on the World Trade Center's North Tower in February 1993 did not beget a global war on terror. 9/11's multiple attacks and all the innocent victims of them did. A single attack on a destroyer or oil tanker? Terrible, but not pressing. In fact, in an odd way the various international maritime agencies have shown considerable restraint over the last half decade in not over-reacting to maritime terrorism. Our ports remain open and seaborne trade continues to flourish without extreme impediments, which is a good thing for economies as interconnected on the global scale as they are today.

Since the 9/11 attacks a variety of measures have been put in place to make international shipping "safer" than it was before. Every major port in the world now has security procedures that are supposed to prevent things from going awry. Anyone who enters a modern facility—be it in Hong Kong, Singapore, Antwerp, Hamburg, Newark, Halifax, Los Angeles, or hundreds of others—is supposed to be cleared by the port authorities. Anyone boarding a vessel bound for foreign waters, and some domestic ones, too, is supposed to be recorded on manifests. Those lists are meant to be available for preclearance by the U.S. Department of Homeland Security and equivalent agencies in other countries. The freewheeling days when someone could get on a ship in Europe, hitch a ride across the Atlantic, and jump off in America are long gone. Passports and mariners' identity cards are now the norm; within a decade we'll see biometric identification becoming routine and, most likely, widely accepted as necessary. So there is a degree of scrutiny going on today that has never existed in the history of seafaring.

But can any amount of surveillance or security measures ever be 100 percent effective?

That's the problem: there's always a "but" involved when you're looking at terrorists. As long as there are men willing to rob, hijack, abduct, and murder on the high seas for profit, there will remain the potential for others to capitalize on this lawlessness for other purposes. The unfortunate truth is that the immense coast-lines of nations like the United States, Canada, or Great Britain, coupled with the vastness of the sea, make it impossible to com-pletely guarantee our safety from the threat of maritime terrorism, let alone piracy. To create a cohesive defense system combining land-based sites, aerial reconnaissance, and marine patrols would bankrupt the wealthiest nation, to say nothing of interfering with global trade and creating an even worse atmosphere of fear.

In the meantime, we will continue to do what we've always done and hope for the best. Hope that the terrorists can be thwarted by our forces, hope they won't smuggle a suitcase containing a dirty bomb aboard a container bound for a city in the Midwest, hope everything will be fine.

As I pack my suitcase in a Mombasa hotel, the anniversary of 9/11 and the terror attacks mounted around this bustling city give me pause. I feel a moment in which the irrational fear of the un-known enemy appears, exacerbated by my having spent my time here poking my nose into piracy and thinking of terrorists. At the airport, I can't help but notice the gaggle of passengers checking in next to me for the flight to Tel Aviv or that the display board shows their flight is due to depart moments before mine. Could it hap-pen? Could someone have slipped ashore in Mombasa and be wait-ing nearby with a missile?

Of course they could. Letting this possibility, which is remote, take control of my emotions is just what the terrorists want, isn't it? So I take a deep breath and watch the Israeli plane safely depart, reminding myself that you can't believe every conspiracy theory out there. And I try to remind myself that there's a lot of lying and misinformation that comes with the territory. The hard part is try-ing to separate fact from fiction.

8

PIRATE TALES

A truth that's told with bad intent
Beats all the lies you can invent.
                    —WILLIAM BLAKE, "AUGURIES OF INNOCENCE"

RETURNING ONCE MORE to Singapore, I'm greeted not by a mysterious lunar eclipse out the porthole of my airliner, but just by the reality of the shipping world. Beneath me, the South China Sea is peppered with ships moving to and fro. By the time the plane nears the airport, the waters surrounding Singapore's various anchorages are filled with dozens and dozens of vessels of all sizes, from immense oil tankers to tiny fishing boats. Somewhere down there is one that awaits me, a merchant vessel sailing from Asia to Europe. I've managed to get a berth on her, the idea being to wrap up my research by sailing through some of the pirate-infested seas, such as the Strait of Malacca, the Indian Ocean, the Red Sea, and the Mediterranean. Departure is slated to occur in less than forty-eight hours, if I recall correctly as I groggily reset my wristwatch to local time.

The airliner creeps in from the north, touching down on a runway still slick from a recent tropical downpour while the sun begins to set off in the west. In my exhaustion, I am mesmerized by the beautiful concentric patterns the jet engines make on the watery tarmac as we taxi to the gate, where my fellow passengers leap en masse to grab their carry-on bags and race for the terminal. As for me, well, I'm in no particular hurry to be enveloped by the humidity waiting outside, the lines at Customs and Immigration, or the drive to my hotel. The idea of a day to recover from jet lag and whatnot is quite appealing to me, though there is one small piece of business I need to deal with before getting on my ship.

Just before leaving Canada, I'd received word from my friend Peter Chin in Singapore, saying he may have found someone I should meet. Knowing that Peter had been trying to set up something with a pirate when I was last here, I was intrigued, to say the least, though my expectations were low. Nothing was confirmed before I boarded my flight in London and there's no text message awaiting me when I turn on my cell phone here, so I assume the worst and head off to my hotel.

My taxi takes me across the north end of Singapore, bound for the Woodlands Causeway, which links the island with the Malayan peninsula. I'm actually not staying in Singapore itself this time but in Johor Bahru, a Malaysian city that's grown up right next door, meaning I've got to fight my way through the crowds at the border crossing. There are thousands of migrant workers heading home from their day jobs on the island and not a few Singaporeans heading across the causeway for the cheaper pleasures of Johor. By the time I arrive at the hotel, it's well after nine at night, though my body clock thinks it's morning in North America. Still, I'm completely bagged and just pulling off my wrinkled clothing when the cell phone does a little vibrating dance across the bedside table.

It's a text message from my friend Peter Chin and simply says:

"We r on tmrow 9pm pls call." I punch in his number and he answers immediately.

"Welcome back," he says curtly—which is not like his usual effusiveness. "Okay, there is someone I think you should see, tomorrow. Can you come?"

I ask for details and Peter gives me some sketchy details. Through the friend-of-a-friend routine, he's found a guy who once worked for a shipping firm Peter dealt with who might have some insights into local piracy. He actually lives not far from where I'm staying in Johor Bahru and worked in a warehouse or something doing manual labor of some sort. The man is willing to talk about some "incidents" he knows of; beyond that, Peter has little information.

My curiosity is certainly piqued, though I'm a bit cautious after Peter's previous attempts to find a pirate for me to meet. Peter's not certain how deeply involved in criminal activities the man is, or was, but says he'll try to find out more. Meanwhile, I agree to meet the mysterious contact tomorrow evening, with Peter coming along to act as a translator, and an extra body. Just in case.

Shortly after eight the next evening, Peter arrives at my hotel with a hired car, saying little besides asking how much money I have on me. He seems somewhat nervous about tonight's meeting, though he won't say why as we wind our way past restaurants and shops lit up and filled with customers. When I ask for more information on the guy we're to meet, Peter can only say he's been told the individual *may* have been involved with a pirate gang.

As we continue on our journey, Peter also tells me that I'll have to pay the man to talk to me, and I inwardly groan.[1] I ask Peter how much should I give the man and he thinks for a moment.

"How about fifty dollars?" I check my wallet to see if I have enough money and reluctantly agree.

We eventually arrive at a restaurant in Pasir Gudong, a satellite port city just east of Johor Bahru. Peter says little to me as we exit the taxi and stand outside the open-air eatery, my friend tapping off a short text message with his cell phone to his contact.

Our intended meeting place seems okay to me: it's not some dank waterfront dive but what appears to be a popular place, open and airy, with little party lights strung along the front, full of people eating, including a number of Westerners. A guy holding menus by the entrance beckons us to come inside, but my friend just ignores him as we continue to wait for our guest.

The man soon arrives and Peter greets him, the two speaking in Malayan to one another as I stand off to one side. The guy is quite thin, even gaunt, and appears to be in his mid-forties, outfitted in jeans and a striped polo shirt that has seen better days, topped off with what has to be one of the worst haircuts I've ever seen: black hair flecked with gray that juts out at a forty-five-degree angle from his head, the ends of which are jaggedly sheared. I sincerely hope that the man cut it himself.

While trying not to stare at the haircut I'm introduced to the man, who shyly shakes my hand and mumbles, "Hallo." He doesn't look particularly fearsome or menacing, not like what I'd expected a pirate to be, if that is what he is. I ask Peter how I should address the man, since I know I can't use his real name, and the two speak with one another for several minutes. Peter then turns to me and says, "He is Musso."

The three of us take a table inside the restaurant and order dinner. Musso must be pretty hungry, because he orders a lot of food, more than Peter and me put together, all of which he happily devours. My initial impressions of the guy, not counting his bizarre coif, is of a nondescript individual who appears relatively relaxed as he dines with two complete strangers. Musso speaks very little English, forcing my friend to translate between us as we eat and get acquainted.

I'm told he was born in the southern part of Sumatra, so he's Indonesian, not Malaysian as I'd first thought.[2] He says his father and uncles had been fishermen, adding, in an offhand manner, that they were killed by the government in the mid-1960s. I ask Peter to clarify what Musso has just said, as I am somewhat shocked and confused about this.

Peter briefly explains the political tumult that wracked Indonesia in 1965–1966: "Several generals or government officials were kidnapped and murdered by those opposed to the government of President Sukarno. It was thought that communists had done this, so a massive campaign was launched against them by the government. Suharto led it.[3] Hundreds of thousands died as the army cracked down, including, it would seem, Musso's family. I think it's safe to say his father was a communist."

Something dawns on Peter and he turns to speak with Musso, who cracks a cautious grin in response. Musso, I am advised, was the name of a famous Indonesian communist leader who was killed after the Second World War, and the strange man sitting opposite me seems to feel that appropriating this moniker is somehow apt. My Musso was just a boy when his father died, which may be why he speaks so dispassionately about his father's death. All he'll say about the aftermath of this is that his family somehow scraped by, he began fishing with a relative as a teenager, and his mother died before he was twenty. He has a sister who lives in Indonesia somewhere.

I ask if Musso has a wife and children and the man nods: "I am married for twelve years. My daughter, she is eleven. But I have not seen them in almost a year." Again, he says all this without any emotion in his voice. Even Peter raises his eyebrow at me: here's a guy whose father was killed by the government, whose mother died years ago, and who hasn't seen his wife and daughter in months yet who offers no sense of remorse about these events. It all sounds just a little too pat, and I'm reminded of what the American journalist Donovan Webster had told me months earlier, about how you can never be certain if those involved with criminal activities are telling you the truth.

Continuing his backstory, Musso says he headed off to the Indonesian capital, Jakarta, while in his twenties in search of more lucrative work. He tried his hand at construction for a while before getting a job in a nearby port. His story then becomes fuzzy: he says he returned to Sumatra to fish, but something happened about which he will not say. What he did through the 1990s is unclear, but by the early part of this century, Musso was becoming financially desperate.

"In my country, things were not well with the economy," he relates, through Peter. "To fish, you had to pay bribes to the police, and I could not afford this. The government is all corrupt; everyone just takes. I think because of my father they ask more. How can I do this? So I find that some people have another idea."

Musso finishes his meal and looks me in the eye for the first time, his features no longer quite so friendly. "You are from a place of wealth. Maybe this is different. I am hungry, just like tonight." He makes a sort of laugh, almost a smirk, and then speaks with Peter. My friend turns to me and says, "He wants to know if you will pay him now."

A moment of truth ensues, for there's nothing that this Musso character has said, so far, that has implied any knowledge of piracy on his part. I'm not very good at bartering, but I know a bad deal when I see it, and this guy seems dubious. Sure I'm about to be fed a load of lies or rehashed stories Musso's heard in some bar, I tell Peter to offer only that I will pay when we're done—and only if this guy is truthful. Peter thinks that's a good approach, though there's a moment of tension as my friend translates and Musso considers the offer. I figure he has nothing to lose and has already gotten a free meal out of the evening. The two of them talk for a bit; then Musso goes quiet, staring at me as he thinks about what I've said. There's a look of disdain on his face now, and certain that the interview is over, I begin looking for the waiter so I can pay the bill and get out of here.

"He agrees," Peter interrupts, "and asks what you want to know."

The noise of the restaurant and its diners recedes as I take a moment to think. Musso pulls out a cigarette, one of the clove-scented ones so popular around here, and lights it up as I wonder where to begin. *Okay,* I decide, *a simple question: Are you a pirate?*

While rolling the lit cigarette between his thumb and forefinger he listens to Peter translate my question. Musso shakes his head in response and says something in his language and I wait for Peter to tell me the meeting is over. Instead, my friend says, "No, he says he is no longer a pirate. But he was."

A million questions now race through my head. I take a breath and then logic finally says to start at the beginning, so I ask how he got started.

"I was in need of work, of money," says Musso. "I tried to find work in Jakarta, in the port, but there was nothing. Then I met some people who said they could use me. This was in Jakarta. I met someone from my village and he says there is a group who go to steal equipment from the ships. Because I was fisherman he knows I can work a boat, and he asks if I would join them, be a driver for them. Handle the boat. He say I can make money, there [will be] no problems. They not murder or hijack. So I say, 'Okay.'"

Musso describes a thriving black market in Indonesia that deals in stolen goods like spare parts for ship engines, tools, lightbulbs, lubricating oil, and even clothing like overalls and hard hats. The gang he fell in with targeted larger commercial vessels anchored around southern Sumatra and western Java, on either side of the Sunda Strait.

The Sunda Strait is a narrow body of water separating the Indonesian island of Sumatra in the north from Java in the south. Barely fifteen nautical miles wide at its eastern end, it is a choke point of maritime navigation that sees heavy traffic heading in and out of nearby Jakarta, the capital of Indonesia and a major regional shipping hub. Though the Sunda Strait sees less vessel movement than the nearby Strait of Malacca, it is still a busy waterway that has been the scene of frequent attacks on ships over the last decade.[4]

Having decided to throw his lot in with these criminals, Musso was invited to come live with them in a three-room place they kept near the sea, somewhere not far from Jakarta, possibly on the Sunda Strait itself. There were certain conditions the gang imposed on Musso: no outside communication was allowed; he had to give up his cell phone until they could trust him and was not allowed to go anywhere on his own. He says this all occurred near the end of the year, which would make it late December of 2006, and Musso only had to wait a week or so until the gang decided to use him.

"I remember the first time was just after the new year started," he says. "I drove the boat with four others, small boat like for fishing but with good engine. Suzuki. It was very late [at night] and we left from shore [on Java], went across the Strait [of Sunda], and headed for some ships anchored in the bay. We cross, pass some ships sailing, and go to Sumatra. In a bay they tell me to drive to very large ship—a tanker, like for oil—and we come around to its stern, very fast. It was very big, black [hull] with red on top [the accommodations]. We come behind [the ship] and some of the men throw ropes with [grappling] hooks to the rails as soon I stop the engine, and they climb to the deck. They have machetes, no guns. One man stay with me and say to be ready to go when he give the order, when the men return from the ship.

"We are there for maybe twenty minutes and all the time watching the ship, to see if the crew see us. There are some lights on the ship, so I worry we will be seen, but nothing happens. Then the three who went aboard begin climbing down the ropes, shouting to start the engine. They throw their machetes into the boat, get in, and I steer the boat away from the ship quickly. Someone saw them [on the tanker] and there was alarm before they could get inside, so we get nothing that night."

Musso says he was very nervous this first time out and hadn't expected they would target such a large vessel. The pirates headed back across the Strait to a small village on the western tip of Java, possibly opting not to push their luck on another vessel that evening. Though they failed to steal anything off the tanker, his new comrades told Musso he'd done an excellent job and said there would be plenty more jobs.

About a week later, Musso headed out with the gang again, this time to scout vessels anchored in the main port north of Jakarta. It was well after midnight, he claims, and the leader instructed Musso to make for a small containership. Using the same tried-and-true technique, they came in from the stern, climbed aboard with their machetes, and left Musso waiting in the attack boat. And, once more, the boarding party quickly returned, shouting for him to get them out of there.

"I start the engine and they say to hurry. They say there are guards aboard the ship, with guns. Everyone is anxious, angry, as I steer the boat away, ducking down low in case they fire the guns. I was told the ships did not have guns, that the crews are unarmed. This was a surprise for me."

A couple more late-night sorties prove no more successful for Musso and his merry gang, leading me to question their competence, as well as wonder if he's telling the truth. After all, there's nothing particularly startling about what I've been told so far, nothing that isn't common knowledge among mariners about how these sorts of attacks are normally carried out. He tells me he cannot remember the names of any of the ships this gang of his targeted and barely remembers what the individual vessels looked like.

The Indonesian seems to take my skepticism in stride, calmly explaining that not every attempt to steal will end up being successful. This he learned from his own experiences and also from the others in the gang, who had already been pirating for a few years by the time Musso joined them. He was cautioned that it might take six, eight, or ten ventures out before they hit pay dirt and there would be little money for the pirates if they failed. He says that the first month he took part all he received in return was meals and a place to sleep, no money. In between nighttime raids, Musso maintained the outboard engine, watched television, played cards, and did some of the cooking and cleaning up at the lair.

I ask Musso to describe the other members of the pirate gang, to tell me where they were from, how long they'd been doing this, and their names. He cups his cigarette between thumb and forefingers, underhanded, and proffers what might be a sneer. No names will be provided, I'm told as Musso takes another drag on his smoke.

As to the makeup of the pirate gang he'd fallen in with, it seems to have varied from time to time. This is another case of me wondering whether Musso is telling the truth or making things up. Sometimes he mentions four others, sometimes five; later still there are more than a dozen involved. If he's not lying, there appeared to be one leader and three other core members, all of whom had broken away from another gang. He implies the pirates were all Sumatrans, though they based themselves in western Java and also enticed Javanese men to join them on later expeditions. No matter how hard I try, Musso refuses to provide the names of his accomplices or specific places they lived and worked out of.

Musso says there was a definite hierarchy to the gang and he thinks it operated independently from any larger group, as he never saw a boss or crime lord in all the time he was a pirate. Yet the gang's leader would decide when the team would stage an attack, and where, which implies to me that he either was getting some directions from above or had connections of some sort that pointed the gang in the right direction. As low man on the totem pole, Musso was required to do all the menial tasks—like the cooking—as well as piloting the boat. It would take a month before the pirate leader allowed Musso to take part in an actual boarding.

"There was a new man who joined us, a youngster," Musso relates, lighting up another cigarette. "So I was to be aboard the next ship [they attacked]. I was given a machete and around midnight they say we go hunting. This was in February, I think, near the east end of the Strait. My job was to keep watch on the deck when we got aboard and signal if the crew [of the attacked ship] was alerted. We went out and there is a cargo ship anchored. Our boat approached from the rear; we make sure there is no one there [on the deck], and throw the ropes up. Then, very fast, we climb—*chook, chook, chook*," he says, miming with his hands how they clambered up the lines and over the rail.

The five-man team made their way to a side entrance into the ship's accommodations, ordering Musso to remain on the main deck as a lookout while the others went inside. Clutching his machete, the Indonesian hid in the shadows while listening for the sounds of anyone approaching. The other boarders had machetes and pistols. After some time—Musso cannot remember exactly how long—his confederates reappeared carrying equipment from inside the ship. They had tools, cordless power drills, and boxes of spare parts for the ship's engines that were stacked on the deck and then lowered into the waiting boat while Musso kept an eye peeled for anyone from the crew who might catch them.

"No one see us. It was strange. No one. It took a long time to get everything into the boat. They keep telling me, 'Make sure no one come,' while they work. I began to worry that maybe they would leave me behind, because I was by the side and they were at the back, so I could not see them. But then one comes up and tells me to go, to get off the ship, so I climb down and we leave. The boat is filled from the ship, we are crowded together, but everyone is happy. My brothers are laughing and we have a party when we get home."

The next few months were a happy time, says Musso. The gang worked hard, heading out once or twice a week in search of victims. He was now a key member of the boarding party team, the eyes and ears the gang relied upon while they ransacked vessels. Though they only managed to successfully rob a couple of vessels during this period—which would appear to be the spring of 2007—the rewards were good enough that Musso was told he would finally be getting a share of the proceeds. After four or five months of pirating he was given a wad of money by the gang leader back at their lair. Musso's dividend amounted to 2 million Indonesian rupiah, equivalent to a little more than $200 U.S.

Having given up his life to become a maritime criminal for almost half a year, Musso held in his hands less than what a law-abiding Indonesian makes in a month. Piracy was not turning out to be quite as profitable a venture as he'd expected. He says he argued with the gang leader about this but was told to keep his mouth shut. For complaining, Musso was not allowed to participate in any attacks for a couple of months, relegated to fixing the motor and feeding the others. He says he felt trapped, unable to go pirating and unable to leave the house. As he was telling me this through my translator, I see a flicker of something in his eyes that might be genuine emotion.

"I keep saying to [the leader], 'Please let me join you again; I am sorry.' He ignore me until one day when he tell me, 'Okay, you can come again.' And I was happy. So now is August, many months since I have been [allowed to join them]. That night, a second group meets us at the beach. We will have two boats now. I do not know these other men, but we all head out, across the Strait. We go to close by my first time, to Teluk Semangka, and again it is a tanker. Four from each boat get aboard, and I am with them now."

I'm told that Teluk Semangka is a bay on the southern coast of Sumatra often used as an anchorage by large merchant vessels. On this August evening in the bay, Musso was told he was not to be a lookout but to accompany the main team as they went inside the ship. The pirates made their way down into the engineering space and found a couple of crew members standing watch in the control room. Waving their weapons and shouting, the attackers ordered the mariners to squat on the deck. While one group of pirates began searching for things to steal, the gang leader ordered Musso to tie the unfortunate crewmen up. And then Musso was forced to prove himself before his accomplices.

"He say in English to the men [the captives], 'Where is the chief [engineer]? Where is the captain?' When they do not answer, he tell me to hit them. To use the [blunt] end of my machete. The others are looking at me, waiting. I have never hit someone like that—never. But I know that if I do not, there will be trouble for me. He say again to beat them. He is angry, maybe at me, maybe at them, I do not know. So . . . I raise my machete above the first man and strike him on the head. Like so—*chook*." Musso makes a slashing gesture with his hand. "Maybe not so hard, but he still has blood on his face. The sailor say [the ship's officers] are in their cabins and pleads for me to stop. My brother laughs and we take the men into a room off the side; then we go to help the others."

The other pirates were hefting large boxes from a storage room, what appeared to be specific items the group was searching for. Musso says they only took what they could carry, but that one of the new men seemed to know which items to take. The boats were again heavily laden as the robbers sped home, and everyone was in a good mood until they reached Java. A man was waiting for them on the beach, someone Musso had never seen before, and after this man reviewed what had been stolen, a disagreement erupted.

"The man say we did not get everything. There is an argument. The others take most of the boxes and leave in their boat, with the man. The man who lead us is very angry. He was a violent man. He turn to me and say, 'Why were you weak? This is your fault.' And he hit me."

Musso feels he became a scapegoat for whatever went wrong that night, though he stresses he had no idea what the overall plan was. He says he did not know what they were supposed to steal off the ship, did not even know if this vessel was a specific or random target. All Musso knew was that the gang's leader was becoming more irrational, possibly because of heroin use, and needed someone upon whom to vent his frustrations.

As several more nighttime raids failed over the coming weeks, Musso felt the harsh brunt of the pirate captain's wrath and decided the time had come to quit the pirate life. Trying to extricate yourself from a life of crime is an age-old dilemma, albeit one to which few law-abiding souls pay much heed. If you decide to cross the line, to "go on account" as pirates of yore once said, it should be expected that the price of returning to our society may be harsh. We admire the lives of the outlaw from afar, gaining some sort of recreational pleasure from hearing of the exploits of Jesse James or Butch Cassidy and the Sundance Kid, to say nothing of Blackbeard or Captain Kidd.

But most of us understand that their lives can never be ours, not for real. We may chafe at the constrictions placed on our daily lives, with all their elements of order and acceptability, yet the vast majority of us are unwilling to toss those restraints aside and become robbers or pirates. This provides the sense of superiority that gives us some meaning, for no matter how far down you are on the rungs of life, you can at least say, "I didn't give in. To temptation or greed. I opted to deal with the unknown of daily life, while these others fled to an apparently easier path." Having eschewed our world, these criminals cannot be easily welcomed home again, for we feel they have forfeited their rights and obligations. This is not a political statement, merely an observation of how some societies have looked upon those they consider criminals.

And those who have crossed the line have long known how we feel about all this. Codes of conduct and expectations have been entrenched in criminal organizations for thousands of years. These not only help organize their operations; they also define who the criminals are, creating a sense of order in what is seemingly a world of disorder. While filling a void created by society, criminal gangs still ascribe to the human sensibility of requiring some parameters to govern themselves. Like any hierarchical structure, it takes time to become accepted within this subculture, and once one is initiated it is extremely difficult to leave and be reaccepted back into our world.

Musso's cell phone rings and he excuses himself to take the call, wandering outside the restaurant while Peter and I sit patiently. My friend quietly asks me what I think about the interview, and I admit to being somewhat skeptical. There's no way to confirm what Musso's told me, at least not until I get back to the research material in my hotel room. For what amounts to a couple of weeks' wages in Indonesia, plus dinner, is Musso just feeding me a pack of rehashed sailor's stories, safe in the knowledge he'll be long gone before I can verify any of it? Neither Peter nor I know for certain, and before we can discuss it further our Indonesian "pirate" has returned, picking up where he left off.

"After the tanker [incident], I am not allowed to go out with them. One [of the gang] say the leader is very angry at me; he blames me for the way things are. They go out several times, but have no success. Now, when we eat meals, I must wait until the others finish; then I get what is left over. I know I must get away from these people. One morning I see a chance. Everyone is asleep. I am supposed to prepare the meal, so I go outside. No one is there. Everyone they sleep. So I walk. I have nothing but my clothes and some rupiah. All day I walk; then I find myself at harbor in Jakarta and a boat going to Malaysia. Here. So I come to Johor. I find job at [shipping firm's warehouse]. I am gone. I am here. I am free."

So . . . you just ran away, I wonder, as easy as that? Musso nods with that quasi-sneer of his. "Why did you come here, and not go to your family?" Now his sneer fades and he speaks in a sharp manner to my friend Peter.

"If he went home," I'm told, "he would be found. And possibly, probably, killed. He says he can never go home now."

The three of us sit there for a while without speaking, Musso glaring off into the distance, Peter staring at the table and me trying to figure out what to do next. The Indonesian finally breaks the silence by speaking to my Malaysian friend.

"He wants to go now. He wants his money," Peter tells me.

Musso's story definitely has elements that could be true, and he hasn't asked me for more money or tried to get me to hang out with him any longer than necessary. His desire to leave is obvious—he's fingering his cell phone and glancing at the street, causing me to become slightly nervous myself. I also note that Peter seems increasingly edgy himself.

I pull two U.S. twenty-dollar bills from my pocket and hand them to Peter. "Tell him that's all I have," I say, trying to show some bravado.

My friend takes the bills, speaks to Musso, and then gives the man the money. The Indonesian stuffs the banknotes into his pocket and stands, preparing to leave.

"Are you really telling me the truth?" I ask him.

"Why would I lie?" he answers.

I can think of a thousand reasons why, but I keep them to myself. Instead, I ask one last question: "Do you regret getting involved with these pirates?"

Musso takes but a moment to ponder this before responding, somewhat angrily, "I thought this would be your first question. Everyone, they think we do this because we like it. We do not like it; we do [it] to survive. I am sorry I did not make the money I thought. I will do whatever I need to do to feed my family. This . . . you do not know."

The man says something final to Peter as he shakes his hand, then limply grasps mine before disappearing into the night.

"He regrets not asking you for more money," Peter tells me. "I think we should go."

In the taxi back to my hotel, Peter is silent for most of the ride, as am I. Arriving at my temporary abode, my friend explains a few details about "Musso" that he'd held back earlier: Musso was part of a group that had been stealing stuff from shipping warehouses here in Malaysia—stuff like TV sets and electronics, what Peter calls port seepage—and the ring had a reputation for being a bit violent. Peter had been warned that Musso was no longer a part of the ring and had made some enemies along the way. He thinks this may be why the Indonesian didn't want to stick around talking to us longer than necessary, and this also explains why Peter figured we ought to head home quickly.

"Were we in any danger tonight?" I ask my Malaysian friend.

"No, I think not. It was good that we left when did, though."

He seems relieved when we part.

It's after two in the morning by the time I make it back to the safety of my hotel room in Johor Bahru. Though I'm supposed to leave for the port in less than seven hours, I need to review my notes from the meeting and, more important, find out if I can corroborate any of the events Musso described.

I begin by checking the IMB's 2007 report on piracy and armed robbery against ships. Musso said the first attack occurred in January sometime, when the gang boarded a tanker anchored in the Sunda Strait. This should make it fairly easy to begin deciphering his tale, and I quickly find that there are records of at least four attacks on tankers in Indonesian waters during that month: One happened in Dumai, an Indonesian port on the Strait of Malacca, so that's not it, while two other tankers were attacked while anchored off Java, so they're also out. But the last one might be it, an LPG tanker that was boarded by three robbers while in the Sumatran port of Plaju on January 7.

Plaju is upriver from the sea, the site of a Pertamina facility (Pertamina is the oil and gas corporation owned by the Indonesian government). This doesn't quite sound like the locale Musso had described, and the report says that the robbers managed to steal some "ship's properties," while he had said the boarders returned empty-handed. Okay, but maybe he lied about that.

I cross-reference the IMB report with that put out by the U.S. Office of Naval Intelligence, but there are no additional incidents similar to what Musso described, so I put his description of the first attack into the questionable pile.[5]

His next apparent attack was about a week later on a containership, so I scour the records for incidents from January and February near Jakarta. There's only one, an attack on a vessel on January 27, 2007, while she was anchored about where Musso had mentioned. The IMB report says that robbers boarded the ship from the stern and entered the engine room, where they stole spare parts. But Musso had said that the pirates he'd been with had not made off with anything and, in fact, had encountered armed guards on the ship. The IMB report makes no reference to this, nor does the ONI, so I consider this another story that's questionable.

I continue to run down the supposed pirate's list of attacks, scouring every database I can access and hoping to find a match between Musso's assertions and any officially recorded incidents. I try to give the guy as much latitude as possible, checking every month, every real or attempted attack, even looking at surrounding countries' real incidents in case there were errors made by the various reporting authorities, though things keep failing to mesh. He spun some good tales, but I cannot find one incident confirmed by reputable sources that corroborates anything Musso told me.

A half-dozen supposed attacks sit in the questionable pile, while nothing makes the verified list, so by five in the morning I am forced to shut down my laptop, clear the reams of paperwork off my bed, and accept the reality of the night.

Before turning the light off and grabbing a few hours of sleep, I sum up my feelings in a text message to Peter Chin typed out in anger: "Musso full of shit. Lies all lies. BS. BS. BS."

9

REVELATIONS

The drop of rain maketh a hole in the stone,
not by violence, but by oft falling.

— HUGH LATIMER, FORMER BISHOP OF WORCESTER, 1549

OF ALL THE places I've ventured, Southeast Asia has been the wettest by far, so perhaps I shouldn't be surprised that Mother Nature has decided to send me off with a deluge of epic proportions. The skies have been overcast and oppressive all day, threatening a tropical downpour that waits until the very moment the mooring lines of the MV *Emma Maersk* are finally cast off late on a Thursday afternoon.

By the time my temporary floating home engages her starboard side thrusters to edge away from the pier, visibility has been reduced to less than a thousand yards. As the harbor pilot orders the captain to execute a 180-degree turn and make for the nearby shipping channel, the ship is engulfed in pelting rain that washes against the wheelhouse windows. Our speed increases to 11 knots as we pick our way gingerly through the other vessels in the harbor, heading for the main sea-lanes in the Strait of Malacca.

Standing on the starboard bridge wing, I find that the unsettled weather matches my mood, for I'm still thinking about last night's meeting with the so-called pirate "Musso," certain he enjoyed bilking a foreigner of some cash by telling me what he guessed I wanted to hear. I will have two weeks to mull it over, for whatever that's worth, since the containership I'm aboard will take that long to reach Spain, where I can disembark. I only hope that I don't let Musso's con job hang over me like the dark clouds outside the wheelhouse windows, ruining my trip.

The MV *Emma Maersk* is the one of the largest vessels afloat today, surpassed in length only by an oil tanker that no longer travels.[1] The Danish ship is leaving the Malaysian containerport of Tanjung Pelepas, just across the waters from Singapore and slightly south of Johor Bahru, bound for Europe with nearly twelve thousand shipping containers stuffed full of all manner of Asian commercial goods. To make the journey, the *Emma Maersk* must sail through the Strait of Malacca, across the Indian Ocean, past Yemen and Somalia into the Red Sea, through the Suez Canal, and across the Mediterranean Sea before making landfall in Algeciras, Spain, opposite Gibraltar.

The chance to sail through some of the most important waters affected by piracy is one I jumped at, even if the chance of an actual attack on the ship is pretty remote. The *Emma Maersk* is an awfully large vessel—longer than an aircraft carrier, wider than a football field, and as high as a twelve-story building—and she is, quite frankly, too large a target for any sensible pirate to consider taking on. The crew's main concern while transiting waters like the Strait of Malacca is that someone might board the ship and pry open one of the containers, hoping to steal whatever they might find inside.

Chief Officer Niels Larsen has already explained to me that they'll be taking standard anti-piracy measures through the Strait and, later, in the Red Sea: fire hoses will be deployed along the sides and aft to deter any boarders by spraying thousands of gallons of seawater overboard, lights will be turned on to illuminate the deck, and every hatch and door leading inside will be secured.

An immense bear of a man with closely cropped hair and a trim mariner's beard, Larsen wears a crisp white officer's shirt bearing the three stripes on his epaulettes of the second-in-command of the *Emma Maersk*. Despite his size, the Dane speaks in a gentle voice tinged with just a touch of disdain for the vessel's anti-piracy efforts.

"To be honest, you would have to be a complete idiot to try attacking us while we're at sea. Company policy is very strict about these situations, so we will take all measures required. But really, with our freeboard and speed—we should be making about twenty, twenty-two knots in the Strait—there's no chance we'll encounter pirates up close."

As the containership finishes executing a gentle turn to starboard and enters the Strait of Malacca proper, I watch Singapore slip away over the stern. I am almost glad to be leaving behind the duplicity, lying, and false tales I found there. The *Emma Maersk* is soon making 22 knots through the main northbound sea-lane and the crew settles into their normal rhythm, even though anti-piracy measures are under way.

A few hours later, I stand on the far starboard wing of the bridge scanning the Malaysian shoreline through binoculars. It's just past nine and the wheelhouse's digital map says we're passing the city of Melaka and coming up on the fishing village of Tanjung Kling, where I'd been months earlier. According to the second officer, this is the closest to the Malaysian coast that vessels get in the Strait, with only eight nautical miles separating me from the fishermen I met. I strain to pick out Tanjung Kling, but it's not easy because the *Emma Maersk* is lit up like a Christmas tree—part of the anti-piracy measures—though I eventually spy lights on-shore that must be the village.

In the time since I was last in these waters, major piracy incidents have been few and far between. The increased presence of naval and coast guard vessels from Malaysia, Singapore, Indonesia, and Thailand has, overall, proven an effective deterrent to attacks on shipping in the region. Indeed, things have improved to the point that a senior Malaysian military officer said there were no attacks whatsoever in the Strait for all of 2007. That may just be hyperbole, for even the IMB counted at least two pirate attacks in these waters, but it is still a sign that putting warships out there does have an effect.

Unfortunately, the smaller-scale incidents I heard about while in Tanjung Kling—those thefts of fishing boats and equipment—continue to occur. A few weeks earlier I'd received an e-mail from a Malaysian contact telling me there'd been an assault on a community farther up the coast resulting in the loss of several boats. "Nothing that would be of foreign interest," he wrote, referring to the various international organizations that keep an eye on pirate incidents. The big vessels may be safer, but not the fishermen.

As the lights of Tanjung Kling slip behind us, the rain finally abates and the Moon comes out, illuminating waters that look peaceful. The ship's radar picks out other merchant traffic and several fishing boats. The second officer watches the radar screen intently.[2] Irinel Neamtu is a dark-haired young Romanian with a serious disposition. While he stoops over a chart to plot the ship's course, a bank of menacing clouds off to the west explodes violently with streaks of lightning. Neamtu barely glances at the dramatic display as he traces his calipers across the chart and marks off the *Emma*'s position with a pencil.

"Eh, is humidity in the air," he tells me, "like the electrical storms up north in my country. Sailor see this all the time."

For the next couple of hours as we transit through what had once been the most notorious stomping ground for modern-day pirates, my efforts at engaging the young officer in a discussion about sea robbers fail. He's either too shy to speak to a stranger or simply uninterested in the topic, so I head off to my berth and leave him to keep an eye on our progress.

Dawn on the Indian Ocean is one of the most beautiful sights I've ever seen. The seas are almost flat and there's barely a cloud in the skies as the sun rises behind the *Emma Maersk*. The wake churned up by her propeller streams out astern and glistens as the light catches it, the waters colored a blue that merges seamlessly with the darkened horizons on either side. We've left the Strait of Malacca behind us and passed the northern tip of Sumatra, our course set for Sri Lanka. The placid seas off the port side reveal nothing of the deadly tsunami that emanated from these parts, and there's no other vessel traffic in the immediate vicinity, nothing but an endless expanse of sea.

We're following an ancient trade route that has been used by Arabian, African, Chinese, Indian, Portuguese, Dutch, and English mariners for half a millennium, and are now sailing through waters where one can relax from the threat of violent attack. The antipiracy measures mounted the previous evening have been ended, and the containership's crew falls into the regular, mundane routine of life aboard a merchant vessel.

Up on the bridge, I run into the *Emma Maersk*'s captain, Jørgen Sonnichsen. He's an amiable Dane in his late fifties with a relaxed and gregarious manner that masks having spent forty years at sea as a professional mariner, the last sixteen bearing captain's stripes. We make small talk while sipping coffee and take in this morning's pleasant interlude. The captain knows I'm looking into the world of piracy and eventually asks me what I've learned through my various travels, chuckling as I recount some of my misadventures. But he grows noticeably more serious when I talk of being in Kenya and meeting with those who have endured hijackings off the coast of Somalia.

"The situation there is not good," Captain Sonnichsen says while staring out the wheelhouse windows. "I wonder, have you found that sometimes [mariners] do not like to talk about these pirates? . . . Yes, you have, eh? Do you know why? It is because we do not like to speak of the bad things that can happen. Storms, accidents, pirate attacks . . . why bother worry about these? We know these are possibilities, but to always think of them is not good, I think. It is like . . . if the person at home thinks all the time about the chance of an automobile accident. Yes, it can happen and the statistics are bad. But if you let this become something that interferes with everything else, that is not good. You must, eh . . . what is the word? 'Compartmentalize,' yes, that is it, like this ship. Be aware of the dangers out there but not let them control you."

Captain Sonnichsen refills his mug and shows me the most current piracy reports received by the ship.

"I read these reports. All my officers do. We know the threat, but this is just something else for us, like the weather reports. I do not mean to sound unconcerned about piracy. I know it affects many people, just not us. I hope." He laughs and then adds, "You know I come from a people some considered to be pirates or whatever. My ancestors were Vikings, and they were [a] fearsome group. Brave, adventurous, very good mariners. They opened up the world. These pirates today? Criminals. They are the worst kind; they offer the world nothing. Maybe this is another reason we do not like to speak of this. They are not deserving of our respect. These . . . pirates, they are not true mariners."

Captain Sonnichsen glances at his wristwatch and heads below to his office, to deal with the day's paperwork, leaving me to mull over his comments on pirates. Though the experienced Danish seafarer may not consider them true mariners, there have always been pirates who have shown great prowess at seamanship. When the likes of Captain Kidd made the Pirate Round over two hundred years ago from the northern Atlantic to Madagascar in the southern Indian Ocean, they exhibited skills unmatched by few other mariners in an era when there were hardly any reliable nautical charts and only the crudest forms of navigational aids to guide them.

Some of today's pirates are equally proficient at seafaring, ranging far from land to engage in their dark endeavors. Not all of them, mind you, and only a minority ever bother to venture more than a few nautical miles away from safety. But the tales of Somali sea robbers cruising well offshore show that some of today's pirates can handle a vessel with considerable aplomb.

But Sonnichsen's derisory sentiments are emblematic of one of the problems we face when dealing with modern-day piracy: how much respect does the issue merit? On the one hand there are those—like the captain—who feel we should not become overly concerned, fearing too much attention gives pirates more credence than they deserve. I have heard this view on numerous occasions from otherwise well-informed individuals. Yes, they argue, there are places where it needs to be addressed (such as the Horn of Africa and the Gulf of Guinea), but to make piracy an important issue on a global scale takes a marginal issue and amplifies it far beyond its real merit.

On the other hand, there are those who believe this avoidance is a failure to address a serious situation. From their perspective, sweeping it under the rug only allows piracy to continue to exist. In fact, sidelining the issue actually helps these maritime criminals, for they can wage their wars against mariners with the knowledge that no larger organization will mount any effective opposition. Whether someone climbs aboard an anchored ship to steal some ropes or a group hijacks an entire vessel on the high seas, the issue is a criminal act committed against innocent victims.

Here, in the middle of the Indian Ocean, I realize that my support falls to the latter group. Having seen what I've seen and talked to so many people about piracy, I cannot feel otherwise. To my very core I believe that any act carried out by a maritime criminal needs to be addressed. The stakes are simply too high to shrug it off, as that only emboldens criminals to continue preying on the innocent.

There are signs that the lax attitude toward piracy is changing among those who hold influence. The United Nations' Security Council considers it to be a serious problem, albeit mostly in the context of Somalia. The White House has condemned piracy, as have the French president and a number of other Western leaders. Before leaving for Asia to join the *Emma Maersk*, I spoke with the outgoing commander of Canada's Atlantic naval forces, Rear-Admiral Dean McFadden, who summed up a perception of piracy gaining weight in some quarters. And though he was speaking about piracy's impact on my homeland, his views are relevant to many nations that think little of the subject.

"Why should we, in Canada, be concerned about piracy? Well, the defense and security of Canada starts a long, long way from our shores. One of the consequences of globalization is that instability anywhere has an effect on us. When that instability leads to lawlessness in certain parts of the world, it can lead to more dangerous situations—such as failed states or failing states—in which the problem is not just local piracy but an outright threat against the commercial interests of those of us in the West. The fact that it is occurring in some places is a definite threat to the security of Canada. It actually does affect the economy. But from a security perspective, it reinforces lawlessness in certain parts of the world, and that breeds destitution. And that is a bad thing for us, both here at home and because I think we do believe we have a responsibility in the world to assist. So we're going to go to those places."

The Canadian admiral agrees that there is a direct correlation between maritime crime and those three elements I've seen time and again wherever pirates roam: greed, lawlessness, and opportunity. And unless we address the root causes, such as endemic poverty and unstable governing structures, any attempts at suppressing piracy may amount to little more than short-term solutions to the problem. Admiral McFadden is not advocating large-scale military intervention anywhere, merely hoping that a broader approach to the issue can be taken. Canada has dispatched naval warships to the Horn of Africa several times over the last few years, as have the United States, Holland, France, and other nations. Generally speaking, the mission mandates have been to keep an eye on the safety of passing vessels, but the warships have also been tasked to assure the delivery of humanitarian aid to the Somali people as well. That's of vital importance in preventing famine and disease, but it only addresses the immediate needs of the Somali people. Until someone can find a way to restore stability to the country and curtail the powers of the gangs that run rampant there, piracy will continue to flourish off the Horn of Africa.

Two days later, the *Emma Maersk* is nearing Sri Lanka and from the open deck atop the wheelhouse I can see the coastline off our starboard quarter. We're passing Dondra Head, the island's southernmost point, with numerous fishing boats working the surrounding seas. I feel a certain sadness glimpsing this nearby landfall, for there seems no end to the fighting that continues to wrack the island.

Though the Sri Lankan government and the separatist Liberation Tigers of Tamil Eelam agreed to a Norwegian-brokered cease-fire in 2002, the initiative has had little real effect on stopping the violence.

In late December of 2007 there was a fierce sea battle off the Jaffna Peninsula in the north end of the island, which resulted in the deaths of at least forty Sea Tigers and one government naval officer. Shortly thereafter, the government in Colombo terminated the cease-fire agreement, leading many to believe that both sides would resume even more active operations against one another. And since control of the waters around the island is crucial to the ability of each side to maintain contact with the rest of the world, it's safe to say that there will be many more attacks in these seas in the coming months.

The next few days are spent steaming ever westward across calm seas, skirting the tip of India, winding between the Lakshadweep islands and the Maldives through Eight Degree Channel and then making for the Red Sea and the Suez Canal. I use this time to review some of the material I've gathered and collect my thoughts. As I do so, I keep returning to the words of those I've met on four continents, individuals whose own recollections are far more dramatic than any official accounts. Some may have been liars, others no doubt exaggerated things, but the majority spoke with honest passion, helping me to see the situation through their eyes.

A week after departing Malaysia, the *Emma Maersk* is nearing landfall again. The first officer, Remus Galiatatos, another Romanian mariner, has the bridge watch. He's an outgoing young man, one of the friendliest among the crew. Galiatatos tells me we're coming up on Socotra, a Yemeni island lying 190 nautical miles south of the Arabian Peninsula, and adds that the captain has adjusted our course to pass north of the island. Normally they would pass Socotra to the south, as it's a shorter route across the Arabian Sea, burning less fuel, but the threat from Somali pirates has prudent mariners keeping as far as possible away from the Horn of Africa.

Galiatatos shows me the most recent piracy report, received a few hours ago, showing there to be no incidents in our area for the last month. "The captain and the company know it is quiet now, but we still take precautions," says the first officer. "We will maintain our speed"—the vessel is steaming at 21.9 knots (about average for a vessel as large as the *Emma Maersk*)—"keep an eye on the radar for small craft, and listen for any radio traffic from other ships. I think is good. Nothing will happen to us, but we remember what happened to the *Danica White*."

Several months earlier the cargo ship MV *Danica White* was hijacked by Somali pirates while en route from Dubai to Kenya. The ship and her crew were held hostage for eighty-three days until her owners paid a ransom claimed to be $1.5 million (U.S.).[3] The *Danica White* is a Danish vessel, like the one I'm currently on, which may also explain why the crew of the *Emma Maersk* kept this particular incident in mind.

The first officer also shows me the paperwork he's preparing for the captain's approval that will be e-mailed to NATO and the British Maritime Trade Operations center in Dubai. The forms give the ship's name, call sign, registry, speed, destinations, and other particulars and are collected by offices set up in the aftermath of 9/11 to monitor shipping traffic in the Arabian and Red seas, Suez Canal, and Mediterranean. The idea was to keep an eye on vessel traffic in order to differentiate legitimate shipping from anyone engaged in smuggling or other activities that could be related to international terrorism. It's a voluntary program for merchant mariners and is supposed to have the added benefit of giving coalition naval vessels a ship's position in case she is attacked by, say, pirates. The first officer has his doubts, though.

"If we were attacked, and again, I think it not very likely, but if we suddenly saw some small boats approaching us, I do not think that the coalition could help us. Not immediately. They would have to be in our vicinity. And even then, what would they do? Board us with commandos to arrest pirates?"

The Romanian shrugs his shoulders, resigned to the hope that any pirates out there will stalk something smaller than this immense containership. Twenty-four hours later, that wish will unfortunately come true.

To our starboard, the coastal mountains of Yemen loom, while Somalia can just be made out off our port side as we near Aden. The *Emma Maersk* is nearing the narrow channel that marks the entrance to the Red Sea, a ten-nautical-mile-wide channel known as the Bab el Mandeb, but the activity I encounter on the bridge has nothing to do with the tight squeeze coming up.

It's First Officer Remus Galiatatos who explains the quiet tension in the wheelhouse: "The ship has received a report that pirates have attacked and hijacked a ship two days ago. It is tug, oceangoing tug, called *Svitzer Korsakov*, and it was sailing near where we just were. Very bad business and there has been contact with head office [in Copenhagen] because tug was with company that is owned by Maersk."

Turns out that the *Svitzer Korsakov* is a brand-new tug built in Russia for the Svitzer firm, which is part of A. P. Moller-Maersk Group, who also operate the *Emma Maersk*. The tug was sailing with a crew of six from St. Petersburg to the Pacific, where she was to be used servicing the oil and gas fields off Sakhalin Island. The pirate attack appears to have been carried out with a certain amount of skill, for Galiatatos says there were no Maydays sent nor was there any other radio traffic from the crew of British and Russian mariners.[4]

There's little the *Emma Maersk* crew can do to help their fellow mariners, so we plod on toward Bab el Mandeb. The captain and watch officers are keeping a more vigilant eye out for small-vessel traffic, scanning the seas with both radar and binoculars. Captain Sonnichsen calls me over to the bridge wing to point out a small island that they use as a navigational reference when making the southern approach to Bab el Mandeb. It's a speck of land the charts label as Mayyun, which Sonnichsen remembers was once used during the cold war as a Soviet military base of some sort.

In fact, the little island with a large harbor in its middle has been used as a base of operations for much longer. Mayyun is also known as Perim, but hundreds of years ago European pirates called it Bab's Key, a handy little refuge to hide out on when working the surrounding seas for plunder. In *The History of the Pyrates,* Captain Charles Johnson writes that Captain Kidd was here in 1697 at what he called "[A] Place upon a little Island at the Entrance of the *Red Sea*; here it was that he first began to open himself to his Ship's Company, and let them understand that he intended to change his Measures." That is, it was here at Mayyun that Captain Kidd made the public decision to become a buccaneer.

As the sandy isle passes astern, First Officer Galiatatos is at my side, whispering that there's something interesting I should see: there's a mystery ship out there somewhere. By the radio station, he shows me a communiqué the ship has just received from the nearby search and rescue center, reporting a missing ship in the Red Sea ahead of us, the cargo ship *Badr One*. It reads in full:

RCVD FROM SEARCH AND RESCUE CENTER
DATE 24/01/08 AT 1445 UTC
THERE IS A SHIP ID 667719000 NAMED BADR ONE
ITS NATIONALITY SERALION

CALL SIGN 9LYG25

IT IS A CARGO SHIP, PSN NEARLY NORTH EAST BRANES

ON BOARD 14 PERSONS,

THERE IS NO CONTACT, NO INFMS. ABT. SHIP

ETS 09/01/08 FM SUES ·

PROCEIDING PORTSUDAN,

ALL SHIPS IN MENTIONED AREA PSE CONTACT SUK ON CH 605,
CH1221 HF

AND ON CH16 VHF IN CASE OF GETTING ANY INFORMATIONS

TKS

A ship that goes missing with fourteen crew while sailing from Port Suez to Port Sudan—one of the busiest waterways in the world—is a serious matter. But Galiatatos is confused.

"I have checked all the lists we have, with registered call signs, vessel names, IMO [identification] numbers, but there is no *Badr One* anywhere. The search and rescue center is strange, too. Is maybe El Quseir, in Egypt, but I do not know for certain."

I help Galiatatos go through the shipping binders in the wheelhouse a second time, but the *Badr One* seems to not exist. We look again at the printout with its bad English typos—"SERALION" must mean Sierra Leone—trying to figure out where it could come from. He's already radioed to another nearby merchant ship to see if they have any news on this mystery ship, but they're as confused as we are. The ship could be an unregistered vessel, and she might have sunk or been pirated. Another theory the officer puts forward is that the message itself could be a fake, sent by pirates who hope that a passing vessel receives it and deviates course to provide assistance in searching for *Badr One*. Captain Sonnichsen decides that unless we receive more credible information about the mystery ship no action will be taken by his crew, so it becomes another of the many small mysteries one encounters at sea.

The *Emma Maersk* continues to steam north through the Red Suez, Captain Sonnichsen hoping we'll arrive at the Suez Canal before midnight. Somewhere off our starboard side lies the Muslim holy city of Mecca, hidden behind the dusty hills of the Arabian Peninsula. Sudan's coast is clearly visible off our port quarter, soon to be replaced by Egypt. The amount of traffic on the sea has increased and the watch officers on the bridge are busy keeping an eye on other containerships, tankers, freighters, and fishing boats, plus the odd warship, heading to or coming from Suez. All this activity is a reminder that we've left the solitude of the sea behind us and are getting closer to civilization again.

One of the joys of being at sea is the ability to pause the information deluge that so many of us deal with on a daily basis. Since most commercial vessels today are equipped with satellite phones and Internet access, this really requires a conscious decision not to check e-mails every hour rather than any real inability to communicate with the rest of the world. If you wish, you can go for days, even weeks, without talking or writing to anyone, safe in the knowledge that everyone will assume you're at sea and unable to keep in touch. For most of my trip on the *Emma Maersk* I was happy to consider myself out of reach, content to let the rest of the world carry on without me. I knew they'd all be there whenever I opted to rejoin the global village, which would not be soon enough, in my estimation.

By the time we make the Suez Canal, we've been sailing for nine days, so I figure I should check in on the world. I wander down to E-deck where the containership's Internet access room is. It's nightfall as the vessel anchors at the Canal's southern terminus, where the Sinai Peninsula meets the African continent proper. We are about to begin a twelve-hour transit north toward the Mediterranean. I suppose it's being back in the embrace of dry land that compels me to log on, where I discover two weeks' worth of e-mails awaiting my attention. Scrolling through the junk mail, I find an e-mail from Peter Chin in Singapore.

It's a lengthy note, written a week earlier in response to my angry text message about Musso having lied to me. Peter says he's surprised I thought the Indonesian had misled us, since he was assured by certain unnamed individuals that Musso was legitimate. "Are you certain—CERTAIN—it was all BS, as you said?" Peter writes. "I am told he was involved in things. Can you check again?"

I consider asking the captain if I can use the satellite phone to call Peter directly, to say that I did check Musso's tales out and found them full of shit. Instead, I save Peter's e-mail and go back to my cabin and do due diligence by rechecking the information. I scour the records of incidents from 2007 in case I had missed something. Nothing's changed.

Then a light goes off. I had only checked pirate attacks from 2007, not the previous year. So I pull out the IMB report for 2006 and begin scanning the reported attacks. As I read through the narrations of incidents, I become somewhat uncomfortable.

On January 6, 2006, at 0040 hours local time, the Norwegian tanker *Torm Ingeborg* was attacked while anchored at Teluk Semangka, southwest of Sumatra on the Sunda Strait between Sumatra and Java. The IMB report says: "Three robbers armed with long knives boarded the tanker at poop deck. Duty A/B raised alarm, crew mustered and robbers escaped empty handed in a waiting boat."

A week later, on January 13, a Panamanian-flagged containership, the *Iberian Express*, was attacked at 0148 local time while anchored in Tanjung Priok, Jakarta's main harbor. "Two robbers armed with long knives boarded the ship at stern from an unlit boat. D/O raised alarm and crew mustered. Four shore security guards on board pointed their guns at the robbers who jumped overboard and escaped empty handed in their boat waiting with three accomplices."

On February 1 at 0130 local time, a Malaysian bulker—the *Eco Vision*—was boarded while anchored at Merak, just west of Jakarta. "Five armed robbers boarded the ship via poop deck and entered engine room. They attacked duty oiler and tied him up. They stole a large quantity spares and escaped."

Oh, crap.

Musso had told me the first time he actually boarded a ship was in February, somewhere on the east side of the Sunda Strait, when five of his group stole some equipment from the engine room.

Gnawing anxiously on a pencil, I run down the list of other incidents Musso told me about and find, to my shock, that they keep matching up with what he'd said:

An attack came at 0815 in the morning April 1 on Panamanian vehicle carrier *Orange Breeze* while anchored at Tanjung Priok: "Four robbers boarded the ship at stern using a rope. They entered the engine room and held hostage C/E. Alarm was raised and crew mustered. Robbers stole engine spares and escaped in their speedboat."

At the end of May, the bulker *New Guardian* was targeted at 0340 hours while anchored at the same port: "Five robbers armed with long knives boarded the ship. They tied up two crewmembers and threatened them with knives. They stole engine spares and escaped in a speedboat."

And then the capper: "August 11, 2255 LT: Liberian tanker *Morning Lady* boarded while anchored at Teluk Semangka. Eight robbers armed with knives boarded the tanker. They entered engine room, tied up and assaulted two duty crew. Robbers stole generator spares and escaped."

Musso had said the last attack he participated in occurred in August, when they used two boats and a large team to target a tanker in Teluk Semangka. This was the incident in which he was made to beat a man on the tanker, though Musso claimed to find it distasteful and it led to his deciding to escape from the pirate gang afterward.

I have gnawed my pencil to pieces and my fingers are twitching as I push the piracy reports aside and stare for the longest time out my porthole at the twinkling lights cast on the anchorage here at Port Suez from other ships waiting to transit the canal.

Up in the Internet room, I log on and write a note to Peter Chin: "Musso's story appears to check out. You were right. I was wrong, I think. Can you please contact him again and ask if he remembers any of these ships' names?" I type out the list of vessels reported to have been attacked in the IMB report, ask Peter to get back to me as soon as possible, and hit the send key. As much as I'm enjoying the trip, I suddenly wish I were back in Singapore.

Our anticipated twelve-hour transit of the Suez Canal turns out to be much longer, owing to a delay ahead of us in the canal.[5] This gives me lots of time to check my e-mail, but I find no word from Peter about Musso. The *Emma Maersk* eventually enters the Mediterranean Sea and heads west toward Spain. It'll take three days to reach Algeciras, the port across the harbor from Gibraltar where the containership is to unload part of her cargo, including me.

The Mediterranean Sea is a blank expanse of water to many people, but to mariners it is filled with character and history. From

Port Said at the northern terminus of the Suez Canal, our course will take us halfway between Europe and Africa, past Egypt and Libya, then through the Malta Channel. We then skirt Sicily and Sardinia on one side, Tunisia and Algeria on the other, until we reach Gibraltar and its namesake strait.

Though piracy is essentially nonexistent in these waters today, the Mediterranean was one of the places where nations first felt compelled to act against the scourge. As international bodies and nations today struggle to figure out how best to confront piracy—and in which strategic locales—I can't help thinking how it was piracy in these waters that compelled a young American republic to first send its military forces across the seas to engage Muslim warriors.

Within a year of the 1783 peace treaty being signed between a nascent United States of America and Great Britain, American commercial ships were being hijacked and held for ransom by Barbary corsairs. By 1795 so many American vessels were being targeted that the government of President George Washington was forced to sign a peace treaty with one of the most notorious gangs, based in Algeria, to the tune of $1 million. But as the attacks continued in other places, the United States was finally left with no option but to send naval ships across the Atlantic and into the Mediterranean. It was the Barbary War of 1801–1805 that saw the first postindependence American military incursion against foreigners. After a force of U.S. Marines attacked the Tripolitian-controlled city of Derna in 1805, it was immortalized in the first line of the Corps hymn: "From the halls of Montezuma to the shores of Tripoli . . ."

Long before the marines made their mark, Walter Raleigh is reported to have said, "Whosoever commands the sea, commands the trade; whosoever commands the trade of the world, commands the riches of the world and, consequently, the world itself." He was referring to the belief that Elizabethan England should assume the mantle of a world power by engaging itself militarily and commercially upon the oceans, something that nation eventually achieved temporarily before being overtaken by other nations, most notably the United States of America. But in today's world, can any one nation actually assert global dominance based solely on maritime power?

For the time being, America remains the world's reluctant policeman, with much of her prominence based on a military prowess engendered by staggering defense expenditures, coupled with an economic clout that, no matter how battered it appears, still commands great respect in foreign capitals. Protection of its financial interests was the reason the United States battled Barbary corsairs in the nineteenth century, for the pirates were posing a direct threat to the economic security of the republic. That's why piracy runs rampant today off Somalia and West Africa, while not being much of an issue in the strategic Strait of Malacca anymore. Should Nigerian pirates begin to have a serious effect on oil and gas shipments destined for America, they would find themselves encountering a lot more American warships in the area.

The Rock of Gibraltar rears its head on the horizon, signaling the imminent end to my two-week journey. I'd spent the morning packing up my stuff while listening to a Moroccan radio station in my cabin, then went to check my e-mail one last time. There are two e-mails waiting from Peter in Singapore. Both say he's been unable to reach Musso and ask me to call whenever I get to a phone.

As the *Emma Maersk* ties up alongside the container terminal in Algeciras, I make my hasty good-byes to the crew. Most are busy with the unloading that will keep them occupied for the next twelve hours, so there's little time for idle chitchat. Captain Sonnichsen shakes my hand and wishes me luck with my investigations; Chief Officer Larsen jokes that the real pirates I should be worried about are ones selling all that illicit computer software ashore. The two Romanian officers—Neamtu and Galiatatos—thank me for keeping them company on the trip, with Galiatatos personally escorting me to the gangway.

"No good comes from this piracy, eh?" the first officer says while guiding me down to the pier. We shake hands one last time and he waves farewell, shouting, "Hey, if I hear anything about that mystery ship, I'll call you, okay?" (A few weeks later, the *Badr One* was reported to have been found drifting in the Red Sea near Port Sudan. Her crew was all accounted for, though how the ship's engines and communications systems became disabled remains unclear.)

I leave the *Emma Maersk* and her crew to their Sisyphean work, traveling in an endless cycle back and forth between Asia and Europe through waters sometimes filled with pirates, and make my way to Málaga, Spain, and a hotel near the waterfront. Settling into my room, I grab a cold beer from the minibar and relish the taste after two weeks' aboard a dry ship, while firing up my laptop to check e-mails. There's a note from Peter titled "Musso News" that I'm glad to see.

I open the e-mail: "Musso dead. Call me."

My cell phone has maybe enough prepaid airtime for me to place a brief call to Singapore, where it's early morning. As I fumble at the keys, my first call goes to a wrong number, but my second finds Peter Chin having coffee in his apartment. I tell him to call me back on the hotel phone, and, once he does, listen to his news.

"I've been trying to get in touch with Musso for a week, since before you e-mailed me to say his story was okay. There was no answer on his mobile [phone], no response to my text messages. So then I tried the guy who set our meeting up, but he wasn't answering, either. So then I tried the person who put me in touch with him, and he got back to me yesterday night. Guy said that Musso was dead. Someone found a body that matched Musso's description, in Johor."

Peter says the body was found six days ago, about when I finally believed the former pirate's tales. He tried checking with the local police, but they had no information. The incident never made the news, never merited any attention; it was just another nobody found in an alley somewhere. Maybe he died in an altercation with someone; maybe he had an accident. Maybe Musso's actually still alive and the body found was not his, though Peter assures me that that is just wishful thinking. Musso's dead, probably buried in a pauper's grave somewhere in Malaysia, forgotten by almost everyone.

There's no great statement to make after learning that someone I met, someone who was a pirate, has been killed. I had no relationship with Musso beyond asking him about what he did as a criminal. He's a man I spent dinner with one evening, someone who admitted to robbing and beating people. I am sorry that someone died and feel a bit of remorse, for Musso did leave the business of being a pirate, if he was indeed telling me the whole truth. And for a moment I consider the chance that Musso hoped to start over again and reunite with his family. The reality, though, is that once you "go on account" it's almost impossible to turn back.

Musso did not appear to have lived a good life, and certainly it was not an easy one. I assume there must have been moments of happiness and joy in his life, such as his meeting his wife or the birth of his daughter. But my memories of Musso are of someone unhappy, someone who rarely smiled, whose features were tired and anxious, and who felt left behind by the world around him. His life was framed by the crime, poverty, and politics of Indonesia, and he could never be free of their influence. All Musso wanted to do, he said, was feed his family. Now I wonder if they even know he's dead.

The impact of thousands of years of piracy on the maritime community cannot be underestimated. It has caused the deaths of untold numbers of mariners and civilians, at sea and ashore. It has affected the economies of nations, towns, and villages and shattered the lives of families around the world. The seafaring community—whether professional mariners, pleasure boaters, or those who make their lives from fishing—places great trust in those with whom they sail and those they may encounter, and the longer you are at sea, the greater that reliance becomes. To be preyed upon by pirates shatters that belief.

Months earlier I went to the site of London's Execution Dock to see where figures from history met their demise, pirates whose stories had become a part of folklore and popular myth. It was the names of famous pirates that people remembered from when Execution Dock was busy dispatching the condemned three hundred years ago, the likes of Blackbeard, Captain Kidd, Calico Jack Rackham, and Black Sam Bellamy.

We have a fascination with pirates that keeps these names alive, even though they were violent criminals whose real actions were abhorrent. Perhaps after a few hundred years it becomes more acceptable to give them a measure of attention. But I'm thankful that today the names of individual pirates are rarely mentioned. Children may continue to dress up like seventeenth-century buccaneers for Halloween, but I pray that future generations never assume the costume of today's pirates, brandishing toy machine guns, rocket-propelled grenade launchers, and black balaclavas.

Joe Casalino, the Brooklyn-born seafarer who had been attacked by Iraqi pirates, put it to me like this: "When people talk about pirates and dress up like them and fly the skull and crossbones, well, sometimes that bothers me. That glorifies criminals. You know, when I see that skull-and-crossbones flag, to me it's no different than seeing a Nazi swastika."

Casalino's probably not far off the mark, and I'm sure there are thousands of mariners who have felt similar emotions when they've encountered pirates throughout history. I'm sure that victims like Casalino won't shed a tear on hearing that someone like Musso is dead, no matter how bad the Indonesian felt about his actions. Because they and other mariners know that there will be someone else to take the pirate's place.

One of the oddest things that I discovered while looking into this murky world is that no one believed piracy could ever be eradicated. Not a single person I met said it would ever go away, not the senior naval officers, government officials, piracy observers, security experts, or professional mariners. While there are many who talk of eventually eradicating poverty, malaria, HIV and AIDS, infant mortality, and other issues, piracy never makes the list. As one maritime security authority put it, "The best we can ever hope for is to contain it to acceptable levels. Piracy will never go away."

There will always be those disposed to the criminal mind, whether on land or at sea. They will prey on the weak, take advantage of situations, and think only of themselves. Mariners inherently dislike this type of people, for seafarers live in a world in which reliance on those around you for your safety and well-being is paramount. One needn't be in the middle of the Pacific Ocean to experience the sense of isolation and solitude that comes from being away from dry land; just venture over the horizon. For at that point one passes a psychological barrier engendered from millennia of living as communities ashore, a barrier that has kept the vast majority of humans from ever setting out on the seas.

But it's important to understand that modern-day piracy is not just a maritime issue. It occurs on the seas, but it germinates ashore. Its ranks are filled with the disaffected, the impoverished, the impressionable, and, yes, the greedy. Why would anyone risk his life for a few hundred dollars? I can see why the leaders do it, but they rarely—if ever—set foot on a boat, brandish a weapon, or take part in an attack. They share little of the risk. But most low-level pirates often have no other options.

Unless something drastic happens to change the way wealth is distributed on this planet, this century will see increasing divides between rich and poor nations, between have and have-not societies, between communities with resources and communities without. One group will become more protective of what it has, while the other will become more envious. And it will drive many more of those desperate ones living near the sea to become pirates.

Combating piracy at sea must begin by addressing the root causes onshore. Stabilize lawless nations, improve the local economies, re-build decaying infrastructure and people may choose not to set out to sea with Kalashnikovs. Remove the need to become a pirate and we will make the waters of the planet far safer than they have ever been. These solutions might also be much cheaper than we realize. Comparatively, the cost of designing, building, equipping, manning, training, and deploying a single warship can run into the billions of dollars. To patrol the world's piracy hot spots effectively would require hundreds, if not thousands, of warships, something few expect to happen given the cost expenditure involved and political will required.

None of this is to advocate a reduction in naval patrols through waters prone to piracy. Far from it, for maritime criminals understand implicitly that the presence of warships willing to engage them is one of the few things that will cause pirates to think twice before attacking vessels. But there must be a political plan to not only allow those warships to take on these gangs but also reduce the root issues that make piracy appealing.

This will not happen overnight, but the next few years could see some crucial changes in the way the West looks upon the issue. For instance, in 2008 the French responded forcefully to the activities of Somali pirates, twice sending in commandos to rescue hostages captured at sea. Meanwhile, the Canadian navy was given permission by the TFG of Somalia to escort UN WFP ships inside the country's twelve-nautical-mile sovereignty to the port of Mogadishu, assuring the aid ships were not attacked. Small signs, to be sure, but positive ones nonetheless.

Still, for the foreseeable future, few observers expect piracy to ever fade completely from the high seas. As long as there is poverty and lawlessness in any coastal region, passing vessels seen on the horizon will remain tempting targets. Some liken it to a maritime cold war, a low-level conflict that will simmer from place to place, decreasing in one area as force is applied, only to reappear somewhere else. And like the cold war, piracy is a global issue that needs to be treated as such.

For those who go to sea today it's become an unfortunate part of their daily lives—the cost of doing business or another risk to be endured. But piracy should never be considered an acceptable risk nor should it be glorified, not when lives are at stake. By ignoring or downplaying the issue, history is truly repeating itself on the waters of our planet today. Our failure to address piracy will only prove a grave mistake, bequeathing to future generations a problem that should be dealt with today.

AFTERWORD

ALMOST THREE YEARS ago, at the onset of my investigation into the world of modern-day piracy, the prevailing notion of more than a few was that this was an issue on the wane and perhaps I had missed the proverbial boat when it came to investigating the situation. Certainly there were incidents of note being recorded around the world, but overall it appeared that piracy had leveled off, or, in places like the Strait of Malacca, was in serious decline.

Yet, as I discovered on my travels and have shown here, pirates were far from ready to give up their criminal endeavors. To the surprise of many, piracy reappeared in Southeast Asian waters and expanded as never before off the coasts of East and West Africa; the seas around Sri Lanka became a high-risk zone thanks to the civil war raging between the government and Tamil Tigers; and recreational boaters from the Caribbean to the Pacific have been dealing with a deadly upsurge in attacks.

Piracy is both ever changing and ever constant. Reports of attacks filter in from all over the planet on a near daily basis, such that keeping abreast about the current situation can be difficult. Indeed, throughout the last part of 2008, as I was finishing this book, it seemed that piracy was exploding on a scale not seen in centuries. And by the time the International Maritime Bureau released its official figures for pirate incidents in 2008, that supposition had turned into a harsh reality. The IMB counted 293 reported attacks, up 11 percent from 2007, with more than a thousand acts of violence committed by pirates around the globe. Some 889 individuals were taken hostage, with 11 mariners killed and 21 still missing as I write this. The number of hostages captured by pirates in 2008 is the highest recorded in well over a century, and the majority occurred in the waters off the Horn of Africa, which saw pirate incidents increase 200 percent in just a year.

The audacity of Somali pirates became ever more brazen as the year progressed, highlighted first by the seizure of the freighter MV *Faina* in late September of 2008. At the time of her hijacking, the ship was en route from Ukraine to Mombasa, Kenya, with a cargo that included thirty-three Soviet-made T-72 main battle tanks, plus anti-aircraft weapons and munitions, as well as a crew of twenty-one mariners. The vessel's capture by pirates—who soon demanded a ransom of $20 million—elicited a furious response from foreign governments, with American warships pursuing the pirates as they sailed the hijacked vessel into Somali waters. The warships set up a blockade around the *Faina* to prevent its departure, while Moscow dispatched a frigate of its own to add to the firepower arrayed against the attackers, such that there were at least a dozen armed ships from a variety of nations in the waters off the Horn of Africa and making this the most forceful response taken against pirates in several hundred years.

But as the warships stood by and the negotiations dragged on with the pirates holding the *Faina* and her crew, another Somali gang managed to capture the most valuable prize ever seized in the history of maritime piracy: the supertanker MV *Sirius Star*. A lynchpin in the global economy, the tanker was hijacked in mid-November while carrying some two billion barrels of crude oil to the United States from Saudi Arabia, a cargo that represents about a quarter of the latter country's daily oil production. Together, the *Sirius Star* and her crude oil were worth close to a quarter of a billion dollars, to say nothing of the value of the lives of the nineteen mariners also being held hostage. Having forced the supertanker's crew to sail into Somali waters, the pirates asked for $25 million in ransom, the largest sum ever demanded.

The *Sirius Star* incident was notable not only for the moneys involved, but also for the immense size of the supertanker—she's as big as a nuclear-powered aircraft carrier—and the fact that the attack occurred about 420 nautical miles offshore, in an area where piracy had never been seen before. By successfully attacking a vessel so big she was considered virtually impossible to board at sea, and by doing so essentially under the noses of heavily armed warships patrolling that part of the world, the pirates marked the zenith of their modern-day capabilities. Of course, for mariners this marked the nadir in their lives, as it was clear that no one, anywhere, was safe from the predations of maritime criminals.

Both vessels were eventually released, the *Sirius Star* on January 9, 2009, and the *Faina* a month later on February 5. In each case, a small plane flew over the captive vessel to make a parachute drop of the cash ransom finally agreed upon by the parties involved. The *Faina*'s captors received $3.2 million, while the supertanker was freed for $3 million (though some of the latter's pirates were unable to enjoy their share of the loot for very long: five of the Somali men drowned when their small boat overturned while heading for home, with one body washing ashore laden down with $153,000 in cash).

But as these, and other, incidents played out in the waning months of 2008, it also became clear that even reporting on piracy has now become fraught with perils. Much of the information reported in the media about the seizure of the munitions-laden freighter MV *Faina* initially came from Andrew Mwangura, the Kenyan piracy expert I'd met in Mombasa. The hijacking of a ship carrying thirty-three tanks by at least fifty well-armed pirates seemed just a little too organized to be a lucky accident, and word soon spread that the weapons were perhaps not intended for the Kenyan military, as the government in Nairobi claimed, but meant to aid rebels in Southern Sudan. (One theory was that Sudanese officials in their capital, Khartoum, had tipped off the Somali pirates about the vessel, possibly wanting to embarrass whoever was arming the rebel forces.)

U.S. Naval officials and other journalists corroborated Mwangura's comments about the cargo's intended destination, but his forthrightness in speaking out about the situation placed him at odds with powerful elements among the Kenyan authorities. As such, he was arrested in early October in Mombasa and charged with making false statements about the hijacking of the *Faina*.

Released after seven days in detention, Mwangura has made almost a dozen appearances in court trying to clear his name, while continuing to be watched by Kenyan authorities. The charges brought against him are clearly a signal from those in positions of power that some aspects of piracy are better left unspoken. Unbowed by his experiences, Andrew Mwangura continues to report on the plight facing seafarers and to highlight the threat posed by pirates off East Africa, a brave voice in the midst of what often seems a global sea of silence.

DANIEL SEKULICH
Toronto, Canada
March 2009

NOTES

PROLOGUE: HASSAN'S STORY

1. According to the 2007 CIA World Factbook (www.cia.gov/library/publications/the-world-factbook/index.html), the national unemployment rate in Kenya is 40 percent, with 50 percent of the population living below the poverty line, and the per capita GDP is $1,200. In interviews, the local Seafarers Assistance Programme says there are at least three thousand professional mariners out of work in the Mombasa area.

2. Khat is a plant native to East Africa, and chewing its leaves produces an effect not unlike amphetamine. Popular in Somalia, it is considered a controlled substance in Canada and the United States but legal in Britain.

3. The full Convention may be seen via the United Nations Division for Ocean Affairs and Law of the Sea Web site (www.un.org/Depts/los/index.htm).

1. THE BRETHREN OF THE COAST

1. William Kidd's tale, including his plea of innocence, is described in the second volume of the *History of the Pyrates*, by Captain Charles Johnson, first published in London in 1728. His earlier bestseller, *A General History of the Pyrates,* was released in 1724. The author was later thought to really be Daniel Defoe, who wrote *Robinson Crusoe,* but this has recently been questioned by researchers, and the true identity of the author of one of the most comprehensive accounts of piracy from that time remains uncertain.

2. IMB statistics are from their reports "Piracy and Armed Robbery Against Ships" for the period January 1–June 30, 2007, as well as the annual reports for 2006, 2005, and 2004.

3. Daniel Sekulich, *Ocean Titans: Journeys in Search of the Soul of a Ship* (Toronto: Penguin Canada, 2006).

4. Statistics on the number of merchant vessels and the amount of world trade they carry come from the United Nations' International Maritime Organization (IMO) and the International Chamber of Shipping/ International Shipping Federation (Marisec).

5. IMO, or International Maritime Organization, is the UN agency responsible for improving maritime safety and preventing pollution. It is headquartered beside the Thames across the river and just upstream from the Houses of Parliament.

6. Statistics relating to pirate attacks on Vietnamese Boat People come from the United Nations High Commission for Refugees. In a report by managing editor/principal author Mark Cutts, *The State of the World's Refugees 2000: Fifty Years of Humanitarian Action* (New York: UNHCR/Oxford University Press, 2000), the plight of Indochinese refugees is detailed in the fourth chapter.

7. In all, UNHCR calculates that over 3 million fled Indochina between 1975 and 1995. The United States, Canada, and Australia took in the largest numbers of refugees.

2. SEA GHOSTS

1. "Melaka" is the Malay-language spelling of "Malacca." Melaka is the name of the local state as well as its capital city. The Strait of Malacca is known as Selat Melaka in Malay, but I use the English version as that is what most mariners call the waterway.

2. The durian is a football-sized fruit native to Southeast Asia with a prickly armored skin shielding a pulp inside. Its taste is not offensive, but its smell is, and of those who know durians, they either love the fruit or abhor it. Some liken the pungent scent of the pulp to that of dirty socks, and there are signs at Singapore's subway stations warning passengers not to carry durians aboard the system.

3. Statistical information on the Strait of Malacca and the countries in the region comes from the London-based International Institute for Strategic Studies (www.iiss.org), the U.S. government's Energy Information Administration (www.eia.doe.gov), and the CIA World Factbook (www.cia.gov).

4. PETRONAS is the acronym for Petroliam Nasional Berhad, the oil and gas company owned by the Malaysian government. It is most famous for its headquarters in Kuala Lumpur: the PETRONAS Twin Towers, the world's tallest twin buildings.

5. There will be those who take exception to my use of the term "fisherman" or its plural form, feeling it may be somewhat sexist in tone, so I would like to clarify this. In my experience, the vast majority of those who make their income from fishing are men, but even the

women I've met who do this prefer to be called fisher*men*. The sentiment expressed to me on several continents is that the word is not sexist, merely a way of describing their job, and all have reacted with unrestrained disdain to being called fishers.

6. Aceh Province is at the northwestern tip of Sumatra and has been the focus of a long-running conflict between local separatists, Gerakan Aceh Merdeka (Free Aceh Movement), and the Indonesian government. It was also the most severely devastated area hit by the Boxing Day tsunami of 2004.

7. Zheng He, also known as Cheng Ho, was called the Admiral of the Western Seas by the Ming emperor and set out on a series of voyages in the early fifteenth century. His expeditions took him to Vietnam, present-day Singapore, Melaka, Sri Lanka, India, and even East Africa, where he procured a giraffe and a zebra for the emperor. Zheng He used Melaka as a local trading base, bringing Chinese immigrants to the area who intermarried with the Malay population; Malaysia still has a large ethnic population descended from these early arrivals, known as Straits Chinese, Peranakan, or Baba-Nonya. A Muslim eunuch, Zheng He is also credited by some with helping to bring Islam to the region. The admiral remains a venerated figure in communities along the Strait of Malacca, with a museum dedicated to him in downtown Melaka (the Cheng Ho Cultural Museum).

8. Francis Xavier was born in what is now Spain but set off for the Far East after entreaties from the king of Portugal to help evangelize the natives. Xavier was a regular visitor to Melaka during the mid-sixteenth century, while traveling as far as Japan on his missionary work. He died in 1552 off the coast of China and was temporarily interred in St. Paul's Church (also known as Bukit St. Paul), which overlooks Old Town Melaka. His body was eventually moved to Goa,

India, where it remains to this day, except for his right arm, which was severed at the elbow and sent to Rome.

9. Much of this information comes from the National Museum of Singapore, the National Library in Singapore, and the Maritime Museum and Malaysia Royal Navy Museum in Melaka.

10. Hours before the bombing of Pearl Harbor on December 7 (Hawaiian time), 1941, Japanese troops landed on the northeastern coast of Malaysia and began a march down the peninsula toward the British stronghold of Singapore. Imperial Japanese troops under General Tomoyuki Yamashita passed through Tanjung Kling in January of 1942 and by mid-February had taken Singapore and secured the region. The Japanese occupation saw many atrocities committed against the local Malay population, especially those of ethnic Chinese background. Yamashita was executed for war crimes after the war ended.

3. PIRACY, INC.

The source for the epigraph is Project Gutenberg's ebook (www.gutenberg .org).

1. Blackbeard was killed in late November 1718 by the Royal Navy in North Carolina's Ocracoke Inlet, after barely two years of pirating. Kidd, as mentioned earlier, was captured and hung in England in 1701. The Barbarossa brothers were leaders of the North African corsairs on the Barbary coast; the elder died in battle against the Spanish, while the younger became admiral-in-chief of the Ottoman sultan and died in present-day Istanbul.

2. Material taken from Captain Charles Johnson's *General History of the Pyrates* (London, 1724; repr., edited by M. Schonhorn, Mineola, N.Y.: Dover Publications, 1972).

3. Though it surprises many, Malaysia is actually a net exporter of oil and gas and of great importance to the economies of Japan, South Korea, and Taiwan. According to the U.S. government's Energy Information Administration (www.eia.doe.gov), Malaysia ranks among the top fifteen sources of liquefied natural gas in the world.

4. See also the International Chamber of Shipping's facts on the industry (www.marisec.org/shippingfacts/worldtrade). These figures only cover professional mariners on merchant vessels. The number of people employed in the fishing industry is much harder to firmly calculate, as there are many individuals working on small, unlicensed craft in countless coastal communities around the world. The United Nations International Labour Organization (http://laborsta.ilo.org) believes there to be about 15 million fishermen working on all manner of vessels, from factory ships to dugout canoes.

5. The Piracy Reporting Centre is financed by twenty-two different groups, which include shipping companies, insurance firms, the government of Cyprus, and the International Transport Workers' Federation.

6. GMT is Greenwich mean time, also known as Coordinated Universal Time or Zulu time. It is the unchanging time at the Royal Observatory in Greenwich, a suburb of London—it does not alter for daylight savings time. Because of the number of time zones around the world, mariners (and many others, such as the military) use GMT to avoid confusion when recording information. Every commercial ship that sails on the planet maintains a chronometer (clock) on its bridge that is kept on GMT.

7. The IMB's Piracy Reporting Centre's weekly updates may be viewed at www.icc-ccs.org/prc/piracyreport.php.

8. Information on Nigeria's economic and security issues comes from the Congressional Research Service Report for Congress, "Nigeria: Current

Issues," updated January 30, 2008 (www.fas.org/sgp/crs/index.html). See also the CIA World Factbook (www.cia.gov).

9. The impression that most of us have of "walking the plank," gleaned from movies and books, is generally considered to be not how pirates of old actually acted. There are few, if any, corroborated stories of pirates forcing people to do this. However, throwing individuals overboard is another thing altogether, and a common enough occurrence in the annals of piracy.

4. THE DRAGON'S TEETH

The source for the epigraph is The American Presidency Project (www .americanpresidency.org).

1. The Persian Gulf is also referred to as the Arabian Gulf, primarily by those living in Arab nations across the waterway from Iran (formerly known as Persia).

2. See the IMB piracy report for 2005 and U.S. Office of Naval Intelligence warnings from the same period.

3. To protect his privacy, the name Peter Chin is an alias.

4. Donovan Webster's interest in piracy also extends to its fabled golden age, as he has written about recovery of treasure from the *Whydah Galley* for the May 1999 issue of *National Geographic*. Flagship of the pirate fleet of "Black Sam" Bellamy, the *Whydah* was laden with treasure and sailing past Cape Cod on April 26, 1717, when a powerful nor'easter sank the ship, killing Bellamy and most of his crew. It should also be pointed out that when Webster went to the Philippines in 1994 he was accompanied by photographer Nitin Vadukul.

5. The IMB's piracy reports do, in fact, list only twelve actual or attempted attacks in the Strait of Malacca throughout all of 2005

and only eleven in 2006. By comparison, there were thirty-eight in 2004.

6. The actions of the USS *Potomac* and her landing parties did not, in fact, make the waters here completely safe for American merchant vessels. Barely six years after the destruction of *Kuala Batu,* another American merchant vessel was attacked by pirates and the U.S. Navy was again dispatched to mete out punishment for the deed. Once more, landing parties went ashore to kill the pirates and burn their homes to the ground.

7. There is a myth that Singapore's guns, like those at Labrador Park, were "facing the wrong way" and did not contribute to the defense of the city when the Japanese attacked from present-day Malaysia. This is completely untrue: the batteries along Singapore's southern coast saw action during the battles that raged in February 1942, firing on enemy vessels that tried to approach from the sea and, in the case of the guns in Labrador Park, even shelling Japanese troops on nearby Pasir Panjang Road.

5. NEW LIBERTALIA

The source for this epigraph is the second volume of Captain Charles Johnson's history of pirates, originally published in London in 1728 as *The History of the Pyrates,* also known as the second volume of *A General History of the Pyrates.*

1. See Marcus Rediker in *Pirates: Terror on the High Seas—from the Caribbean to the South China Sea* (North Dighton World Publications Group, 1998) and Kevin Rushby's *Hunting Pirate Heaven: In Search of Lost Pirate Utopias* (New York: Walker, 2001).

2. Just past daybreak on March 18, 2006, the guided-missile cruiser USS *Cape St. George* and the guided-missile destroyer USS *Gonzalez*

encountered a suspicious boat while on patrol about twenty-five nautical miles off the Somali coast, in the Indian Ocean. As a boarding party prepared to inspect the vessel, the Americans noticed the suspected pirates brandishing rocket-propelled grenade launchers. The Somalis then opened fire on the U.S. warships with automatic weapons, striking the *Cape St. George*'s hull. In retaliation, the commanding officer of the *Gonzalez* ordered the destroyer's port-side guns to target the Somali vessel, causing her to erupt in flames, killing one of the attackers and wounding five more aboard the suspicious craft.

3. "A Description of Magadoxa," from Captain Charles Johnson's *History of the Pyrates,* vol. 2, chapter 11.

4. A detailed look at the American involvement in Somalia from 1992 to 1994 can be seen in a brochure produced by the U.S. Army viewable at their Center of Military History Web site (www.history.army.mil/brochures/Somalia/Somalia.htm).

5. ICC-IMB Piracy and Armed Robbery Against Ships Report—Annual Report 2007.

6. Press gangs were groups of naval sailors whose job it was to find able-bodied men to become crew on naval warships, whether the men liked it or not. A common practice several hundred years ago in British and other European cities, this was usually done by trolling the waterfronts of seaports and forcibly grabbing anyone unlucky enough to be around. It was a drastic measure, to be sure, but navies felt it necessary to overcome their manpower shortages. This was yet another reason many naval sailors opted to become pirates when the opportunity arose, for the conditions were generally better on pirate ships than aboard government vessels.

7. Somewhat anachronistically, the Mombasa chapter still calls itself the Mission to Seamen, though Reverend Sparrow emphasizes it has

nothing to do with any sexual bias. "Things change slower here," he told me.

6. FEASTS AND FAMINES

The story of the Mukunga Mbura monster was told to me by a Kikuyu man in Nairobi.

1. For the WFP's two-year Protracted Relief and Recovery Operation in Somalia that ended in July 2008 the top five international donors were the United States, Canada, the Netherlands, Saudi Arabia, and Japan. Their combined contributions topped $44 million (U.S.), with the Americans alone donating $23 million. By comparison, the United States was spending about $329 million in Iraq every day at the time. (Source: Congressional Research Report for Congress, *The Cost of Iraq, Afghanistan, and Other Global War on Terror Operations Since 9/11*, July 16, 2007.)

2. While Somali waters have seen the most frequent attacks on ships carrying relief cargoes, it should be noted that Indonesian sea robbers boarded two different vessels under contract to the United Nations in the Strait of Malacca in July 2007. In both cases, the pirates stole money, equipment, personal belongings, and fuel but did not hold the civilian crews hostage or pillage the cargo, which was intended for Indonesian victims of the December 2004 tsunami.

3. The attackers were eventually caught by Brazilian authorities and in June of 2002 received prison sentences ranging from twenty-six to thirty-six years, with Blake's murderer, Ricardo Colares Tavares, receiving the longest punishment.

4. The first European definition of territorial waters was adopted in the early eighteenth century by a Dutch jurist, Cornelis van Bynkershoek, and was based on how far out to sea a nation could defend itself

from shore. (It was decided that this would be three miles, the maximum distance that cannons could be fired at the time.) The 1994 UN Convention on the Law of the Sea codified territorial waters as extending to the twelve-mile limit.

5. Resolution 1772 (2007), adopted by the UN Security Council at its 5,732nd meeting, on August 20, 2007, states that "the situation in Somalia continues to constitute a threat to international peace and security in the region" and encourages "Member States whose naval vessels and military aircraft operate in international waters and airspace adjacent to the coast of Somalia to be vigilant to any incident of piracy and to take appropriate action to protect merchant shipping, in particular the transportation of humanitarian aid, against any such act, in line with relevant international law."

6. See the report of the United Nations Monitoring Group on Somalia from May 4, 2006 (www.un.org/sc/committees/751/mongroup.shtml).

7. See the IUCN's "Ocean Blues: Threats and Responses Fact Sheet" from June 2006 (downloadable at cms.iucn.org/index.cfm).

8. The United Nations Monitoring Group on Somalia managed to get their hands on a so-called fishing permit issued by something called the National Fishing Authority of Jubbaland State, possibly part of the National Volunteer Coast Guard's operations. It was believed that the owners of the East Asian fishing boat paid $80,000 for the permit.

9. See the UNEP post-tsunami reports (www.unep.org/tsunami/).

10. The June 14, 2007, Memorandum from the President does not, in fact, mention Somalia. It does state: "The United States strongly supports efforts to repress piracy" and "Piracy endangers maritime interests on a global scale." But it also says that the policy of the United States to repress piracy needs to be "consistent with U.S. law and international

obligations" and affirms that the responsibility for dealing with piracy does not rest solely with the United States.

7. SIX DEGREES OF SEPARATION

Bin Laden's comments came in a recorded statement broadcast by Arab news channel al-Jazeera on October 6, 2002.

1. See the U.S. Congressional Report that looked into the activities of the American intelligence community in connection with the 9/11 attacks (www.gpoaccess.gov/serialset/creports/911.html).

2. Canada deployed at least forty members of its elite Special Forces unit Joint Task Force Two (JTF2) to Afghanistan in December of 2001. This has been little known to many, even in Canada. The unit's Web site is www.jtf2.forces.gc.ca.

3. See *The Guardian*, October 15, 2001, in Brian Whitaker's dispatch, "Piecing Together the Terrorist Jigsaw" (www.guardian.co.uk).

4. When she was attacked, the *Limburg* was under charter to the Malaysian firm PETRONAS, carrying crude oil from Iran, and stopping off in Aden to top up her tanks before heading to Malaysia. She was later repaired and renamed the *Maritime Jewel*.

5. See Jane's Information Group's assessment at www.janes.com/security/international_security/news/jdw/jdw060929_1_n.shtml.

6. See www.whitehouse.gov/news/releases/2002/10/20021007-5.html.

8. PIRATE TALES

William Blake (1757–1827) is thought to have written "Auguries of Innocence" circa 1800–1803. Excerpted from *The Penguin Book of English Verse*, John Hayward editor, 1956.

1. The issue of paying money for interviews is one that troubles all journalists. Standard procedure is to not pay anyone, as it opens up the possibility that an individual is merely telling what you want to hear, rather than offering a supposedly unbiased perspective. However, in truth, payment for interviews happens all the time, though it's often camouflaged as "professional fees" of some sort. Indeed, it's normal practice for media outlets to pay an honorarium to those who appear on news and information programs as pundits or experts. A good deal of common sense must be used when you're put in situations like this, and it's not going too far to give someone in a Third World country a few dollars for their time. For the record, at no point in the course of working on this book did I solicit interviews by offering money. This was the only time that paying for someone's interview occurred, and it was arranged without my knowledge.

2. The Malay and Indonesian languages—Bahasa Malaysia and Bahasa Indonesia—are essentially the same, though with enough regional dialects to differentiate the way they are spoken. Malay has more English words incorporated into it, while Indonesian uses more Dutch, both as a result of the colonial influences of the Europeans.

3. In October 1965 Suharto was a major general in the Indonesian Army, while Sukarno was the president, the country's first since gaining independence from the Netherlands after the Second World War. Early on the morning of October 1, 1965, groups within the government and military tried to stage a coup d'état, though the exact details of who was involved and what their motivations were remain mired in controversy more than forty years later. General Suharto appeared to not have been involved in the putsch, but he later ousted Sukarno to become president of the country in 1967, holding office until 1998. He died in January 2008. Sukarno died in 1970. For more insights, see former BBC correspondent Roland Challis's book *Shadow of a*

Revolution: Indonesia and the Generals (Thrupp [Stroud], U.K.: Sutton Publishing, 2001).

4. Almost smack in the middle of the Sunda Strait lie the remains of Krakatoa, the mighty volcano that erupted in 1883. It continues to be an active volcano, having erupted as recently as October 2007.

5. The Office of Naval Intelligence publishes weekly reports on worldwide threats to shipping through the Web site of the U.S. government's National Geospatial-Intelligence Agency. These reports may be seen at www.nga.mil/portal/site/maritime/ and clicking on ONI Reports.

9. REVELATIONS

The epigraph comes from Latimer's seventh sermon to Edward VI and may be read, in whole, on the Project Canterbury Web site (www.anglicanhistory.org).

1. The *Emma Maersk* is part of a series of nine PS-class containerships built and operated by the Danish firm Maersk-Moller. She was the first built and the series is surpassed in size only by the *Knock Nevis,* a supertanker now used as a floating storage unit in the Persian Gulf. The *Knock Nevis* is 458 meters (1,504 feet) long, while the *Emma Maersk* and her sisters are 397 meters (1,302 feet) long.

2. Aboard the *Emma Maersk* the officer ranks differ slightly from other merchant fleets. What many know as the first mate is referred to on her as the chief officer. The second mate is the first officer, and the third mate is called the second officer. The captain remains the captain.

3. The actual amount of the ransom paid for the release of the *Danica White* and her crew has been disputed. Danish media reported the owners paid out $1.5 million, but while I was in Mombasa a number of well-placed shipping insiders believed the real ransom was $765,000.

4. The *Svitzer Korsakov* would eventually be released after forty-five days in captivity. The ransom paid was reported to be between $700,000 and $1.5 million. Partway through her incarceration at the hands of Somali pirates, the U.S. Navy fired on boats attempting to resupply the hijackers. An unnamed individual was also reportedly speaking to a news outlet in the Puntland region of Somalia, Radio Garowe, and claiming to represent the hijackers, who he said were not pirates but, rather, environmental activists called the Ocean Salvation Corps. The spokesperson told the radio station that the tug was part of the environmental destruction of Somalia's marine resources. And while it is true that illegal fishing and waste dumping are a problem there, the passage of a tugboat bound for Russia's east coast cannot be construed as part of any multinational assault on Somalia's maritime assets. This was but a pirate operation attempting to cloak itself in the guise of social responsibility.

5. Vessels transiting the Suez Canal do so in convoys, two heading southbound from the Mediterranean and one northbound each day. Because of the narrow confines of the canal, vessels rarely make the journey at night.

BIBLIOGRAPHY

Ayres, Chris. *War Reporting for Cowards*. London: John Murray, 2005.

Burnett, John S. *Dangerous Waters: Modern Piracy and Terror on the High Seas*. New York: Dutton (Penguin Putnam), 2002.

Challis, Roland: *Shadow of a Revolution: Indonesia and the Generals*. Thrupp (Stroud), UK: Sutton Publishing, 2001.

Conrad, Joseph. *Heart of Darkness & Other Stories*. Ware, UK: Wordsworth Editions, 1995. First published as *Youth: A Narrative, and Two Other Stories* in 1902.

Cordingly, David, consulting editor. *Pirates: Terror on the High Seas—from the Caribbean to the South China Sea*. North Dighton, Mass.: World Publications Group, 1998.

———. *Under the Black Flag: The Romance and the Reality of Life Among the Pirates*. New York: Random House, 1995.

De Villiers, Marq. *Witch in the Wind*. Toronto: Thomas Allen Publishers, 2007.

Dyer, Gwynne. *Future: Tense*. Toronto: McLelland & Stewart, 2004.

Gottschalk, Jack A. *Jolly Roger with An Uzi: The Rise and Threat of Modern Piracy*. Annapolis, Md.: Naval Institute Press, 2000.

Gutman, Roy, and David Rieff. *Crimes of War: What the Public Should Know*. New York: W. W. Norton, 1999.

Herman, Arthur. *To Rule the Waves: How the British Navy Shaped the Modern World*. New York: HarperCollins, 2004.

Hympendahl, Klaus. *Pirates Aboard!: Forty Cases of Piracy Today and What Bluewater Cruisers Can Do About It*. Sheridan House, Dobbs Ferry, N.Y., 2006.

Ireland, Bernard. *History of Ships*. London: Hamlyn, 1999, 2002.

Johnson, Charles. *A General History of the Pyrates*. London, 1724. Reprint, edited by Manuel Schonhorn. Mineola, N.Y.: Dover Publications, 1972.

Kaplan, Robert D. *Eastward to Tartary: Travels in the Balkans, the Middle East, and the Caucasus*. New York: Random House, 2000.

———. *Hog Pilots, Blue Water Grunts*. New York: Random House, 2007.

Langewiesche, William. *The Outlaw Sea: A World of Freedom, Chaos and Crime*. New York: North Point Press, 2004.

Lobley, Douglas. *Ships Through the Ages*. Secaucus, N.J.: Octopus Books, 1972.

Long, David F. " 'Martial Thunder': The First Official American Armed Intervention in Asia," *Pacific Historical Review* 42, no. 2 (May 1973): 143–162.

Lye, Keith, ed. *World Factbook*. Richmond Hill: FireflyBooks, 2006.

Petrie, Donald A. *The Prize Game: Lawful Looting on the High Seas in the Days of Fighting Sail*. New York: Berkley Books, 1999.

Rediker, Marcus. *Villains of All Nations.* London: Verso, 2004.

Royal Canadian Navy. *Boatswain Trade Training Manual for Trade Group One BRCN 3039(64),* rev. ed. Ottawa: The Queen's Printer, 1964.

Rushby, Kevin. *Hunting Pirate Heaven: In Search of Lost Pirate Utopias.* New York: Walker, 2001.

Rutter, Owen. *The Pirate Wind: Tales of the Sea Robbers of Malaya.* London: Hutchinson & Co., 1930.

Talty, Stephan. *Empire of Blue Water.* New York: Crown Publishers, 2007.

Tripp, Edward. *The Meridian Handbook of Classical Mythology.* New York: New American Library, 1970.

Watson, Paul. *Where War Lives.* Toronto: McLelland & Stewart, 2007.

Williams, Neville. *The Life and Times of Elizabeth I.* London: George Weidenfeld & Nicolson and Book Club Associates, 1972.

Woodward, Colin. *The Republic of Pirates.* Orlando, Fla.: Harcourt, 2007.

INDEX

Abdalla, Hassan, 2–6, 13, 146, 153
Abu Sayyaf, 212
Aceh Province, 52, 129–31, 282n6
Achille Lauro, cruise ship, 203
Aden, 206
Afghanistan
  insurgency movements, 191
  invasion of, 206, 290n2
  under the Taliban, 194
Afweyne, Abdi Mohamed, 186
AK-47, 10, 150, 151
Albemarle, merchant ship, 146
Albuquerque, Alfonso de, 60
Alfa Gemilang, MV, 105
Algeciras, 266, 268
Ali (fisherman), 57–58
al-Nashiri, Abd al-Rahim, 207–8
Alpi, Ilaria, 190
Al Qaeda, 10, 199–202, 210
Alvarado, Arnulfo, 212
American embassy bombings (1998), 200
American mariners, 179

American privateers, 8
anti-piracy measures, 37, 87, 90, 256–57,
  268, 274
  of the United Nations, 40, 87, 256
A. P. Moller-Maersk Group, 260, 292n1
Arabian Gulf (Persian Gulf), 285n1
Arabian Sea, 181
armed guards on ships, 180
armed robbery against ships, 11
arming of mariners, 52, 178–80
articles of piracy, 82–84
assassins, 201
attacks. *See* pirate attacks
Avery, Long Ben, 139

Bab el Mandeb, 260
Bab's Key, 261
Badr One, MV, 261–62, 269
balaclavas, 126, 132
Bali, 202
banca (Philippine boat), 125
Bandah Aceh, 70

Bangladesh, 21, 23, 170
Barbarossa brothers, 283n1
Barbary coast, 283n1
Barbary corsairs, 267
Barbary War of 1801–1805, 267
Bay of Bengal, 170, 218, 221
beaches, nighttime raids on, 56
Beavis, Captain William, 146
belacan cakes, 64–65
Belawan, 52
Bellamy, "Black Sam," 271, 285n4
bin Laden, Osama, 197, 201, 205, 207
bin Laden family, 205
Blackbeard, 8, 58, 271, 283n1
Black Hawk Down incident, 147
Blake, Sir Peter, 178–79
Blake, William, 229, 290chap 8
boarding any ship with the intent to
    commit a crime, 11
Boat People (Indochinese), 38–41, 280n6
Bolivia, 103
Boston, 18
bribes, 176
Britain
    in Afghanistan, 206
    "cod war" with Iceland, 69
    in war on terror, 201
British colonialists, 61, 136
British Empire, 61–62
British Maritime Trade Operations, 259
buccaneers, French, 8
Buddhism, 76
Bush, George W., 195
Bynkershoek, Cornelis van, 288n4

Canada
    in Afghanistan, 206, 290n2
    anti-piracy efforts, 256–57, 274
    "turbot war" with Spain, 69
    in war on terror, 201
Cape St. George, USS, 171, 286n2
Caribbean
    conflict between England and Spain
        in, 32
    piracy in, 61, 220
Casalino, Joe, 115–20, 179–80, 271–72

Catholic Church, 31
Cavite City, 124
Central America, 32
Chaplin, Gord, 151–52
Charleston, S.C., 58
Cheng Ho Cultural Museum, 282n7
Cheng I Sao, 81
Cherry 201, MT, 52–53
Chin, Peter, 120–22, 135, 230–33,
    245–46, 264, 266, 269, 285n3
China
    age of exploration, 58–59
    confronting of piracy, 104
    piracy from, 104
Chinese, ethnic, in Malaysia, 282n7
Chittagong, 170
Choong, Noel, 91–101, 105
Cicero, 12
City of Liverpool, MV, 220–21
clothing, traditional, 57
coastal communities, pirate attacks on,
    58–59
cod wars, 69
Colares Tavares, Ricardo, 288n3
cold war, 31, 126, 147
Cole, USS, 206–8
colonial maritime powers, 60, 85, 130,
    154
Combined Task Force 150 (CTF 150),
    180–81
containers, 225, 227
containerships, 292n1
convoys, Spanish, 32
corporate espionage, 109
corsairs, 8, 267, 283n1
crews
    dumping of, 145
    executions of, 52–53
criminals
    mind of, 243–44, 272
    pirates as, 9, 254
Cuba, 58

Danica White, MV, 259, 292n3
Danish ships, 259
Dar es Salaam, 200

Defenders of Somali Territorial Waters, 186
Defoe, Daniel, 280n1
Department of Homeland Security, 226
Dewi Madrim, MT, 209–10, 225
dirty bombs, 227
Dondra Head, 257
Dong Won 628, trawler, 181
Dragon's Teeth Gate, 137–38
Drake, Sir Francis, 18, 29–33
    circumnavigation of the globe, 30
drunken sailors, no longer exist on shipboard, 179
duku fruit, 65
durian, 281n2
Dutch
    colonialists, 60, 130
    freebooters, 8

Eco Vision, bulker, 265
Egypt, 262
Elizabeth I, 31–33
e-mails, 262
Emma Maersk, MV, 249–69, 292n1
England
    colonial expansion of, 85
    Elizabethan, 268
    seafaring history of, 30
    struggle with Spain, 31–33
English corsairs and privateers, 8, 32
Ethiopia, 194
Execution Dock, 17–18, 271

failed states, 148, 173, 193
Faina, MV, 276, 278
Farah 3, MV, 221–24
Farquhar, William, 136
fiberglass boats, 55
Fifth Fleet, U.S. Navy, 181
Filipinos
    Islamists, 203
    pirates, 123
    terrorists, 10
fire hoses, 51
fires, 67
fishermen

Malaysian, 43–47
number of, worldwide, 284n4
pirate attacks on, 46, 51, 53, 55–57, 187, 252
the term, 281n5
fishing, 67–71
    illegal, 187–89
    tradition of, 66
fishing boats
    being out in one, 43–47
    stolen, 56–58
    victimized by pirates, 187
fishing permits (from pirates), 188, 289n8
fishing villages, traditional, Southeast Asia, 65–66
flag of convenience states, 103
food aid, 171–77
France, 85, 257, 274
freebooters, Dutch, 8
freedom fighters, 225
French Revolution, 202
Friendship, merchantman, 130
Fu Yuan Yu 225, trawler, 218–19

Galiatatos, Remus, 258, 260, 269
Gambia Castle, pirate ship, 83
gangs of armed robbers, 95
    evolutionary stages of, 192–93
Germany, 201
global economy, 224
gold, 32
Golden Hinde, pirate ship, 29–33
Gonzalez, USS, 286n2
government, by gangs, 192–93
Gray, "General," 157–58, 186
Greenwich mean time (GMT), 284n6
Guantánamo Bay, 208
guillotine, 202
Gulf of Aden, 147, 181, 208
Gulf of Guinea, 96, 255
Gulf of Oman, 181
Gulf of Siam, 26
Guyana, 37

Haikou, 104
Haradheere, 186

Havana, 18
Henry VIII, 31
high seas, 11
hijacking of ships, 25, 143
    a case of, 26–27
    of entire vessels, 95–96
Hindus, 4, 59
Holland, 85, 257
Horn of Africa, 93, 147, 171–72, 188,
    255, 257, 259
hostages, freeing of, 99–100
hostis humani generis (enemies of the
    human race), 12
humanitarian aid, 174

"Ian," 28–37
Iberian Express, containership, 264–65
Iceland, 69
identity cards, 226
improvised explosive device (IED), 213
Inabukwa, MV, 109–10
India, 21, 46, 62
Indian Ocean, 129, 140, 147, 181, 182,
    189–91, 253
Indians, 161
Indonesia, 48–49, 52, 93, 108, 126
    civil war in, 129, 233, 291n3
    piracy in waters off, 23, 24, 37, 148
    territorial waters of, 68–69
Indonesian language, 291n2
Indonesians, 56, 69–70
    Islamists, 203
insurance companies, 35
insurance rates, 35
insurgency, 60–61, 191–93
International Chamber of Commerce, 18
International Maritime Bureau (IMB),
    11–12, 18–28, 178, 246, 276
    Asia Regional Office, 90
    Piracy Reporting Centre (Kuala
        Lumpur), 19, 22–23, 90–101,
        284n5, 284n7
    piracy reports, 35–36, 37, 142
international maritime law, 181–82
International Maritime Organization
    (IMO), 35–36, 178, 184, 280n5

International Union for Conservation of
    Nature (IUCN), 187
international waters, 5, 181–82
Internet, pirates' monitoring of, 26
interviews, paying money for, 291n1
Iraq
    insurgency movements, 191
    piracy in waters off, 115, 119
Iraq War (2003 onward), 196, 288n1
Islamic Courts Union (ICU), 194–95
Islamists, 96, 129, 203, 212
Islamist states, U.S. nonsupport of, 194
Israeli vessels, 179
Issa, "Captain," 157

Jabbar, Ramaz Abdul, 221–23
Jackson, Andrew, 113, 130
Jaffna, 220–21
Jaffna Peninsula, 258
Jamaica, 37, 220
Japanese, 64, 136, 283n10, 286n7
Java Sea, 105
Jewish rebels, ancient, 201
Johnson, Captain Charles, 140–41, 146
    The History of the Pyrates, 139, 261,
        280n1
Johor, 122, 130
Johor Bahru, 230

Kamarudeen, 44–45, 54–57, 63–71, 75
Kenya, 1, 171, 181, 278
    peaceful reputation of, 141–42
    statistics about, 279n1
    terror attacks in, 199–201
khat, 4, 194, 279n2
Khawr 'Abd Allah waterway, 115
Kidd, Captain William, 8, 15–18, 81,
        139, 255, 261, 271, 280n1, 283n1
    life of, 16
    trial and execution, 16–18
kidnapping
    of fishermen, 53
    of senior officers, 94–95
    a tale of, 2–6
    of workers for ransom, 96
Kisauni, Kenya, 1

Knock Nevis, MT, 292n1
Krakatoa, 292n4
Kuala Batu, 130–31
Kuala Lampur, 88–90, 281n4
Kudrati, Karim, 160, 162–63, 176, 177
Ku Klux Klan, 202

Labrador Park, 286n7
Larsen, Niels, 250, 269
Latimer, Hugh, 249
law enforcement, maritime, 48
Lee, Mr. (of Singapore), 102, 105–11,
    121
legitimate businesses, 111
letters of marque, 16, 33, 85–87
Liberation Tigers of Tamil Eelam
    (LTTE), 214–23, 258
Libertalia, 140–41
Liberty Service, pollution control vessel, 97
Limburg, MV, 208, 290n4
Liverpool Packet, privateer, 86
Lloyd's, 35
London, 17–18, 202
Lowther, George, 83
lunar eclipses, superstitions about,
    46–47, 76

machetes, 55–56
Madagascar, 139–41
Madrid, 202
Maersk line, 260
Mafia, 190
Mahalingam, Captain Sellathurai, 156,
    157–59
Makcik ("Auntie"), 63
Malabar coast, 15
Malacca Strait. *See* Strait of Malacca
Malay language, 44, 291n2
Malaysia, 46–77, 88–90, 93, 250, 282n7,
    283n10, 284n3
    piracy in waters off, 24
    traditional story from, about a sea
        ghost, 76
Malaysians, 43–47, 56, 69–70, 72
Manila, 211
Manwaring, Dr. Max, 192–93, 195

Marcos, 126
mariners
    arming of, 52, 178–80
    community of, and reliance on each
        other, 12, 272
    number of, worldwide, 284n4
maritime crime, leading countries in,
    148
Maritime Security Program (MSP), 115
maritime sovereignty, redefining the limits
    of, 195
maritime terrorism, 202–27
    differences from piracy, 225
    not over-reacting to, 226
Marka groups, 186
Mayyun, 261
Mbura, Mukunga, 169
McFadden, Dean, 256–57
media, little attention given to piracy, 27
Mediterranean Sea, 266–67
Melaka, 46, 59–61, 130, 154, 251,
    281n1, 282n7
MEND (the Movement for the
    Emancipation of the Niger
    Delta), 98
Merak, 265
merchant vessels
    arming of, 52, 178–80
    attacks by privateers, 16
    number of, 33–34
    rarely carry weapons, 52
    trade carried by, 224
militants, 97
Miltzow, MV, 155
Ming Dynasty, 59
Mission to Seafarers, 163–64, 287n7
Mission to Seamen, 287n7
Misson (French buccaneer), 140–41
Mogadishu, 147, 171, 194, 274
Mohamed, Garaad, 185–86
Mombasa, 1, 143, 153–55, 197–99, 200
Mongolia, 103
monsoon season, 184–85, 197
Morgan, Sir Henry, 18, 58, 220
Morning Lady, MT, 265
mosques, 198

Motaku Shipping Agencies, 160–63, 175
mother ships (pirates'), 25, 149–50
mugging at sea attack, 25
Mukalla, 208
Mukundan, Pottengal, 18–28
Mullaittivu Lighthouse, 221
Muslims, 4, 76, 90, 200
Musso (sometime pirate), 232–48, 264,
    266, 269–71
Mvita, Juma, 158–59
Mwangura, Andrew, 144–46, 148,
    152–56, 159, 163–66, 184–85,
    188–89, 190–91, 278
Myanmar, 108

Nairobi, 171, 200
Nassau, 18, 170
National Volunteer Coast Guard
    (NVCG), 185–86, 289n8
NATO, 259
naval escorts, 180–84
Neamtu, Irinel, 252, 269
negotiating with shipowners, 4–16
New Guardian, bulker, 265
New York City, 18
Nigeria, 21, 23, 96–98
9/11 attacks, 201, 226
    security environment after, 194,
    205–6
Nova Scotia, 86

Ocean Atlas, MV, 115–18
Ocean Salvation Corps, 293n4
Office of Naval Intelligence, 292n5
Oklahoma City bombers, 202
Operation Anaconda, 206
Orange Breeze, vehicle carrier, 265
organized-crime syndicates, 25, 104
Outside magazine, 123

Palestine Liberation Front, 203
Palestinian radicals, 203
Panama, 58
Parameswara, 59
Paris, Treaty of 1856, 87
passports, 226

Pelican, pirate ship, renamed the
    Golden Hinde, 32
Pelli, César, 90
Penang, 61
People's Liberation Army Navy, 104
perahu (Malaysian boat), 44, 55
Perim, 261
perompak (Malay pirates), 55
Persian Gulf, 115, 285n1
PETRONAS, 49, 281n4
Petronas Towers, 90
Petro Ranger, MV, 103–4
phantom ships, 25, 102–5, 108
Philip II, 31
Philippines, 108, 110, 126, 211–13
piracy
    articles of, 82–84
    as a business endeavor, 80, 81
    considered a quasi-legitimate form of
      maritime life, 18
    cost to society, 271
    cover-up of, 36
    doubts about prevalence of, 101–14
    ebb and flow of over time, 79–80
    effects on land-dwellers, 38
    eradication of, considered not
      possible, 272
    eradication of, goal of Islamists, 194
    golden age of, 82
    in history books, 7, 82
    hot spots of, 23
    information on, 19–28
    as insurgency, 60–61
    legal definition of, 10–12
    losses every year, 80
    mariners' nonchalance about, 254
    planning and execution of, 27
    policing and prosecuting, 87–88
    prevalence of, worldwide, 6–7,
      101–14
    profit from, 80
    reappearance of, 275
    reporting of, 8–9, 90–101
    root causes of, 23, 196, 257,
      273–74
    state-sanctioned, 85

three factors required to flourish
(greed, lawlessness, and opportunity),
48, 257
unconcern about, 255–57
unfortunate victims of, 27–28
unwritten rules of, 169–71
piracy enterprises, shareholders in, 82
Piracy Reporting Centre. *See under*
International Maritime Bureau
pirate attacks
description of, 236–38
distinct types of, 24–25, 94–96
failed, 150
going out on one, 125–26, 133–34
government protection from, 46
and insurance rates, 35
planning of, 25, 27
statistics on, 20–22, 28, 276
tales of, 3
three types of (mugging, ransoming,
hijacking), 25
unreported, 20, 28, 34–37
the Pirate Round (of legendary pirates),
140, 255
pirates
combatting, 62
as criminals, 9, 254
death of, 127, 134
difficulty they have of quitting the
pirate life, 243–44
fascination with, 271
firsthand experience with, 114
gangs, sophistication of, 9–10
home communities of, 169–71
an interview with one, 123–34
legendary, 7–8, 12, 182
lynching of, 170
and maritime terrorists, differences, 225
meeting one, 121–22
reasons for becoming, 19, 119–20, 126
recruits, in legendary times, 82–85
reluctant, 124
ruthlessness of, 19, 150
spies for, 75, 166
violent death an occupational
hazard of, 127

pirate vessels
mother ships, 25
small boats, 125
Port Kelang, 101
Port Royal, 170, 220
ports, loading and unloading on, 224–25
Portuguese
colonials, 60, 154
seafaring history of, 30
Potomac, USS, 130–31, 286n6
Prabhakaran, Velupillai, 215
prawns, 64
press gangs, 287n6
privateers, 16, 86–87
American, 8
English, 32
protection rackets, 164
Puntland groups, 186

quitting the pirate life, 243–44

Rackham, Calico Jack, 271
radio frequencies, pirates' monitoring
of, 26
Raffles, Stamford, 136
raiders, Spanish, 8
Raleigh, Walter, 267
ransom
amounts paid, 143, 148–49, 259,
292n3
demands for, 52, 95–96
payment of, 5–6, 99–100, 277,
293n4
planning of an attack for, 25
policy not to pay, 176
rape, 39
"Ratnam" (Tamil interviewee), 215–16
Rawlins, Michael, 127–29
recreational boaters, attacks on, 275
Red Flag Fleet, 81
Red Sea, 10, 23, 181, 260
red snapper, 45
refugees, 38–41
régime de la terreur, 202
rocket-propelled grenade launchers, 10,
150, 151

Rogers, Mike, 151–52
Roosevelt, USS, 181
Royal Africa Company, 83
Royal Navy, 62, 84
Royal Thai Navy, 40
Rozen, MV, 155, 175
Russia, 276
Russian vessels, 179
Rutter, Owen, 61

Salleh, Abdul, 44–45, 54–57, 66–71
Santa Maria, cruise ship, 203
Santos, Brazil, 23
Sarkozy, Nicolas, 184
Scottish pirates, 8
Seabourn Spirit, cruise ship, 150–53, 171
Seafarers Assistance Programme (SAP),
    144–45
seafaring
    ancient, 8
    dark side of, 8, 37
    secrecy of, 33–34
    See also mariners
seajacking, 103
Seamaster, research vessel, 178–79
Sea Tigers, 217–23
security procedures, 194, 205–6,
    226–27
Selat Melaka, 281n1
Semlow, MV, 148, 155–59, 160,
    162–63, 171
Shabelle, Middle and Lower, 173
Sharia law, 194
shipowners, negotiating with, 4–16, 25
shipping business
    competitive and secretive, 28, 122
    customers of, 34
    global boom in, 10, 36
    security procedures, 226–27
shipping containers. *See* containers
ships
    registration, 103–4, 108
    renaming, 25
    renaming and changing registration,
        103–5
Siad, Sheikh Yusuf Mohamed, 186

silver, 32
Singapore, 24, 47, 48, 59, 61, 93, 102,
    113–14, 120–21, 135–38, 229,
    283n10, 286n7
Sinhalese, 214–19
Sirius Star, MV, 277
skull and crossbones, 271–72
Smerdon, Peter, 172–78
Socotra, 258
Somalia
    conditions conducive to piracy, 23
    criminal organizations in, 184–89
    dangerous reputation of, 142–43
    as a failed state, 93, 193
    marine resources of, 293n4
    media inattention to, 172
    piracy in waters off, 37, 145–50
    relief efforts in, 4, 147
    territorial waters, 181–82
    threat to U.S. of piracy from,
        195–96
    trade with, despite piracy, 160–66
    types of pirate attacks in, 94–96
    typical case of piracy in, 22
    United Nations and, 147–48
Somalians
    pirates, 171, 256, 259, 276, 289n5
    terrorists, 200
Somali Marines, 186, 193
sonic blaster, 152
Sonnichsen, Jørgen, 253–54, 269
South Africa, 20
South America, 20, 32
South China Sea, 39–41, 81, 125, 126
Southeast Asia, 24
    corruption and crime in, 122–23
    traditional fishing village life,
        65–66
sovereignty, 193
sovereign waters, 11
Soviet Union, 31, 126, 147, 179
Spain, 85, 201
    seafaring history of, 30
    struggle with England, 31–33
Spanish Main, 32
Spanish raiders, 8

Sparrow, Reverend Michael, 163–66, 287n7
spies, for pirates, 75, 162–63, 166
Spratly Islands, 21
Sri Lanka, 10, 214–24, 257–58
Strait of Malacca, 23–24, 35, 37, 43–77, 93, 94, 128–29, 130, 180, 209, 220, 249, 252, 285n5
  one of the world's major shipping lanes, 49
  pirate attacks in, 50–51
Straits Settlements, 61–62
Sudan, 262, 278
Suez Canal, 262, 266, 293n5
Suharto, 126, 233, 291n3
Sukarno, 233, 291n3
Sumatra, 48, 52, 67, 70, 130–31
Sunda Strait, 236, 264, 292n4
Super Ferry 14, ferry, 211–13
supertankers, 277
Svitzer Korsakov, tug, 260, 293n4
Swahili, 2

Taliban, 194
Tamils, 214–19
  separatists, 10, 203
Tanjung Ketapang, 47
Tanjung Kling, 47–48, 53, 58, 65–66, 95, 251
Tanjung Pelepas, 250
Tanjung Priok, 265
Tanzania, 23
Teluk Semangka, 264, 265–66
Temasek, 59, 136
territorial waters, 288n4
terror attacks, in Kenya, 199–201
terrorism
  definition of, 11
  involvement with modern piracy, 10
  no statutes defining, 225
terrorists
  Filipino, 10
  Somalian, 200
Tew, Thomas, 139
Thailand, 26, 40, 48–49, 108
Thanadol 4, MT, 26–27

thugees, 201
Tim Buck, MV, 150
Torgelow, MV, 155
Torm Ingeborg, MT, 264
Toronto, 217
Toronto, HMCS, 183
tourist attractions, 29
trade, volume carried by merchant vessels, 224
trade routes, ancient, 253
Transitional Federal Government (TFG) of Somalia, 173, 194–95, 274
tsunami of 2004, 69–70, 129, 162, 189–91, 219–20, 282n6
Turbot War of 1995, 69

Umm Qasr, 115
United Kingdom. *See* Britain
United Nations
  anti-piracy program, 40, 87, 256
  countries from which piracy has been reported, 20
  humanitarian missions, 4, 165, 177
  office in Nairobi, 171
  pirate attack on ships under contract to, 288n2
  policy not to pay ransom, 176
  and Somalia, 147–48
United Nations Convention on the High Seas, 87
United Nations Convention on the Law of the Sea (UNCLOS), 10–11, 183, 289n4
United Nations Environment Programme (UNEP), 189–90
United Nations High Commissioner for Refugees (UNHCR), 40
United Nations Monitoring Group on Somalia, 289n8
United Nations World Food Programme (WFP), 154, 162–63, 171–77, 184, 274, 288n1
United States
  in Afghanistan, 206
  anti-piracy efforts, 257, 268
  in the cold war, 31, 126

United States *(continued)*
  letters of marque issued by, 86
  territorial waters, 128
  threat of piracy to, 195–96
  in the war on terror, 201
U.S. Navy, 181

vacation resort complex, 65
Vadukul, Nitin, 285n4
Victoria, MV, 176
Victorio, Rande, 124–27
Vietnam, 38
Vikings, 254

"walking the plank," 110, 285n9
Wang Da Yuan, 137
Wapping, 17–18
war, asymmetrical, 195
warlords, 164, 193
War of 1812, 86
war on terror, 201–2
Washington, George, 267

waste, dumping at sea, 189–91
Water Rats, 179
waterways, busy, 49
Webster, Donovan, 123–27, 234,
  285n4
West Africa, 20, 23, 35
West Coast, U.S., labor dispute of
  October 2002, 224–25
Whydah Galley, pirate ship, 285n4
Winston S. Churchill, USS, 181
wood boats, 55
World Trade Center, 1993 attack, 225
World War II, 136, 283n10, 286n7

Xavier, Francis, 60, 282n8

Yamashita, Tomoyuki, 283n10
Yemen, 206–8, 260

zealots, 201
Zeven Provincien, HNLMS, 181
Zheng He, Admiral, 58–59, 282n7